MODERN ORTHODOXY IN AMERICAN JUDAISM

The Era of
Rabbi Leo Jung

Studies in Orthodox Judaism

Series Editor:
Marc B. Shapiro (University of Scranton, Scranton, Pennsylvania)

Editorial Board:
Alan Brill (Seton Hall University, South Orange, New Jersey)
Benjamin Brown (Hebrew University, Jerusalem)
David Ellenson (Hebrew Union College, New York)
Adam S. Ferziger (Bar-Ilan University, Ramat Gan)
Miri Freud-Kandel (University of Oxford, Oxford)
Jeffrey Gurock (Yeshiva University, New York)
Shlomo Tikoshinski (Jerusalem)

MODERN ORTHODOXY IN AMERICAN JUDAISM

The Era of
Rabbi Leo Jung

MAXINE JACOBSON

Boston
2016

Library of Congress Cataloging-in-Publication Data:
A bibliographic record for this title is available
from the Library of Congress.
Copyright © 2016 Academic Studies Press

All rights reserved.
ISBN 978-1-61811-437-2 (cloth)
ISBN 978-1-61811-521-8 (paper)
ISBN 978-1-61811-438-9 (electronic)

Cover design by Ivan Grave.
Book interior design by Kryon Publishing
www.kryonpublishing.com

Published by Academic Studies Press in 2016
28 Montfern Avenue
Brighton, MA 02135, USA
press@academicstudiespress.com
www.academicstudiespress.com

To my husband, Stephen
With love always

TABLE OF CONTENTS

List of Illustrations | vii
Preface | viii

Introduction | 1
1. Modern Orthodoxy in the 1920s | 29
2. Modern Orthodoxy in the 1930s | 75
3. Modern Orthodoxy in the 1940s | 119
4. Modern Orthodoxy in the 1950s | 171

Conclusion | 220
Bibliography | 231
Index | 243

LIST OF ILLUSTRATIONS

1. Rabbi Dr. Leo Jung as a young man. Courtesy of Anne Etra, granddaughter of Rabbi Jung

2. Rabbi Jung with his wife, Irma and three of his four daughters Erna, Rosalie, Julie. Fourth daughter, Marcella was not yet born. Early 1930's. Courtesy of Anne Etra, granddaughter of Rabbi Jung

3. Dedication of the new building, the main building of Rabbi Isaac Elchanan's Theological Seminary and the Yeshiva College. Courtesy of Yeshiva University Archives

4. Bernard Revel at his desk. Courtesy of Yeshiva University Archives

5. Bernard Revel –founding President of Yeshiva University, close friend of Leo Jung. Courtesy of Yeshiva University Archives

6. Bidding farewell with Torah scrolls and moving to new headquarters 1928. Courtesy of Yeshiva University Archives

7. Samuel Belkin, President of Yeshiva University from 1943 to 1976. Courtesy of Yeshiva University Archives

8. Leo Jung after receiving an honorary degree. 1949. Courtesy of Yeshiva University Archives

9. Rabbi Jung and President Truman. Courtesy of Anne Etra, granddaughter of Rabbi Jung

10. Rav Soloveitchik with students. 1960-s. Courtesy of Yeshiva University Archives

PREFACE

Before the 1980s and 1990s, there was a paucity of books on American Modern Orthodoxy. At that time, a new stirring of scholarly attention reflected that there was something interesting occurring. Jeffrey Gurock, Saul Bernstein, William Helmreich, Charles Liebman, Gilbert Klaperman, and Aaron Rothkoff-Rakeffet have written about some aspect of Orthodoxy. This book gives an expanded look at the phenomenon of Modern Orthodoxy, which will also be referred to as "American-style" Orthodoxy.[1]

---

1 Saul Bernstein, *The Orthodox Story: A Centenary Portrayal* (Northvale, NJ and Jerusalem: Jason Aronson Inc., 1997); Saul Bernstein, *The Renaissance of the Torah Jew* (New York: Ktav Publishing House, 1985); M. Herbert Danziger, *Returning to Tradition: The Contemporary Revival of Orthodox Judaism* (New Haven and London: Yale University Press, 1989); Jeffrey S. Gurock, *American Jewish Orthodoxy in Historical Perspective* (New York: Ktav Publishing House Inc., 1996); Jeffrey S. Gurock, *Men and Women of Yeshiva: Higher Education, Orthodoxy and American Judaism* (New York: Colombia University Press, 1988); Jeffrey S. Gurock, ed., *Ramaz: School, Community, Scholarship and Orthodoxy* (Hoboken, NJ: Ktav Publishing House, 1989); William Helmreich, *The World of the Yeshiva: An Intimate Portrait of Orthodox Jewry* (New York: Free Press and London: Collier MacMillan, 1982); Gilbert Klaperman, *The Story of Yeshiva University* (New York: MacMillan, 1969); Aaron Rakeffet-Rothkoff, *Bernard Revel* (Philadelphia: The Jewish Publication Society of America, 1972); Aaron Rakeffet-Rothkoff, *The Silver Era in American Jewish Orthodoxy: Rabbi Eliezer Silver and His Generation* (New York: Yeshiva University Press; Jerusalem: Feldheim Publishers, 1981).

Up to and including the 1950s, scholars told the story of Modern Orthodox history in America from the viewpoint of decline. Dr. Meyer Waxman, an editor for the Orthodox journal *Jewish Forum*, wrote in 1924: "In fact voices are being heard in the Jewish press and especially in the Zionist press—that Orthodox is disappearing, that whoever speaks in the name of Orthodox Jewry speaks in the name of fiction."[2] Many Socialist Yiddish newspapers actively participated in discrediting religion and Orthodoxy in particular, winning over huge numbers of religious Jews to their socialist cause.[3]

Mordecai Kaplan, the founder of Reconstructionist Judaism, wrote in 1920 that Orthodoxy was out of keeping with the march of modern thought and that the fundamental doctrine of Orthodoxy was repugnant to the thinking man of the time.[4]

Oscar Fasman, a former head of Hebrew Theological College, remembered one of his confreres remarking (when he graduated in 1929) that he, as a rabbi, would be able to recite to a generation or so later the final *kaddish* for Orthodoxy.[5]

Marshall Sklare, perhaps the most influential exponent of this notion, saw Conservative Judaism as the only possible alternative for American Jewry, and saw Orthodoxy as alien to the American environment. He wrote in the 1950s that the history of Orthodoxy in America could be written in terms of a case study of institutional decay.[6] Amidst all the tales of woe and doom and gloom, this book presents an optimistic and positive view.

---

2 Dr. Meyer Waxman, "American Orthodoxy—The Fifth Unknowable," *Jewish Forum* 7, no. 5 (October 1924): 652.
3 Tony Michels, *A Fire in their Hearts: Yiddish Socialists in New York* (Cambridge, MA, and London: Harvard University Press, 2005), 12.
4 Mordecai Kaplan, "A Program for the Reconstruction of Judaism," *The Menorah Journal* 6, no. 4 (August 1920): 182.
5 Oscar Fasman, "After Fifty Years an Optimist," *American Jewish History* 69, no. 2 (December 1979): 227.
6 Marshall Sklare, *Conservative Judaism: An American Religious Movement* (Glencoe, IL: Free Press, 1955), 43.

Dr. Marc Shapiro, editor of the Academic Studies Press series on Orthodox Judaism and Professor at the University of Scranton, suggested that I make my doctoral thesis into a book; this is the result. The thesis, "Trends in Modern Orthodoxy as Reflected in the Career of Rabbi Dr. Leo Jung" (which was completed in 2004 at Concordia University in Montreal), deals with Modern Orthodox Judaism in America from 1920 to 1960.

My thesis supervisor was Dr. Ira Robinson; in the many years since I have graduated, I have not stopped working with him, seeking his advice, his constructive criticisms, and helpful suggestions. He continues to share his wide knowledge base and experience with me, and I continue to think of him as teacher and mentor. His help in writing this book is greatly appreciated.

I thank the members of the Institute for Canadian Jewish Studies for their assistance and support. The institute encourages and enables research, publications, and educational programs for academics, students, and the community at large. In these areas, they have many accomplishments.

I also wish to thank Shulamit Berger, chief archivist at Yeshiva University, for her help and attention throughout many years.

My husband, Stephen, has been a fine example in his devotion to ongoing learning and professional excellence. He has always been patient, encouraging, and has taken pride in my accomplishments. My children, Edie and Allen, Natasha and Morris, Ronit and Avi, and Elka and Eitan, have also stood as additional stimulus to my work, as I admire their many achievements. I am grateful for their love and support.

INTRODUCTION

This work presents the issues—from the 1920s to the 1960s—of a particular Orthodox group in America that would become known as Modern Orthodox, by looking at the activities and involvements of one of its leaders, Rabbi Dr. Leo Jung. Rabbi Jung's career as a pulpit rabbi, community leader, and avid writer spanned over 60 years, beginning in the 1920s. This Orthodox group went from being a threatened entity on the American scene to a well-recognized, respected force in Judaism. The phenomenon of Modern Orthodoxy will be examined in the context of Orthodox invigoration and change.

The chapters appear in chronological order, beginning with the 1920s. Though time frames can be artificial and certain issues are ongoing, chronological treatment does give a full picture of the movement, its involvements, concerns, and achievements at a given time. The goal is to understand the issues and challenges that Modern Orthodoxy faced in each decade.

The chapters deal with progress in organizational activity, educational programs, and capable leadership as they are instrumental in developing Modern Orthodoxy and reflect progress in the movement. The chapters will also demonstrate how the economic, social, and political influences impacted Modern Orthodoxy and how they influenced Rabbi Jung's activities and philosophy.

Rabbi Jung's path crossed with some of the most interesting people of his time. He collaborated with Chaim Weizmann (the first president of Israel) on Zionist issues, and he worked with Albert Einstein to promote Yeshiva College. Herman Wouk, an American author and Pulitzer Prize winner, studied with Rabbi Jung, who exposed him to the classics of Judaism; Wouk claimed that Rabbi Jung was a profound influence on him. In Rabbi Jung's search for universal peace and a major role for religion, he planned a project with Pearl Buck, a Nobel Prize laureate and Pulitzer Prize winner.

Rabbi Jung is a fulcrum around which many issues can be explored. This book does not focus on him exclusively, but rather on the significance of his interests and activities and its impact on his surroundings. As noted by Samuel Heilman, "the notion of using the rabbi as an indicator of the Jewish state of being is useful as a tool for tracing the development of Orthodoxy."[1]

Rabbi Jung was one of the spokesmen for an American-style Orthodoxy; he combined the religious faith of Orthodoxy with the American way of life. He was involved in almost everything that was going on in American Orthodox Judaism, either in a major or minor way. He was involved in institutions that articulated the Modern Orthodox position; these organizations are part of the history of American Orthodox Judaism.

Modern Orthodoxy in the 1920s lacked hard lines and clear concepts, and was floundering as it tried to adjust to its new environment. These concepts became somewhat clearer over time. Modern Orthodox institutions were weak; there was a lack of adequate facilities necessary for an Orthodox community to exist and a lack of adequately trained educators. There was a widespread laxity in observance of the most basic Judaic laws among Jews espousing Modern Orthodoxy. For the most part, its adherents were transplanted Eastern Europeans, religiously uneducated, unobservant, and in awe of America and the modern world.

---

1 Samuel C. Heilman, "The Many Faces of Orthodoxy," *Modern Judaism* 2, no. 1 (1982): 26.

By 1960, a foundation had been laid for a movement to the "right," which was marked by the tightening of religious standards, more identification with the tenets of *halakhic* Judaism, stricter piety, and more distrust of the secular world. Though this pursuit of stringency rather than leniency, known as the movement to the "right," has been noted by scholars (such as Saul Bernstein, Haym Soloveitchik, and Jeffrey S. Gurock), this book will try to make clear some of the factors leading to this shift.[2]

What Is Modern Orthodoxy?

First, there was no agreement on the use of the term "Modern Orthodoxy"; the term itself has caused discomfort to many scholars and rabbis. Rabbi Jung pointed out that the term "Orthodox" had a Christian connotation, referring to those who clung to the official tenets and dogmas of their respective churches. He preferred the term "Torah-true Judaism," but it was never widely used and Rabbi Jung used "Orthodox" in some of his writings.[3] Rabbi Jung wrote:

> And in want of a better word in English we may use it [Orthodox], provided we know it as a means to designate the genuine Jew, the man or woman who lives in strict accordance with Jewish law.[4]

---

[2] Saul Bernstein, *The Renaissance of the Torah Jew* (New York: Ktav Publishing House, 1985), 2–6, 54, 274–275; Herbert M. Danziger, *Returning to Tradition: The Contemporary Revival of Orthodox Judaism* (New Haven, CT and London: Yale University Press, 1989), 1–3, 335–338; Ralph Pelcowitz, *Danger and Opportunity* (New York: Steingold Publishers, 1976), 20–26; Shlomo Riskin, "Conservatism and The Orthodox Resurgence," in vol. 8 of *The Alteration of Orthodoxy*, ed. Jacob Neusner (New York: Garland Publishers, 1993), 231–233; David J. Schnall, "Orthodox Resurgence," in vol. 8 of *The Alteration of Orthodoxy*, ed. Jacob Neusner (New York: Garland Publishers, 1993), 234–240; Haym Soloveitchik, "Rupture and Reconstruction: The Transformation of Contemporary Orthodoxy," *Tradition* 28, no. 4 (Summer 1994).

[3] Leo Jung, *The Path of a Pioneer: Autobiography of Leo Jung*, Jewish Library, Second Series, vol. 8 (London and New York: Soncino Press, 1980), 4.

[4] Leo Jung, *The Essentials of Judaism*, Jewish Library, First Series, vol. 2 (New York: Union of Orthodox Jewish Congregations of America, 1924), 11.

Though Rabbi Jung spoke always of Americanization and tradition, he failed to give the followers of this type of Judaism a lasting name. One of the earliest uses of the term "Modern Orthodox" was found in a 1924 article in the *Jewish Forum*, an American, Modern Orthodox, monthly journal that was published from 1918 to 1962. It appears more prominently again in the *Jewish Forum* in August 1937, in an article entitled "Neo and Modern Orthodox Judaism".[5]

Briefly, this group is fully committed to the Torah tradition and is open, at the same time, to the wider culture of the modern world. Rabbi Jung described Orthodoxy as *Torah im derekh eretz* (Torah along with the way of the world), offering all the intensity and true beauty of true Judaism plus decorum and a system of modern method; that was the goal to which he devoted his life. Rabbi Jung's response was not unique; his responses and attitudes are typical of a specific group, which today is widely known as Modern Orthodoxy.

Jacob Breuer, in his introduction to *Nineteen Letters*, by Rabbi Samson Raphael Hirsch, said that the term "Torah-true" had been used to refer to this group, and only later when their opponents called them "Orthodox Jews" was that term used.[6] Rabbi Mordecai Kaplan, as well as others, used the term "Neo-Orthodoxy" because it was felt that Rabbi S. R. Hirsch's *Torah im derekh eretz* philosophy deviated from that of traditional, premodern Judaism. This conception of Judaism was, in fact, different from traditional practices of preceding generations. The term "Jewish Jews" was also used, but infrequently. The cover of Jung's book, *Living Judaism*, dated 1927, states that he is the rabbi of the Jewish Center, a synagogue for "Jewish Jews." Jung begins an article, "Modern Trends in American Judaism," written in 1936,

---

5   Isaac Marks, "The Phenomenal Growth," *Jewish Forum* 7, no. 4 (April 1924): 240–241; Joseph Barondess, "Achievement and Failings of Borough Park," *Jewish Forum* 7, no. 4 (April 1924): 243. Phineas Israeli, "Neo and Modern Orthodox Judaism,"*Jewish Forum* 20, No.8 (August 1937):140-141. Also mentioned in Jenna Weissman Joselit, *New York's Jewish Jews: The Orthodox Community in the Interwar Years* (Bloomington, Indiana: Indiana University Press, 1990), 21.

6   Jacob Breuer, introduction to *Nineteen Letters*, by Samson Raphael Hirsch (Jerusalem: Feldheim Publishers, 1969), 4.

with the motto for "Jewish Jews."[7] Jenna Weissman Joselit, author of *New York's Jewish Jews*, wrote that the term was used to show that this group was superior, as well as in a defensive way; therefore, its usage was private and not often found in print.[8]

The dilemma of the term "Modern Orthodox" has never been completely resolved. Norman Lamm, a former president of Yeshiva University (1974–2003), wrote in 1969: "...To use the two dreadfully inadequate words which describe us as a distinct group, we are both 'modern' and 'Orthodox.' I shall be using these terms only with the greatest hesitation."[9] Like his predecessors, he tried unsuccessfully to define this group.

The *Torah im derekh eretz* philosophy is associated with Rabbi S. R. Hirsch, one of Rabbi Jung's influences. *Torah im derekh eretz* was a novel and influential approach to Torah-true Judaism in the nineteenth century, when the emancipation of Western European Jewry confronted Jews with unprecedented challenges and dangers.[10] Emancipation meant that Jews could partake in the general society. This change was either welcomed or rejected to some degree, which divided the Jewish community.

Only in response to the Reform movement did Orthodoxy, as a whole, have to think about defining itself and its response to Emancipation.[11] The Reform movement was the first to embrace the Enlightenment by reforming classical Judaism and abandoning most of *halakhah*, or Torah-based Jewish law. It became a powerful force to contend with by the end of the nineteenth century in Western Europe. Rabbi S. R. Hirsch's book, *Nineteen Letters*, first published under the pseudonym "Ben Uziel" in 1836, was written in defense of Orthodox

---

7 Leo Jung, "Modern Trends in American Judaism," in *Harvest: Sermons, Addresses, Studies*, ed. Leo Jung (New York: Philip Feldheim Inc., 1956), 219. "Modern Trends in American Judaism" first appeared in Mizrachi Jubilee Publication in New York in 1936 and is available at the Jewish Center Synagogue Archives in New York.
8 Personal interview with Jenna Weissman Joselit, November 11, 1996.
9 Norman Lamm, "Modern Orthodoxy's Identity Crisis," *Jewish Life* (May–June 1969).
10 S. R. Hirsch, *The Nineteen Letters* (Jerusalem: Feldheim Publishers, 1969), 112–116.
11 Jung, *The Essentials of Judaism*, 11.

Judaism and was addressed to those who were turning to Reform. In this book, Rabbi S. R. Hirsch showed how modernity could be reconciled with Judaism and he welcomed Emancipation; at the same time, however, he defended Orthodox Judaism. The *Nineteen Letters* offered an alternate to the Reformers' approach with the *Torah im derekh eretz* philosophy, which stated that Jews must not only live among gentiles, but with them, and that they must learn the language and adopt the culture of the land while keeping intact the *halakhic* tradition.[12]

Rabbi S. R. Hirsch introduced changes in the synagogue, including aesthetic changes, in keeping with some of the modern demands, which had been attractive to Reformers. He felt that isolation from worldly activities was not a Torah precept and was therefore unjustified.[13] The philosophy applied to an educational system established by Rabbi S. R. Hirsch; Jewish studies could exist alongside secular studies.[14] The Hirschian philosophy of Modern Orthodoxy is that interpretation of *halakhah* is nourished when drawn from life's experiences.

Rabbi S. R. Hirsch's Orthodox group abandoned special Jewish dress, speech, and mannerisms. In Frankfurt am Main, Rabbi S. R. Hirsch had a devoted following, who remained loyal and apart from other Modern Orthodox groups, even when they came to America as refugees in the 1930s and became known as the Breuer Community. Rabbi Jung befriended this group when others did not.

Rabbi S. R. Hirsch's philosophy was a new interpretation of tradition, reflecting bourgeois norms, universal aspirations, and a worldly emphasis. This type of Orthodoxy was presented as compatible with the modern values of individualism, autonomy, and tolerance. Rabbi S. R. Hirsch had a Kantian understanding in keeping with nineteenth-century moral sensibilities. He thus affirmed free will, and he felt that humans had the ability to decide between good and evil.[15] He negated the virtue of pure literalism; the words were open to different

---

12 S. R. Hirsch, *The Nineteen Letters*, 107–111.
13 Ibid., 107–110.
14 Ibid., 123, 127.
15 Ibid., 45.

interpretations.¹⁶ For him, Judaism was fully up to the most advanced standard of modern thought. Rabbi S. R. Hirsch affirmed the need for the rejuvenation and reformulation of Judaism while maintaining the Jew's commitment to *halakhah*.

However, according to the historian and rabbi Zev Eleff, Rabbi S. R. Hirsch never set out a clear program of how to achieve the goals of *Torah im derekh eretz*, and for many reasons, his disciplined, scientific, and Germanic approach never resonated with great success in America.[17] First, American Jews were emancipated from the start, thus had no need to respond to Emancipation. Most German Jews that came to the United States turned to Reform Judaism, and Reform leaders condemned Rabbi S. R. Hirsch.[18] In America, a large percentage of Jews were from Eastern Europe, where Rabbi S. R. Hirsch's work was relatively unknown; hence, many of the Eastern European rabbis were not interested in spreading his work. As America's Orthodox Jews were too illiterate to access Rabbi S. R. Hirsch's writings on their own, his work remained largely unknown.[19] Among the exceptions were Rabbis Bernard Drachman, Bernard Revel, Leo Jung, Phillip Klein, and Shraga Feivel Mendelovitz.[20] Rabbi Drachman translated Rabbi S. R. Hirsch's *Nineteen Letters*, hoping it would help stem the tide to Reform. Bernard Revel, the president of the Rabbi Isaac Elchanan Theological Seminary (RIETS) and the founder of Yeshiva College, wrote about Rabbi S. R. Hirsch but had reservations about his teachings for American Jews, and Revel's seminary differed from Rabbi S. R. Hirsch's philosophy. Rabbi Jung wrote about Rabbi S. R. Hirsch and cited his work as a model message for Orthodox Judaism; he championed the legacy of Rabbi S. R. Hirsch in the 1920s and 1930s with his sermons, publications, and Jewish Library series.[21] Rabbi Jung learned of Rabbi S. R. Hirsch's

---

16 Ibid., 83–87.
17 Zev Eleff, "American Orthodoxy's Lukewarm Embrace of the Hirschian Legacy, 1850–1939," *Tradition* 45, no. 3 (2012): 36.
18 Ibid., 37 and 41.
19 Ibid., 40 and 44.
20 Ibid., 40 and 48-49.
21 Leo Jung, "What is Orthodox Judaism?", in *Essentials of Judaism*; Leo Jung, *The Path of a Pioneer*, 20; Leo Jung, ed., Preface, *Guardians of Our Heritage: 1724–1953*,

message when he was a student at Hildesheimer Rabbinical Seminary; he came from Moravia, the birthplace of Rabbi S. R. Hirsch, and Rabbi S. R. Hirsch had had an influence on Rabbi Leo Jung's father, Rabbi Tzevi Jung, therefore on Rabbi Leo Jung himself.[22]

Rabbi Ezriel Hildesheimer had much in common with Rabbi S. R. Hirsch; yet there were also significant differences between Rabbis S. R. Hirsch and Hildesheimer.[23] Both men were strong opponents of Reform, and both felt that without adjustments and innovations in Orthodox practice, Orthodoxy would not survive the onslaught of modernity. However, for Rabbi S. R. Hirsch, secular and religious studies could only exist side by side. Unlike Rabbi S. R. Hirsch, Hildesheimer integrated or synthesized secular and religious studies.[24] Rabbi S. R. Hirsch advocated coexistence, not synthesis. In other words, the Modern Orthodox individual lives in two civilizations by either synthesizing secular and Torah learning or by assigning each to a specific area of thought and action. Since Yeshiva University, which represents Modern Orthodoxy in America, strives to synthesize secular and religious studies, Hildesheimer is a more accurate model for Modern Orthodoxy in America than is Rabbi S. R. Hirsch.[25]

Rabbi S. R. Hirsch was an anti-Zionist; from the start, American Jews had misgivings about such a stance. In light of recent history, few Jews would identify with this anti-Zionist philosophy.[26]

Jewish Library, First Series, vol. 7 (New York: Bloch Publishing Co., 1958).

22 Leo Jung, *Jewish Leaders: 1750–1940*, Jewish Library Series, First Series, vol. 6 (Jerusalem: Boys Town Jerusalem Publishers, 1953 and 1964); Leo Jung, *Guardians of Our Heritage*.

23 Jacob Katz, *A House Divided: Orthodoxy and Schism in Nineteenth Century European Jewry* (Waltham, MA: Brandeis University Press, 1998), 125–126 and 128.

24 Ibid., 97–100; Michael K. Silber, "The Emergence of Ultra Orthodoxy: The Invention of Tradition," in *The Uses of Tradition: Jewish Continuity in the Modern Era*, ed. Jack Wertheimer (New York: Jewish Theological Seminary of America, 1992), 31–32, 36–37.

25 Marc Shapiro, *Between The Yeshiva World and Modern Orthodoxy: The Life and Works of Jehiel Jacob Weinberg, 1884–1966* (Oxford, UK and Portland, OR: The Littman Library of Jewish Civilization, 1999), 76–79, 130, and 140.

26 Eleff, "American Orthodoxy's Lukewarm Embrace of the Hirschian Legacy, 1850–1939," 52.

Hildesheimer was an active supporter of the idea of Jews working for *Eretz Israel*. For Rabbi S. R. Hirsch, Jews were exiled from the Holy Land to enable them to perfect themselves and to fulfill the mission of the "chosen people" by remaining faithful to the Torah and God. He felt that this mission could only be accomplished when Jews were dispersed throughout the nations.[27] Rabbi S. R. Hirsch would not meet with non-Orthodox Jews to discuss issues of concern to all, as he felt that this accorded them legitimacy; Rabbi Hildesheimer thought that such engagement was necessary.[28]

The differences between the two men are mentioned because the dilemmas they adumbrate persist and are examined throughout the book. For example, Orthodoxy's relationship with non-Orthodox Jews has never been completely solved. The problems concerning how to integrate Judaism and modernity and how to integrate sacred and secular studies likewise have never been completely resolved.

Modern Orthodoxy has no main authoritative body. It has been argued that, because it lacks a clear authority structure, it may not in fact be a movement.[29] Rabbi Emanuel Rackman pointed out that there are certain freedoms in Modern Orthodoxy because of its lack of a central authority.[30] Rabbi Rackman described Modern Orthodoxy as a coterie of rabbis in America and Israel whose interpretation of the tradition has won approval of Orthodox intellectuals, who are knowledgeable in both Judaism and Western civilization. Jenna W. Joselit said: "Modern Orthodoxy was a less coherent ideological or intellectual statement than a system of expressive religious behaviors."[31]

There is no agreement in the contemporary sources on the use of the term "Modern Orthodoxy." This term will be used for the purposes

---

27 S. R. Hirsch, *The Nineteen Letters*, 62–64.
28 Ibid., 104; Katz, *A House Divided: Orthodoxy and Schism in the Nineteenth Century European Jewry*, 103.
29 Chaim I. Waxman, "Dilemmas of Modern Orthodoxy," *Judaism* 42, no. 1 (Winter 1993): 59.
30 Emmanuel Rackman, "Orthodox Judaism Moves With The Times: The Creativity of Tradition," *Commentary* 13, no. 6 (June 1952): 547.
31 Jenna Weissman Joselit, "Of Manners, Morals, and Orthodox Judaism: Decorum Within the Orthodox Synagogue," in *Ramaz: School, Community, Scholarship and Orthodoxy*, ed. Jeffrey S. Gurock (Hoboken, NJ: Ktav Publishing House, 1989), 28.

of this work, as it is the most descriptive of the dilemmas that will be discussed and because it is most commonly used and recognized. The combination of words conveys the potential tension between the will to maintain Jewish integrity and the will to play a full part in the world. "Modern" and "Orthodox" seem to be a contradiction in terms, because Orthodox bespeaks traditional values and therefore not modernity.

The Modern Orthodox Jew has been pulled in two directions: the direction of the secular world and the direction of the religious world. Opposing sides, the religious and the modern, were both critical of Modern Orthodoxy: one side felt that it was not religious enough, the other side that it was not modern enough. Rabbi Jung reported: "…As we proceed to the right, we will be told that Torah-true Judaism is dead, and on the left that it is not fit for modern life…"[32] The word "modern" evokes negative reactions for traditionalists, as modernity negates the traditional worldview; the absolute status of religious norms and values are challenged. The concept of divine revelation of Torah and Oral Torah, which is to be accepted without debate, without empirical proof, can be a problem for "moderns," who are also Orthodox.

Orthodoxy contains many groups that are far removed from one another. However, there are two broad groups in Orthodoxy, Modern Orthodox and Ultra-Orthodox, which include the Yeshiva Orthodox and Hasidic groups.[33] The Ultra-Orthodox, also referred to as Haredi, reject any change to Judaism on the grounds that all new things are forbidden by Torah law. They believe that secular learning is a waste of time and dangerous, as secular ideas are incompatible with Jewish beliefs. For these groups, individual autonomy is denied and decisions rest with the religious leaders. Ultra-Orthodoxy emphasizes the glorious past and its own leaders' interpretation of Torah. Within the Orthodox movement in America, Modern Orthodoxy prevails,

---

32　Leo Jung, "Jew and Jewishness in America," *Jewish Forum* 9, no. 3 (May 1926): 132.
33　Samuel Heilman, "The Many Faces of Orthodoxy, Part I," *Modern Judaism* 2, no. 1 (February 1982): 26. Heilman identified two trends in Orthodoxy, Modern Orthodoxy and traditional Orthodoxy, though he is not the first or only one to do so.

although the Ultra-Orthodox—newer on the scene—are increasing in numbers.

Modern Orthodoxy has core beliefs that distinguish it from Orthodoxy generally. The goal of Modern Orthodoxy is to harmonize the secular and religious aspects of life in ways that are compatible to both. The Ultra-Orthodox group seeks to exclude modernity. At one end of the spectrum is the insistence on the meticulous and punctilious observance of the commandments in the context of separate and segregated communities. Unlike Modern Orthodoxy, the Ultra-Orthodox usually avoid cooperating with other Jews. For these Jews, there is conflict between commitment to Torah and full participation in the scientific and cultural activities of modern society. Most traditionalists believe in the self-sufficiency of the Torah, written and oral, and the observance of *halakhah*, or Jewish law.

Historically, there have always been some Jewish scholars opposed to the comingling of sacred and secular learning. The lines of the division between groups are not so simply marked, as there are degrees, in each group, as to how much modernity is accepted or rejected, and as to how much coexistence or synthesis there should be between the secular and the sacred.

In America, the traditionalist "right" coalesced organizationally in 1902 and was originally represented by the Agudath Harabbonim (Union of Orthodox Rabbis of the United States and Canada). It spoke mostly for first-generation European rabbis, who found it harder to acclimate to the American environment. The Agudath Harabbonim tried to curb the influence and growing power of the American Orthodox rabbinate. The Agudath Harabbonim felt that American Modern Orthodox rabbis were not up to the required standards of Judaic knowledge that they themselves had acquired.[34] Modern Orthodox Judaism is very much worldly, with its validity determined by its personal and social significance in the here and now, but conversely with the premise that all the Torah law is God's revealed will. Rabbi Jung thus addressed real and rational issues such as honesty in business,

---

34 Jonathan D. Sarna, *American Judaism* (New Haven and London: Yale University Press, 2004), 191-193.

ritual food, sexual purity, industrial fairness, and commercial integrity.[35] He said that Judaism even promised prosperity.[36] There is a respect for human reason along with the acknowledgment of faith. There is acknowledgment of personal autonomy, human responsibility, and activity rather than passive submission and fatalistic resignation. Rabbi Jung thus presented Modern Orthodoxy as a religion of reason, and he denied that it conflicted with the findings of science.[37] He wrote that superstition was opposed to the meaning of Judaism.[38] One had to take every advantage of science and the ingenuity of the human mind.

Openness to new interpretations is one of the things that separate Modern Orthodoxy from other groups within Orthodoxy. Rabbi Jung's message was that "on every occasion we must contribute our own endeavour first and only after we have done all in our power to get well, should we beseech God to aid our work."[39] Rabbi Jung wrote: "Human history is the plan of God for the perfection of man by his own free will."[40] He also said: "When practice is not undermined, interpretation is a religious duty."[41] No interpretation is definitive, and as he said, any worthwhile interpretations that shed new light on the scriptures are "welcomed by modern rabbis as long as they are based on the unchanging foundation of Jewish life—the belief in *Torah min ha-Shamayim*, or the divinely revealed Torah."[42] This helps to keep the Torah "a Book of Life" relevant to all ages, young and dynamic.[43]

A key issue in Modern Orthodoxy is the belief that Jewish studies can exist harmoniously with secular studies. This facilitated the possibility of integrating Jews into secular society. For many Orthodox Jews,

---

35 Leo Jung, *Towards Sinai: Sermons and Addresses* (New York: Pardes Publishing House, 1929), 27.
36 Ibid., 218.
37 Ibid., 23.
38 Yeshiva University Archives, Jung Collection, Box 1, Folder 1—letter to Albert Einstein, April 15, 1943, in German.
39 Leo Jung, "Judaism and Health," *Jewish Forum* 7, no. 5 (May 1924): 304.
40 Leo Jung, *Foundations of Judaism*, Jewish Library, First Series, vol. 1 (New York: The Jewish Center, 1923), 40.
41 Leo Jung, *The Path of a Pioneer*, xvi-xvii.
42 Yeshiva University Archives, Jung Collection, Box 41, Folder 4—letter from Leo Jung to Isaac Rosengarten (editor of the *Jewish Forum*), March 16, 1937.
43 Ibid., Box 1/4—a letter to Albert Einstein, April 15, 1943, in German.

Rabbi Dr. Leo Jung as a young man. Courtesy of Anne Etra, granddaughter of Rabbi Jung

there is no attempt to integrate secular and religious studies; for others, the challenge is to integrate the two in a creative, fruitful way.

Rabbi Jung was sensitive to modernity and aware of his mission, which was to show that Orthodoxy could hold its own in the modern world.

Some Biographical Details

The following is not intended to be a complete biography of Rabbi Leo Jung. The social, communal, and intellectual aspects of his life from the 1920s to the 1960s are discussed as the book progresses.[44]

Rabbi Jung was born on June 20, 1892 in Ungarish-Brod in Moravia, then part of the Austro-Hungarian Empire, and died in 1987 at the age of ninety-five, in New York.

---

44 For a more complete biographical sketch, see Marc Raphael, "Rabbi Leo Jung and the Americanization of Orthodox Judaism," and Monty Noam Penkower, "From Catastrophe to Restoration: The Response of Leo Jung," in Jacob J. Schacter, ed., *Reverence, Righteousness and Rachmanut: Essays in Memory of Rabbi Dr. Leo Jung* (Northvale, NJ and London: Jason Aronson Inc., 1992); see also Jung, *The Path of a Pioneer.*

He received a secular and Talmudic education. Cambridge was his alma mater; he received his doctorate from the University of London.[45] In 1910, he attended the *yeshiva* of Eperies, Hungary (present-day Prešov, Slovakia). In 1911, he went to study in Galanta, Hungary (now also in Slovakia). He also attended the Hildesheimer Rabbinical Seminary in Berlin, the prized enterprise of Rabbi Hildesheimer, which was the first Modern Orthodox rabbinical seminary. Rabbi Jung claimed that he received three rabbinic ordinations—from Rabbi Mordechai Tzevi Schwartz, Rav (Rabbi) Avraham Yitzhak Hakohen Kook, and Rabbi David Tzevi Hoffman of Berlin.[46] He regarded his *semikhah*, or rabbinic ordination, from Rabbi Hoffman as "his last and most cherished *semikhah*."[47] These luminary figures were Rabbi Jung's mentors, along with Rabbis S. R. Hirsch and Hildesheimer, all regarded by historians as founders and leaders in the Modern Orthodox movement. Their writings and philosophy served as Rabbi Jung's examples, and he helped spread their influence in America.

Certain attitudes and perspectives emerged from the works of Rav Kook that influenced Rabbi Jung and Modern Orthodoxy. Rav Kook became the first Chief Rabbi of Palestine, and had worked together in London with Rabbi Jung's father, Rabbi Meir Tzevi Jung.[48] Rav Kook's religious philosophy was one of tolerance; he extended a hand of friendship to all, including his ideological adversaries. Rav Kook's writings are a guide pointing the way toward a synthesis between Orthodox tradition and secular values, though he comes from Eastern Europe, where Modern Orthodoxy did not develop until later.

---

45 Milton R. Konvitz, "Leo Jung—Rabbi For All Jews," *Midstream* 39, no. 6 (August/September 1993): 38.

46 Schacter, "Rabbi Dr. Leo Jung: Reflections on the Centennial of His Birth," *Jewish Action* 53, no. 2 (Winter 1992–1993): 22; Yeshiva University Archives, Public Relations (PR) File, Leo Jung, 1985–1988; Konvitz, "Leo Jung—Rabbi For All Jews," 38.

47 Jung, Preface, *Guardians of our Heritage*.

48 Yeshiva University Archives, Jung Collection, Box 1, Folder 1—notice of a rabbi's conference in conjunction with Kenethiyoth Hayiroelis (that is the spelling on the stationery—Kenethiyoth Hayiroelis). The president was Rav Kook, and the vice-president was Rabbi Dr. Meir Jung, the Chief Minister of the Federation of Synagogues of London.

Rabbi Hoffman, a native of Hungary (and Germany's leading *halakhic* authority in the early twentieth century), was Rabbi Jung's "guiding light at the Hildesheimer Seminary in Berlin before the First World War."[49] Rabbi Hoffman studied at the Hildesheimer Yeshiva in Eisenstadt and was exposed there to a combination of Torah and secular learning. He wrote his doctoral thesis at the University of Tuebingen, one of Germany's oldest and most famous universities. Rabbi Hoffman also studied with Abraham Sofer, son of Rabbi Moses Sofer, known by his main work, the *Ketav Sofer*. Rabbi Hoffman was in a position to evaluate different Orthodox points of view. His choice was Modern Orthodoxy; Rabbi Hoffman became a major figure in that wing of Orthodoxy.[50] When Rabbi Hildesheimer established an Orthodox rabbinical seminary in Berlin, Rabbi Hoffman joined the faculty and became the rector in 1899, the year that Rabbi Hildesheimer died, serving until his own death in 1921.

In London, Rabbi Jung was able to earn his reputation as a wonderful English-speaking orator. He was sought after to fill an American pulpit in Cleveland, where he arrived in January 1920. At this time, American Jews were still going to Europe to look for their rabbis. In Cleveland, he was an "utterly novel phenomenon, the first English-speaking Orthodox rabbi, bearded and a Ph.D."[51] After serving in Cleveland, at the Knesset Israel Congregation for two and a half years, he was asked, in 1922, to be the rabbi at the prestigious Jewish Center Synagogue in New York, where he went with Irma Rothchild, his bride of six months.

A Look at Orthodoxy in America Through the Eyes of Rabbi Jung

This is the story of how a religious group adjusted to the challenges of modernity and a new environment in a country very young in tradition. Rabbi Leo Jung gave an account of what Orthodoxy in America was

---

49 Letter from Rosalie Rosenfeld (Jung's daughter) to Maxine Jacobson, October 29, 1997, in the possession of Maxine Jacobson.
50 Heilman, "The Many Faces Of Orthodoxy, Part I," 44 and 46.
51 Jung, *The Path of a Pioneer*, 47.

Rabbi Jung with his wife, Irma and three of his four daughters Erna, Rosalie, Julie. Fourth daughter, Marcella was not yet born. Early 1930's. Courtesy of Anne Etra, granddaughter of Rabbi Jung

like when he started out as a young rabbi, and of what his goals and plans were to facilitate the adjustment. He wrote:

> I wish to transplant Judaism from the marshy grounds of eastern Europe into the new American mentality, recreating a new unity, a view of life forged out of the two poles—of Jewish ideals and modern method, of Hebrew enthusiasm and Gentile accomplishment, of Torah and *derekh eretz*.[52]

Rabbi Jung sang the praises of America, but at the same time, he talked about the challenges and dangers that the new land presented. America was a land of freedom of religion. The commitment to freedom of religion made Americans sympathetic to those escaping persecution; in return, the Jews were very appreciative of American liberties. Rabbi Jung wrote that it was "a story of Jewish readjustment in a country as young in tradition as the U.S.A. ... in flight from tyranny of a

---

52 Jung's address, 1926 Convention, Union of Orthodox Jewish Congregations of America.

continent of old patterns, both of individual grace and of communal evil."⁵³ As immigrants changed their geographical location, they tore themselves away from an established order of living where they had spiritual and cultural roots.

Jews had lived in lands where they had been mistreated and where they had no opportunity to advance economically, socially, and intellectually. They came to America because they treasured what America stood for and for what they could achieve there. Rabbi Jung expressed the views of many immigrant Jews who felt that America constituted potentially another promised land. He wrote:

> What is America but man's second opportunity, the second chance for culture? What is America but another effort of God's to let man find himself free from the ballast of past wrongs, free for the glory of self-worked salvation.⁵⁴

America, the nation-state, was the product and agent of the process of modernity, which stood for democracy, equality, justice, and progress. For Rabbi Jung, American democracy and the basic ideals of Judaism coalesced. In America, religion was considered a good thing and America stood for cultural pluralism.

Rabbi Jung reminded his congregants that the welfare and ways of the country were binding when they did not interfere with religious principles.⁵⁵ He hoped that the Modern Orthodox could contribute to the American scene.

There was freedom of religion but also freedom from religion. There was freedom to choose, and religious leaders had to win over adherents through intellectual, emotional, and practical appeal. One had the right to arrive at one's own religious belief independently and to practice—or not practice—religion as one felt to be correct. Jews were

---

53 Yeshiva University Archives, Jung Collection, Box 21, Folder 11—Jung, excerpt from sermon, second day of the Jewish New Year (year unknown).
54 Jung, *Foundations of Judaism*, 99.
55 Jung, "Orthodox Judaism," in *Variations of American Religion*, ed. Charles Samuel Braden (Chicago and New York: Willet, Clark and Co., 1936), 242.

not answerable to communal bodies capable of punishing deviant behavior; traditional structures of authority were absent.[56]

Orthodoxy in America had to confront a new environment, which was "modern," materialistic, and secular in nature. Though America was the Promised Land, Rabbi Jung feared that there was a loss of Jewish feeling and devotion on the part of many Jews. Many did not wish to maintain their religious way of life.[57] Some had come to America seeking change, wanting to throw off what they saw as the yoke of their old lifestyle. There was an eagerness to Americanize and to part with customs that were identified as different. For these Jews, America was everything to them and the Jewish past was little.

Jewish education and observance were swept away as the value of material achievement was ranked higher or was seen as a necessity.[58] Many of those who wished to maintain their Jewish traditions and observe the Sabbath were forced to work long hours (often in sweat shops) on the Sabbath and on Sundays. When they were better settled, it was hard to return to religious ways.[59] Many Orthodox among the working class neglected Jewish learning, violated dietary laws, broke the Sabbath, and deserted the synagogue. After work, they sought intellectual advancement. The demands of Torah scholarship were neglected in deference to the demands of secular education. Rabbi Jung wrote:

> When I arrived in New York, I discovered that Judaism (I prefer that term for the classic faith of our people in preference to Orthodoxy, which is a Christian term, or even to Torah-true, a term which I introduced in the United States of

---

56 Tony Michels, *A Fire in Their Hearts: Yiddish Socialists in New York* (Cambridge, MA and London: Harvard University Press, 2005), 12.
57 Samuel Heilman, "The Many Faces of Orthodoxy, Part II," *Modern Judaism* 2, no. 2 (May 1982): 186; Michels, *A Fire in Their Hearts*, 12–16 (identifies the particular problem of the Orthodox); Philip Davis, "'Jewish Working People...Have Lost All Interest in the Synagogue' (1905)," in *Jewish Radicals*, ed. Tony Michels (New York and London: New York University Press, 2012), 168–173; Henry Periera Mendes, "Orthodox Judaism," *Jewish Forum* 3, no. 1 (January 1920): 33; Sarna, *American Judaism*, 161; Michels, *A Fire in Their Hearts*, 17.
58 Sarna, *American Judaism*, 158–159 and 162.
59 Michels, *Jewish Radicals*, 169–170.

America) was generally unknown in theory and too often seen in deplorable practice, a combination of Eastern European culinary habits, considerable superstition, and disorganized, unharmonious, often unintelligent presentation. There was an almost complete lack of available information about the Jewish solution of modern problems.[60]

Status and adjustment in America were associated with the amount of Americanization and the amount of financial gain. For many, the "American dream" was attaining wealth. Americans were seemingly not worried about their souls.[61] Rabbi Jung wrote that there was a "continual looking for… gold."[62] There was rampant disloyalty to Jewish tradition, not because of modern science, according to Rabbi Jung, but because of pleasure seeking.

> No more was God the theme, but, man; no more perfection, but, enjoyment the aim of life. No more fidelity to the ideal, but to the use of our opportunities. No more duty but right. Drink to the full the cup of pleasures, did this new life tell him. Drink and enjoy yourself; tomorrow you may be no more. The hereafter is no concern of yours.[63]

Dedication to material values deadened the capacity for religious experience. Rabbi Jung lamented: "Why indeed does this country save the man and destroy the Jew?"[64] He wrote: "What boots it that we gain all the world if we lose our children; what if our children gain all the world, if they lose themselves?"[65]

Both Jews and non-Jews saw Orthodoxy as a product of Eastern Europe, un-American, and alien.[66] America was not friendly to the

---

60 Jung, *The Path of a Pioneer*, 126.
61 Leo Jung, *Foundations of Judaism* (New York: The Night and Day Press, 1927), 14.
62 Jung, *Toward Sinai*, 178.
63 Jung, *Foundations of Judaism* (1927), 46.
64 Ibid., 80.
65 Ibid., 81.
66 Jung, *The Path of a Pioneer*, 105.

concept of "Orthodoxy." In America, Orthodox Judaism was associated with the "grotesque panorama of unsightly mass habitation."[67] Orthodoxy was not felt to be "modern," and it was seen as medieval; it was designated as out of date. Orthodox Judaism was associated with the past, with old ways. It was associated with the immigrant experience, and it was felt that it would appeal only to the old, the poor, and the unacculturated.[68] Orthodoxy thus had to be presented in a different way, in keeping with the times. It is American conditions that developed the anomaly of the "Orthodox Jew," who neither observed the Sabbath nor followed the dietary laws or any other commandments. Rabbi Jung wrote:

> In this country one may be Orthodox although the Sabbath has departed from one's life and *trefa* (unkosher) food is one's daily fare, the use of this term to designate the law observing Jew, is at least very curious.[69]

Judaism in this context did not seem to have much to do with observing the *mitzvot* (Jewish laws). The term "Orthodox" in America was applied to many of whom were not Orthodox.

Jews were exposed and opened to new ideas. Some were capitalists, but many were socialists. The Orthodox were troubled by young Jews turning to socialism, since the socialists won over huge numbers (including religious people). There was rivalry between the Orthodox and the socialists.[70] The socialists felt that the synagogue had nothing to offer them, that it had no concern for the cause of labor, and that the language of the synagogue was foreign. To the socialists, the synagogue was dead, sterile, and retrogressive.[71] The Orthodox felt that social values stemmed from Torah values. Rabbi Jung espoused socialist ideals,

---

67 Leo Jung, *Living Judaism* (New York: The Night and Day Press, 1927), 5.
68 Jenna Weissman Joselit, "Modern Orthodox Jews and the Ordeal of Civilization," *American Jewish History* 74 (1984): 133.
69 Leo Jung, "Agudath, Zionism and a Modus Vivendi," *Jewish Forum* 7, no. 11 (November 1924): 715.
70 Michels, *A Fire in Their Hearts*, 15; Michels, *Jewish Radicals*, 168–173.
71 Michels, *Jewish Radicals*, 172–173.

but always as part of the basis of Jewish values. He always maintained that social activism was an outcome of traditional Jewish values, saying:

> Instead of deploring the poverty of the poor, the Torah strives to prevent it. Hence, the commandment to support the falling lest he fall, to lend a helping hand—to show brotherhood...[72]

Orthodox rabbis were sympathetic with socialists but felt it was more important to promote their brand of Judaism. Rabbi Bernard Drachman worried that socialism estranged large numbers of Jewish laborers from Judaism and that their only concern was economic improvement with no interest in Judaism.[73]

America introduced many changes in Jewish life. With these changes, the role and status of the rabbi changed drastically; Orthodox rabbis had lost their dominance.[74] An ongoing problem, as Rabbi Jung pointed out, was how spiritual leaders could be authoritative.[75] No one had to listen to the rabbi; there was certainly no social pressure to do so. Rabbis had no coercive power; they could do little more than beseech. The leaders had to stimulate the will to Jewishness. The message had to be appealing, as there could be no coercion. There was also competition in winning adherents and in effective religious leadership. Religious leadership had to keep these things in mind. Rabbi Jung said: "Be very patient with your flock but fight with grit and determination the destroyer of the faith."[76] According to Rabbi Jung, the rabbi had to give "unfailing direction" and had to "translate the creed of Judaism into Jewish life."[77]

There was conflict between Orthodox rabbis who were educated in America and their colleagues of the European school who rejected

---

72 Jung, *Essentials of Judaism*, 7–8.
73 Bernard Drachman, "Plan For the Organization of a Society for the Promotion of Jewish Religious Life," *Jewish Forum* 3, no. 10 (December 1920): 592.
74 Michels, *A Fire in Their Hearts*, 14.
75 Jung, "Modern Trends in American Judaism" (New York: Mizrachi Jubilee Publication, 1936), 6. Available at the Jewish Center Synagogue Archives.
76 Jung, *Living Judaism*, 132.
77 Ibid., 158.

American and modern ways. Orthodox rabbis struggled to preserve Judaism; however, the two groups differed on how to do this. The two groups are described by Jeffrey Gurock as accommodators and resisters. Gurock pointed out that resisters refused to compromise with American society, while accommodators were willing to modify certain aspects of Judaism without sacrificing fundamentals.[78] Many rabbis who had come from Europe were ill equipped, as the role of congregational rabbi in America differed greatly from that of the rabbi in Europe.

From the shores of America, the role of the Old World rabbi seemed uncomplicated, static, clearly defined, and well respected. He was the head of his community, and a last resort to whom all Talmudic and *halakhic* problems were referred for final decision. The European rabbi's main function was solving questions of Jewish law. The community in which the Old World rabbi lived did not seem to experience drastic changes, although in actuality change was inevitable. The premodern Ashkenazi rabbi was expected to deliver but two sermons a year, before Yom Kippur and Passover. As a rule, the Eastern European rabbi did not even attend synagogue, as he had a *minyan* in his own home. The rabbi spent most of his time in study, and his home was a meeting place for scholars. People arose when he walked into a room and stood until he was seated, a sign of the utmost respect.[79]

In Europe, the community paid the rabbi's salary, and he was thus an employee of any particular synagogue. The European rabbi, according to scholar Kimmy Caplan, earned more in the United States than in Europe but was considered to be underpaid in the United

---

78 Jacob Rader Marcus and Abraham J. Peck, *The American Rabbinate: A Century of Continuity and Change, 1883-1983* (Hoboken, NJ: Ktav Publishing House Inc., 1985); Jeffrey Gurock, "Resisters and Accommodators: Varieties of Orthodox Rabbis in America, 1886-1983," *American Jewish Archives* 35, no. 2 (November 1983); Joshua Bloch, "The Orthodox Rabbinate in America: The Older vs. the Younger," *Jewish Forum* 39, no. 11 (December 1956).

79 Max Drob, "The Rabbis' Role in Jewish Life," *Jewish Forum* 24, no. 6 (June 1941): 132; Yeshiva University Archives, Collection—Hazedek, Box 19, Folder 4—Judah Stampler, "What Is The American Yeshiva?," *Hazedek* 11, no. 1 (April 1945). *Hazedek* is a publication of the Student Organization of Yeshiva University.

States.⁸⁰ In many cases, the Old World rabbi was viewed as an outmoded antique. Often in America, the European rabbis were even scorned.⁸¹ His tenure was also uncertain and in the hands of laymen as judges.⁸² Lower salaries and status resulted in a shortage of rabbis. Rabbis had to supplement their income often by supervising over kosher food, providing other religious services, and—to a lesser extent—selling their published material. This they did in Europe also. Reform rabbis had wealthier congregations, earned more money, and therefore earned more respect.⁸³

The Old World rabbi went to *yeshiva* exclusively to learn; there were no courses in homiletics and practical rabbinics in Europe.⁸⁴ In America, the *yeshiva* took on a duality of function, trying to be a professional training school and a school for the sake of pure study.⁸⁵

The education of the American Orthodox rabbi had to be complex; he had to be equipped to master two spheres, the religious and the secular. The rabbi could be called upon to be chaplain, scholar, educator, theologian, philosopher, preacher, preserver, and interpreter of the law. In America, in the early part of the twentieth century, a main function was speaking and organizing communal life.⁸⁶ The American rabbi had to be a preacher, giving weekly sermons and lectures at many other functions. The better he was at preaching, the higher was his social status. He had to be a social director, and he had to raise funds, bury the dead, and visit the sick. The American rabbi also was a public relations person vis-à-vis the gentile public.⁸⁷ He had to battle for observance of the laws, which were either under attack or else not known.

---

80 Kimmy Caplan, "In God We Trust: Salaries and Income of American Orthodox Rabbis, 1881–1924," *American Jewish History* 86, no. 1 (March 1998).
81 Moses Weinberger, *People Walk on Their Heads: Jews and Judaism in New York*, trans. Jonathan D. Sarna (New York: Holmes & Meier Publishers, 1982), 59.
82 Weinberger, *People Walk on Their Heads*, 42–43.
83 Caplan, "In God We Trust: Salaries and Income of American Orthodox Rabbis, 1881–1924."
84 Michels, *Jewish Radicals*, 169–170.
85 Drob, "The Rabbis' Role in Jewish Life," 91–92.
86 Caplan, "In God We Trust: Salaries and Income of American Orthodox Rabbis, 1881–1924."
87 Arnold Eisen, *The Chosen People in America* (Bloomington, IN: Indiana University Press, 1983), 9.

America was a land where respect for Torah scholarship was lost, and emphasis in Modern Orthodox circles was on the rabbi being a good English speaker. Rabbi Jung was articulate, English-speaking, secularly and religiously educated, and proficient in Talmud and Kant—a new and respected phenomenon in the American Orthodox milieu. He was knowledgeable in the ways of the secular world and the ways of America. Rabbi Jung's presentation of American Orthodox Judaism demonstrated that it was relevant and compatible with America and modernity. His Torah education, secular education, social skills, and mastery of speaking made him able to compete with Conservative and Reform rabbis and to influence Jews in America. Rabbi Jung was thus able to appeal to the large group of Jews who rejected European-style Orthodoxy, who were more interested in what America stood for than in Jewish learning, but who still preferred to call themselves "Orthodox."

The interaction of Modern Orthodox Jews and their American environment had an effect on the type of Judaism they practiced. Rabbi Jung pointed out that social conduct had always changed in new conditions, and that there had always been new explanations, derived from the experience of each generation.[88] An accord between Torah and daily life had to be constantly created in times of changes in social conditions.

Orthodoxy, in particular, had to adjust to America; in the process of doing so, it continued to change. Modern Orthodoxy in general had to develop ways to survive and thrive, and to develop and affirm what it stood for. The Orthodoxy of the Eastern European *shtetl* could not be transplanted intact.

Rabbi Jung felt that the best way Jews could contribute to the glorious new country was by being true to their own rich heritage and religion; "the Jew must be a Jew to be American."[89] He wrote:

> We shall not have done our full duty to America unless we have contributed our real selves, unadulterated Jewishness. We have our message for this country, but the message must

---

88 Jung, "Modern Trends in American Judaism," 2.
89 Jung, *Foundations of Judaism*, 101.

come from the fullness of Jewish life. From the colorless abode of assimilation it has no meaning.[90]

He reiterated this message many times through the years: "To the Jew this new America says [that] your greatest contribution to the concert of nations is your religion."[91] Rabbi Drachman concurred that the ideal American Jew was one who was a complete Jew and a thorough genuine American.[92]

The Modern Orthodox approach was that changes had to be made that were both acceptable to Orthodoxy and to American culture. The challenge in America for Rabbi Jung was finding teachers who would transplant Judaism from the marshy grounds of Eastern Europe into the new American mentality, who—with love and foresight—would prepare young souls for the teaching of Torah, and who would systematically sow the seeds of harmonization. They would recreate, in a new unity, a view of life forged out of the two poles of Occidentalism and Orientalism, of Jewish ideals and modern method, of Hebrew enthusiasm and gentile accomplishment, and of Torah and *derekh eretz*.[93]

Rabbi Jung's Jewish Center Synagogue in New York represented something new, with its varied educational, cultural, and social activities. New York was, and still is, the heart of American Jewry and the pulse of its Jewish life; Rabbi Jung was thus in a position to influence all American Jews.

He worked at making Orthodoxy appealing to the American psyche or consciousness, developing an Orthodoxy that would be acceptable to Jews "outside the ghetto." For Rabbi Jung, "Orthodox Judaism…is part of the cosmopolitan society and modern culture."[94]

---

90 Ibid., 100.
91 Yeshiva University Archives, Jung Collection, Box 23, Folder 2—Jung, "The Modern Program for 5701 (1941)."
92 Bernard Drachman, "Jewish Educational Problem in America," *Jewish Forum* 3, no. 9 (November 1920): 515.
93 Yeshiva University Archives, Jung Collection, Box 23, Folder 2—Jung, "The Modern Program for 5701 (1941)," *B'nai Brith Messenger* combined with *Jewish Community Press* (September 1940), 92.
94 Leo Jung, "What is Orthodox Judaism?" in *Essentials of Judaism*, ed. Leo Jung, Jewish Library, vol. 2 (New York: Union of Jewish Congregations of America, 1953), 115.

Rabbi Jung was one of the spokesmen for an American-style Orthodoxy; he combined the religious faith of Orthodoxy with the American way of life. He served as a bridge between the old Eastern European Orthodoxy that did not develop in America beyond the immigrant generation and the Modern Orthodoxy of today.

Why Read This Book?

This book has relevance for further studies in several areas. It is part of the study of religious acculturation, of the interaction of religion with the different social systems, of the conflict between tradition and modernity, and of religious reinvigoration in a secular society.

America prides itself on being an amalgam of various immigrant groups. This is the story of adaptation of one particular group in America and of its accommodation with contemporary society and changing times. Having lost their moorings, the Modern Orthodox looked for a definition of who they were and what they stood for in the land of democracy and freedom of religion. In terms of communal problems, it would be interesting to compare and contrast this group's experience with other groups. This is an immigrant story and an integral part of the history of United States.[95]

A religious system does not exist in a vacuum; it interacts with other social systems. The time period covered depicts an era of change, of new vitality, and of self-confidence and maturity in Modern Orthodoxy. This parallels the change, new vitality, and maturity in the political, social, and economic history of the United States itself. Modern Orthodoxy responded to the cultural, economic, and political challenges presented in America.

The social values of America affected its religious outlook. The 1920s, with its heightened value of material things, had led to a mounting

---

95 Elliot Robert Barkan, ed., *Immigrants in American History: Arrival, Adaptation and Integration* (Santa Barbara, CA: ABC-CLIO, 2013); Richard Alba, Albert J. Raboteau, and Josh DeWind, eds., *Immigration and Religion in America: Comparative and Historical Perspectives* (New York and London: New York University Press, 2009); William A. Scott (with collaboration from John Stumpf), *Adaptation of Immigrants: Individual Differences and Determinants* (Oxford, UK and New York: Pergamon Press, 1989).

permissiveness in society and had set the moral and social tone of the nation, which made for a poor religious milieu. Rabbi Jung and other leaders stressed morality and ethics instead of emphasizing the law, and tried with little success to present the spiritual benefits of Orthodoxy. The economic depression of the 1930s made Modern Orthodoxy focus on the social issues and social justice that were part of the religious tenets of Judaism, and it increased Orthodoxy's need for outreach. The economic recovery, after World War II, accompanied a sense of renewal and revival, which also affected Orthodoxy's religious outlook.

This book is also a study of religious responses to the Holocaust. The Holocaust is an example of modernity at its worst. It is an example of how the abusive Nazi regime led Jews to react with a call for stronger religious leadership and involvement, a call to which Modern Orthodoxy, among other movements, responded. It was clear that assimilation and accommodation had not saved Jewish lives; it was clear that the values of the Enlightenment had been ignored.

Modern Orthodoxy can be included as part of the study of the rightward drift in religion and its implications. A movement to the right can be a sign of rejecting the establishment. When Jews first came to America there was, for the most part, wholehearted acceptance of the status quo of America, making religious adherence a dilemma. By the late 1930s and 1940s, Rabbi Jung (a religio-political activist), as well as other Modern Orthodox leaders, drew attention to the flaws of modernity and of Enlightenment values, and he tried to improve society and reshape American life. The movement to the right is part of the quest for good values. The growth of the right reflects developments in other faiths as well, such as Christianity and Islam.[96] Modern Orthodoxy can be included in the study of those who return to a religious life in the various faiths, called "born agains" or "returnees," or in Hebrew, *ba'alei teshuvah*.

---

96 David Zeidan, *The Resurgence of Religion: A Comparative Study of Selected Themes in Christian and Islamic Fundamentalist Discoveries* (Leiden, The Netherlands and Boston: Brill, 2003); Richard T. Antoun and Mary Elaine Hegland, eds., *Religious Resurgence: Contemporary Cases in Islam, Christianity and Judaism* (Syracuse, NY: Syracuse University Press, 1987).

The "right" has had political spin-offs. Political issues affect religious outlooks, but the reverse is also true. With the reassertion of religious values, there is a decline in the liberal establishment and a trend to more conservatism. The "right wing" has concerned itself with issues such as abortion, homosexuality, and the role of women and family. It embraces issues of religious significance such as store openings on Saturdays or Sundays. Religious variables are important in understanding political behavior. This thesis could lend information to such a study.[97]

The movement to the right, as mentioned, serves as a lens to focus on the conflict of modernity and tradition. While modernity is flawed, most groups are not reactionary and they do appreciate Enlightenment thinking. This study of Modern Orthodoxy presents the dilemmas, conflicts, and choices that have been made in the ongoing quest to coordinate or synthesize modernity and tradition.

---

97 Anita Shapira, Yedidia Z. Stern, and Alexander Yakobson, eds., *The Nation State and Religion: The Resurgence of Faith* (Sussex, UK: Academic Press, 2013); Gilles Kepel, *The Revenge of God: The Resurgence of Islam, Christianity and Judaism in the Modern World*, trans. Alan Braley (Cambridge, UK: Polity Press, 1994); E. J. Dionne, *Souled Out: Reclaiming Faith and Politics After the Religious Right* (Princeton, NJ: Princeton University Press, 2008).

1. MODERN ORTHODOXY IN THE 1920S

...

"What are the roots that clutch, what branches grow out of this stony rubbish?"
(T.S. Eliot, *The Wasteland*)

Introduction

American Modern Orthodoxy began in this decade with the development of its landmark organizations and institutions so that the proper facilities necessary for an Orthodox community would exist. The 1920s was a period of responding to outside criticism, diagnosing the problems, and developing solutions. The new leaders articulated an effective response to the criticisms of the movement, and thereby began to define Modern Orthodoxy. Successes were few; new institutions and new leaders represented only the beginning of the work. Rabbi Jung was involved in building the groundwork; the 1920s, to quote him, was an "uphill road."[1] Modern Orthodoxy was adjusting to the modern American scene.

In the 1920s, Rabbi Jung joined the battle to revive and promote Orthodox Judaism. He began his involvement with his synagogue (the Jewish Center) and with Yeshiva College. Rabbi Jung became active, through his organizational work, in ensuring proper kosher facilities, rights for Sabbath observers, updated educational programs and facilities, and support for *Eretz Israel* (the Land of Israel). His first challenges were to ensure proper facilities for Sabbath observance, basic *kashrut*, and family law.

---

1 Leo Jung, "Modern Trends in American Judaism" (New York: Mizrachi Jubilee Publication, 1936), 5. Available at the Jewish Center Synagogue Archives.

He presented a platform of Torah-true Judaism. In his view, "Orthodoxy was the only legitimate form of Judaism," and those who were not Orthodox were dissenters and misguided. It was their lack of knowledge that led to this dissension, to attraction to the newest fads, one of which was Reform.[2] By the 1920s, Reform was far from being a fad, but this was Rabbi Jung's description.

Always sensitive to American needs and determined to preserve Torah-true Judaism, Rabbi Jung presented Orthodoxy as compatible with modernity and with America. The presentation, not the tenets, of Orthodoxy had to change from the spectacle of disorder associated with the ghetto-style Eastern European service to an aesthetic Americanized modern presentation. He worked to enhance Orthodoxy's image through decorous synagogue service and through a "modern," "harmonious" education that would teach, inspire, and reclaim Jews.

The State of Orthodoxy

American Orthodoxy in the 1920s was undefined. It appeared unlikely to many observers that Orthodox Judaism would remain an important factor on the American scene.[3] By force of numbers, Orthodox Judaism was important; its staying power was nonetheless in question. By the 1920s, Eastern European Jews had been in America long enough to begin to assimilate; as they Americanized, European Orthodoxy (transplanted from Europe) lost its hold since respect for religion weakened.[4]

Though prospects for Orthodoxy's future in America were grim, Rabbi Jung remained optimistic that the future would rest with Torah-true Jews, saying:

Orthodoxy was in "winter's laboratory" in its embryonic stage.
To the one, winter's snowstorms convey enduring decay; to the

---

2   Leo Jung, *Towards Sinai: Sermons and Addresses* (New York: Pardes Publishing House, 1929), 78 and 183.
3   Leo Jung, *Living Judaism* (New York: The Night and Day Press, 1927), 208.
4   Jeffrey S. Gurock, "The Winnowing of American Orthodoxy," in *Approaches to Modern Judaism*, ed. Marc Lee Raphael, vol. 1 (Chico, CA: Scholars Press, 1983), 42–44; Jung, *Living Judaism*, 334; Leo Jung, *Foundations of Judaism*, Jewish Library, First Series, vol. 1 (New York: The Jewish Center, 1923), 45.

other, the most ferocious snowstorm is but the forerunner of spring. The one sees the disintegration of a nation in the coldness of its members, in the indifference to the holiest ideals of their people; the other views such periods from a perspective which reveals bright vistas of revived energies, of reawakened love, of a nation again aware of its soul, again alive to its historic past.[5]

He felt that Jews had a future in America; he wrote:

It hasn't even begun to appear in its clear light. American Jewry has never rejected Orthodox Judaism for American Jewry has never seen what Orthodox Judaism is.[6]

The common complaints of Orthodox leaders were that there were few knowledgeable, inspiring Orthodox leaders, and they lacked proper educational facilities to produce more Orthodox leaders in America. At this time, there were no big centers of Jewish learning in America, though there had been a shift in Jewish settlement. New immigration laws halted immigration after World War I with great effect on education, as religious and intellectual leaders were not able to come to America.[7]

Jewish education was in a shambles; the system needed to be Americanized. Mordecai Kaplan's study of Jewish educational conditions in New York in 1909 showed distressing results. When Isaac Rosengarten—associate editor of the *Jewish Forum*, the first Orthodox journal to be written in English—gave an account of Jewish education, it did not vary from Kaplan's findings.[8] There was no harmony or coordination between secular and religious teaching; the Hebrew schools

---

5   Jung, *Towards Sinai*, 104.
6   Leo Jung, "Jew and Jewishness in America," *Jewish Forum* 9, no. 3 (May 1926): 133.
7   Harris L. Selig, "What Will The Yeshiva Do?," *Jewish Tribune* (March 1926): 46.
8   Isaac Rosengarten, "Order Out of Chaos in Jewish Education," *Jewish Forum* 3, no. 9 (November 1920); Jonathan B. Krasner, *The Benderly Boys and American Jewish Education* (Waltham, MA: Brandeis University Press, 2011), 41, 55, and 75; Meyer Berlin, "Jewish Education in America," *Jewish Forum* 3, no. 9 (November 1920).

were "dusty, malodorous, and utterly unattractive" and were not up to the standards of public schools.[9] Their teachers, inadequately trained, were pedagogically generally inferior to those in public schools.[10] Facilities, materials, equipment, and methods were inadequate, attendance was spotty, and attrition rates were high.[11] Hebrew teachers often were uncommitted to what they taught; teachers in sympathy with the teachings of Judaism and the culture of America were required.

The question of Jewish education included the problem of adjustment, harmonization, and Americanization.[12] Educational materials from Europe had to be adapted to the American scene; as well, new material had to be worked on.[13] If Yiddish was the language of instruction, then the students could not understand the teachers; thus, the teachers were out of touch with the young people. That fact, in addition to outdated and incompetent teaching methods, meant that the youth were not learning what was being taught. Rabbi Meyer Berlin, president of Mizrachi of America, bemoaned the fact that, with the exception of New York, there were few parochial schools anywhere.[14]

Lack of Jewish knowledge and educational facilities as well as the difficulty of living an Orthodox life in America resulted in many members of Modern Orthodox synagogues being unobservant. Religious commitment and observances were at a low level and nonobservance of the Sabbath was the norm.[15] According to Rabbi Jung, they were attached sentimentally to Jewish tradition but lacked a clear identity.[16] Choosing between earning a living or observing the Sabbath meant that a tremendous number of Jews, even the ones who

---

9   Jung, *Living Judaism*, 213; Krasner, *The Benderly Boys and American Jewish Education*, 41.
10 Rosengarten, "Order Out of Chaos in Jewish Education," 520; Krasner, *The Benderly Boys and American Jewish Education*, 32.
11 Krasner, *The Benderly Boys and American Jewish Education*, 41.
12 Jenna Weissman Joselit, *New York's Jewish Jews: The Orthodox Community in the Interwar Years* (Bloomington, IN: Indiana University Press, 1990), 6; Bernard Drachman, editorial, *Jewish Forum* 3, no. 9 (November 1920): 515.
13 Krasner, *The Benderly Boys and American Jewish Education*, 33 and 41.
14 Berlin, "Jewish Education in America," 588; Cyrus Adler, "Dr. Solomon Hurwitz," *Jewish Forum* (June 1923): 370.
15 Jung, *Towards Sinai*, 111.
16 Ibid., 244.

desired to observe the Sabbath, succumbed to the temptation of working on the Sabbath.

The congregants of the Jewish Center Synagogue in Manhattan, where Rabbi Jung was the rabbi, were representative of this trend. Affluent suit and cloak manufacturers from Orthodox immigrant families started the synagogue. The congregants had limited religious and secular educations, but retained a respect for Orthodox Judaism. The congregants remained affiliated with an Orthodox synagogue as a reminder of the Jewish traditions of their parents.[17]

Orthodoxy lacked organization, unity, leadership, institutions, and financial support; this added to its decline. Rabbi Jung wrote that Orthodoxy "had a genius for escaping organization."[18] Similarly, the *Jewish Forum* (an American Orthodox monthly journal) lamented that "all parties in Israel have a united front except Orthodoxy."[19] The different factions, including the Vaad Harabanim, the Rabbinical Board of Greater New York, the Union of Orthodox Jewish Congregations of America (UOJCA), and Mizrachi, were not united. Disorganization resulted in powerlessness and replication of services, which in turn led to extra financial burdens. The chaotic *kashrut* situation was an example of this lack of organization. Without kosher facilities, there could not be any Torah-true Jewish community, thus this was a serious problem.

Orthodoxy did have a central lay organization, the UOJCA; however, unlike the Reform and Conservative movements, the Orthodox group had several seminaries and several rabbinic conferences.[20] The UOJCA was not intimately related to Yeshiva College and the Rabbi Isaac Elchanan Theological Seminary (RIETS), as was the case with

---

17 Jeffrey S. Gurock and Jacob J. Schacter, *A Modern Heretic and a Traditional Community: Mordecai M. Kaplan, Orthodoxy, and American Judaism* (New York: Columbia University Press, 2013), 115.
18 Leo Jung, "Of Orthodoxy in America," *American Jewish Chronicle*, volume and issue unknown (1939, month unknown): 6.
19 Editorial, *Jewish Forum* 10, no. 11 (November 1927), 547. For more about the *Jewish Forum*, see the following article: Ira Robinson and Maxine Jacobson, "'When Orthodoxy was not as chic as it is today': The Jewish Forum and American Modern Orthodoxy," *Modern Judaism* 31, no. 3 (October 2011): 285–315.
20 *American Jewish Year Book*, 39 (1937–1938), 70.

the lay-seminary relationship in other movements, because it had several other seminaries to train rabbis.[21] In contrast, the Reform and Conservative movements each had a central organization with representative rabbinical seminaries and rabbinical conferences, with one seminary each to train rabbis.

Orthodoxy's factions were divided, and they did not have experience in much-needed long-range planning for the future of the Jewish community.[22] Its influence was not felt in national movements; Orthodox leadership was relatively absent in Zionism, the Central Relief Committee of the Joint Distribution Committee, and the American Jewish Congress.[23] Major Jewish institutions were not directed by Orthodox Jews, and the institutions were "at best neutral, at worst uncompromisingly hostile to the principles and obligations of Torah-true Judaism."[24] The Orthodox movement also lacked financial support.[25]

Orthodoxy Faces Competition

Orthodoxy had to compete to exist. The historian Jeffrey S. Gurock stated that denominational competition began in earnest in the 1920s, and the rhetoric grew stronger.[26] They sometimes created Conservative synagogues that they felt had adjusted better to American ways.[27] The boards of Orthodox synagogues often had to fight to remain Orthodox, but still, numerous Orthodox community synagogues converted to Conservative in the 1920s and thereafter.[28]

---

21 Ibid., 71.
22 Jacob Katz, "Orthodox Jews from Passivity to Activism," *Commentary* 79, no. 6 (June 1985): 34.
23 Dr. Meyer Waxman, "American Orthodoxy—The Fifth Unknowable," *Jewish Forum* 7, no. 5 (October 1924): 650.
24 Leo Jung, *The Path of a Pioneer: Autobiography of Leo Jung*, Jewish Library, Second Series, vol. 8 (London and New York: Soncino Press, 1980), 70.
25 Bernard Drachman, "Plan for the Organization of a Society for the Promotion of Jewish Religious Life," *Jewish Forum* 3, no. 10 (December 1920): 593.
26 Jeffrey S. Gurock, "The Orthodox Synagogue," in *The American Synagogue: A Sanctuary Transformed*, ed. Jack Wertheimer (Cambridge, UK, and New York: Cambridge University Press, 1987), 60.
27 Personal interview with Dr. Jeffrey S. Gurock, December 17, 1996.
28 Gurock, *American Jewish Orthodoxy in Historical Perspective* (New York: Ktav Publishing House Inc., 1996), 91.

Though competition between Orthodox and Conservative Judaism intensified in the 1920s, Reform Judaism was considered an even greater enemy. Reform Judaism was powerful in the United States, even in the East, Orthodoxy's stronghold. Rabbi Jung's comments regarding Reform were vitriolic, and this was quite representative of the Orthodox rhetoric. Rabbi Jung said that Reformers "have reformed Judaism until there is nothing left."[29] Rabbi Dr. Henry Pereira Mendes, of Congregation Shearith Israel in New York, referred to Reform as a tide of evil that had to be stemmed.[30] Likewise, Rabbi Dr. David de Sola Pool, who succeeded Rabbi Mendes in 1907 at Shearith Israel, also felt that Reform represented "all kinds of dangerous innovations and amputations by irresponsible surgeons, who did not know, nor did they care to know, what is vital to Judaism."[31] The editorial board of the *Jewish Forum* wrote that Orthodox Jewry was responsible for Reform because it was not organized to cope with modernity.[32]

However, though competition was evident between Reform and Orthodoxy, Conservative Judaism was widely perceived to be similar to Orthodoxy. Perhaps that is why it was easy for some to change allegiance. The separation of Conservatism and Orthodoxy was a slow process that began in the 1920s. Initially, Conservative did not denote a movement but a type of "Orthodox" congregation that was more decorous in form and more American in appearance. Early in the twentieth century, congregations that joined the United Synagogue often identified with the Modern Orthodox. Their social agendas were similar and legal disagreements were often more theoretical than practical. At the start, there was an overall desire to have unity, and most Conservatives were unwilling to alienate, within their own ranks, those who identified as Modern Orthodox.[33]

---

29 Jung, *Towards Sinai*, 13.
30 Henry Pereira Mendes, "Orthodox Judaism," *Jewish Forum* 3, no. 1 (January 1920): 33–34.
31 David de Sola Pool, "A Glimpse into The Development of American Judaism," *Jewish Forum* 5, no. 5 (June 1922): 214.
32 Editorial, *Jewish Forum* 12, no. 2 (February 1929).
33 Michael R. Cohen, *The Birth of Conservative Judaism: Solomon Schechter's Disciples and the Creation of an American Religious Movement* (New York: Columbia University Press, 2012), 102.

Dr. Cyrus Adler, president of the Conservative Jewish Theological Seminary (JTS), was adamantly opposed to mixed seating in synagogues, as was Professor Louis Ginzberg, Chairman of Rabbinical Assembly's Committee on Interpretation of Jewish Law.[34] Nonetheless, congregations in the movement overwhelmingly adopted mixed seating. Ginzberg did not want to tamper with Jewish law.[35] Adler believed that the designation Conservative applied to congregations that had departed somewhat in practice from Orthodox, but not in theory.[36] Rabbi Jung referred to Conservatism as "the other kind of Orthodoxy."[37] He maintained that JTS was originally conceived and conducted along the lines of Orthodox Judaism, but had continued along a somewhat different course.[38]

There are many examples of the overlap of Conservative and Orthodox Judaism. Numerous seminary students had a mix of Orthodox and Conservative training. There were some Orthodox teachers at JTS and some JTS graduates who were placed into Orthodox pulpits.[39] Symbolizing this confusion, the faculty and alumni of JTS founded the Orthodox Young Israel movement.[40] Philosophies and goals seemed to

---

34 Samuel Benjamin, "The Cleveland Center Then and Now," *Jewish Forum* 10, no. 12 (December 1927): 611.
35 Cohen, *The Birth of Conservative Judaism*, 65.
36 Herbert Parzen, *Architects of Conservative Judaism* (New York: Jonathan David, 1964), 99.
37 Leo Jung, "Orthodoxy, Reform and Kaplanism," *Jewish Forum* 4, no. 4 (April 1921): 782.
38 Leo Jung, ed., *Harvest, Sermons, Addresses, Studies* (New York: Philip Feldheim Inc., 1956), 229.
39 Benjamin, "The Cleveland Center Then and Now," 611–612; Jeffrey S. Gurock, "Another Look at the Proposed Merger: Lay Perspectives on Yeshiva and Jewish Theological Seminary Relations," in *Hazon Nahum: Studies in Jewish Law, Thought, and History Presented to Dr. Norman Lamm on the Occasion of His Seventieth Birthday*, eds. Norman Lamm and Jeffrey S. Gurock (New York: Ktav Publishing House Inc., 1998), 8–9; Moses Hyamson, "Hyamson's Sabbath and Festival Addresses" (New York: Bloch Publishing Co., 1936). Rabbi Samuel Benjamin, a graduate of JTS, became the rabbi of an Orthodox synagogue in Cleveland. Rabbi Herbert Goldstein, another JTS graduate, shared a pulpit with Rabbi Moses Sebulun Margolies, the Ramaz, a most prominent Orthodox rabbi who held many leadership positions in the Orthodox community. Rabbi Dr. Moses Hyamson, an Orthodox rabbi at the Orthodox synagogue Or Hayyim, taught codes at JTS and told students not to accept pulpits with mixed seating.
40 Gurock, "The Orthodox Synagogue," 56.

be similar.⁴¹ The Conservative vision of a traditional service with English, decorum, and modern education coincided with that of Modern Orthodoxy.⁴²

Rabbi Joseph H. Hertz, later the Orthodox Chief Rabbi of Great Britain and the Commonwealth, graduated in the first class of JTS—in 1894, prior to the Solomon Schechter era, and before the Conservative movement, as such, was created. This is significant because Schechter introduced important changes in philosophy in the seminary. An Orthodox rabbi, Mendes, had been president of JTS before Schechter, and Rabbi Bernard Drachman had been dean of the JTS faculty in the pre-Schechter period. Both later joined the faculty of Yeshiva College and RIETS.⁴³ Schechter fired both Rabbis Mendes and Drachman, claiming it was because of their scholarly ability, or inability, but both Rabbis Mendes and Drachman suspected personal motives. It is likely that Schechter wanted to start with a clean slate and not have major players around from pre-Schechter days. Both Orthodox men went on to contribute to Modern Orthodoxy. The treatment of these two rabbis had implications in the future for the separation of Orthodox and Conservative Judaism.⁴⁴

However, in the 1920s, the Conservative movement was unwilling to alienate those within their own ranks who identified as Modern Orthodox. There was little to distinguish Schechter's disciples from the Modern Orthodox.⁴⁵ Modern Orthodoxy was true to practices, such as English sermons, decorum, and the cause of women, as was the Conservative movement.⁴⁶ These values put Modern Orthodoxy in contention with the rabbis of Agudath Harabbonim.⁴⁷ Clearly, both movements needed defining.

---

41 Jonathan D. Sarna, *American Judaism* (New Haven and London: Yale University Press, 2004), 237-238.
42 Cohen, *The Birth of Conservative Judaism*, 109.
43 Oscar Fasman, "After Fifty Years, an Optimist," *American Jewish History* 69, no. 2 (December 1979): 227.
44 Cohen, *The Birth of Conservative Judaism*, 22.
45 Ibid., 102.
46 Ibid., 22.
47 Ibid., 64.

Issues that Helped Define Modern Orthodoxy

The following stories have been told, but as they are germane to the development of Modern Orthodoxy and because Rabbi Jung was intimately involved in addressing and solving these issues, they bear telling again.

Provocative Beginning to the 1920s—Mordecai Kaplan's Plan to Reconstruct Judaism and Rabbi Jung's Response

The 1920s began with Mordecai Kaplan publicly presenting his program for the reconstruction of Judaism, which appeared in the August 1920 issue of *The Menorah Journal*, followed by Rabbi Jung's rebuttal in the April 1921 issue of the *Jewish Forum*.[48] Kaplan's proposals for the reconstruction of Judaism were a shock to Orthodox Judaism in that they were inconsistent with his previous position as an Orthodox rabbi. He wrote that:

> Orthodoxy is altogether out of keeping with the march of human thought. It has no regard for the world-view of the contemporary mind. Nothing can be more repugnant to the thinking man of today than the fundamental doctrine of Orthodoxy, which is that tradition is infallible.[49]

Kaplan believed that "any religious idea that has come down from the past will have to prove its validity by being a means of social control and betterment."[50] He maintained that belief in a supernatural God would destroy the Jewish people, saying:

> Unless its mythological ideas about God give way to the conception of divinity immanent in the workings of the human

---

48 Mordecai Kaplan, "A Program for the Reconstruction of Judaism," *The Menorah Journal* 1, no. 4 (August 1920), 181–196; Jung, "Orthodoxy, Reform and Kaplanism," 778–783.
49 Kaplan, "A Program for the Reconstruction of Judaism," 182.
50 Ibid., 188.

spirit, unless its static view of authority gives way to the dynamic without succumbing to individual lawlessness and unless it is capable of developing a sense of history without, at the same time, being a slave to the past, the Jewish people has nothing further to contribute to civilization.[51]

Kaplan felt that Judaism had to be revised from a social viewpoint, as follows:

> The adoption of the social viewpoint is an indispensable prerequisite to a thoroughgoing revision of Jewish belief and practice. That viewpoint will enable us to shift the center of spiritual interest from the realm of abstract dogmas and traditional codes of law to the pulsating life of Israel.[52]

Kaplan wrote that to save Judaism from extinction, Jews must recover their group consciousness. He felt that his main ideas—a naturalistic, this-worldly "God idea," and his concept of Jewish peoplehood—were congruent with modern scientific reasoning and with American ideals and culture.

Rabbi Jung took a very hard line against Kaplan, calling his plan "downright *epikorsut* [heresy]."[53] For Rabbi Jung, the existence of God and His divine revelation were irrefutable, therefore Kaplan's theology and denigration of Jewish law was totally unacceptable. Rabbi Jung's article in the *Jewish Forum* in April 1921 had strongly rebuked Kaplan for his plan to reconstruct Judaism and for his critique of Orthodoxy. It had also catapulted him into the role of rabbi of the Jewish Center Synagogue, replacing Kaplan, who had resigned in 1922.[54] Rabbi Jung

---

51 Mel Scult, ed., *Communings of the Spirit: The Journals of Mordecai M. Kaplan, Vol. 1, 1913-1934* (Detroit: Wayne State University Press, and Philadelphia: The Reconstructionist Rabbinical College Press, 2001), 235.
52 Kaplan, "A Program for the Reconstruction of Judaism," 187.
53 Jung, "Orthodoxy, Reform and Kaplanism," 778.
54 Yeshiva University Archives, Jung Collection, Box 1, Folder 2—letter to Jung from Joseph H. Cohen, president of the Jewish Center, Aug. 18, 1922, expressing joy at his election; Scult, ed., *Communings of the Spirit*, 149.

then had the opportunity to be rabbi of a prestigious congregation in the geographical heartland of Modern Orthodoxy, where his ideas had more fertile ground to grow in than when he had been rabbi at Cleveland's Knesset Israel Congregation.[55]

Kaplan's plan to reconstruct Judaism led to an evaluation of what Modern Orthodoxy was because Orthodox rabbis were obliged to take stock and consider fresh methods or approaches that would become characteristic of Modern Orthodoxy.[56] Kaplan thus became a defining issue for Orthodoxy. His ideas had a significant impact on Rabbi Jung, who wrote that a new epoch for Orthodoxy began when the Jewish Center Synagogue "rallied round the flag of Torah to defend it against the pompous folly of its betrayers." The betrayer, of course, was the rabbi of that synagogue, Mordecai Kaplan.[57] It should be noted that Rabbi Jung was not alone in his condemnation of Kaplan; Rabbi Drachman had also called for his resignation from the Jewish Center Synagogue.[58]

Rabbi Jung vehemently rejected Kaplan's nontheistic stance and endorsement of "folkways" or customs of the people as authoritative. Also, Rabbi Jung maintained that Judaism was not merely a national or racial attitude. For Rabbi Jung and for Orthodox Judaism, the religious connection to Palestine was essential. Palestine could not merely be a national center, as Kaplan had proposed; it had to be a center of Torah Judaism. Cultural or national aspects of Zionism were not sufficient. Rabbi Jung wrote:

> Nationalism, with its brutal Torahlessness, is the worst possible kind of assimilation. It reduces God's chosen people in principle to the level of the Eskimos, the Poles, or the Magyars. We are no more a people created by God for His purpose, as a kingdom of priests and a holy nation, but just a

---

[55] Jacob J. Shachter, "Rabbi Dr. Leo Jung: Reflections on the Centennial of His Birth," *Jewish Action* 53, no. 2 (Winter 1992–1993): 20.
[56] Jung, "Orthodoxy, Reform and Kaplanism," 778–783.
[57] Jung, *Living Judaism*, 223.
[58] Drachman, "Reconstructing Judaism?" *Jewish Forum* 4, no. 1 (January 1921): 645.

nation among many, endowed with wonderful capacities. Palestine is no more the land where Torah and *Abodah* are to be given an example to all mankind but the center, where we are to express ourselves by some concoction of Cincinnati plus Shemaryah Levin. Nationalism, in its radical form, is so absurd a phenomenon, so tactless a joke of history, that it was bound to go down as soon as our people would see clearly through its supermodern phraseology.[59]

Rabbi Jung shared Kaplan's worry that "Judaism in America has not given the least sign of being able to perpetuate itself," but he found that Kaplan's solution was destructive.[60] Yet Kaplan had identified something that needed attention in America. For Rabbi Jung, Kaplan's challenge was a call to action; "the only answer to Kaplanism is: The immediate convention of a living Orthodox body to work out a systematic educational scheme for the re-assertion of Orthodoxy, absolutely faithful in principle, absolutely fresh in method."[61] Rabbi Jung considered that "any rebel might make Orthodoxy more aware of their duties." He believed that Kaplan was correct in believing that social changes were needed. For Rabbi Jung, the solution to the problems was Orthodoxy plus decorum and a modern education of "Torah and *Derech Eretz*." Decorum particularly was the key to halting the erosion of Orthodoxy.[62]

When Kaplan left the Jewish Center in 1922 to become the rabbi of the Society for Advancement of Judaism, a block east of the Jewish Center, half of the families in the synagogue left with him. Gurock and Rabbi Jacob J. Schacter maintain that both Kaplan and Rabbi Jung had reason to fear each other's influence ever since the amalgamation of the

---

59 Jung, "Orthodoxy, Reform and Kaplanism"—Shemaryah Levin was a Russian revolutionist and political Zionist; Scult, ed., *Communings of the Spirit*, 235—confirms Kaplan's view regarding Palestine.
60 Mordecai Kaplan, "A Program for the Reconstruction of Judaism," 182.
61 Jung, "Orthodoxy, Reform and Kaplanism,"783.
62 Yeshiva University Archives, Harris L. Selig Administration Files, Box 12, Folders 2-29—press release, 1925-26, "The Discovery of Orthodox Judaism in America," 2-3—interview with Rabbi Jung.

two synagogues was discussed in 1928, and this remained a live issue even later on. This heightened Rabbi Jung's resolve to stop the spread of Kaplanism, for Orthodoxy and for his own sake.[63]

There was an added effect of Kaplanism for the Jewish Center Synagogue and other synagogues.[64] The congregation accepted Rabbi Jung's demand that he have complete authority in matters touching the school and synagogue services and that religious activities would conform to *halakhic* ideals.[65] Kaplan had affiliated the Jewish Center with JTS, and one of the first acts taken by Rabbi Jung was to replace it with affiliation to the RIETS Yeshiva.[66] This avoided any change of the Center's mode of worship. Other Orthodox synagogues followed his example.[67] Rabbi Jung wrote that:

> The fight for Torah in which the Center leadership had earned triumphs and scars, evoked profound interest throughout the country and served as a spark plug for the reassertion of Torah-True Judaism throughout the country. Although the congregation avoided the fanfare of publicity, its insistence on time-hallowed principles, its willingness to ignore every handicap and inconvenience in the process, and the fact that its leaders represented socially and financially successful personalities, lent it a significance which is hard to exaggerate.[68]

It was important that not only the old, poor, and uneducated support Orthodox Judaism. The victory had been for Orthodox Judaism and for the image of Orthodox Judaism. According to Rabbi Jung, it was important that the leaders of the Jewish Center Synagogue had stood up to the nontheistic tendencies of Dr. Kaplan in 1921.[69]

---

63 Gurock and Schacter, *A Modern Heretic and a Traditional Community*, 130 and 134.
64 Hyman B. Grinstein, *A Short History of the Jews in the United States*, ed. Leo Jung, Jewish Library, Second Series, vol. 7 (London and New York: Soncino Press, 1980), 102–103.
65 Jung, *The Path of a Pioneer*, 69.
66 Ibid., 124.
67 Grinstein, *A Short History of the Jews in the United States*, 103.
68 Jung, *The Path of a Pioneer*, 67.
69 Ibid., 74; Scult, ed., *Communings of the Spirit*, 150—this is an example showing that leading congregants did not support Kaplan.

Reaction to Kaplan's philosophy thus helped define Modern Orthodoxy and traditional Orthodoxy; in some cases, it was a point of departure for Orthodox defenders.[70]

Meeting a Threat—Merger Proposal

The proposal for the merger of JTS and RIETS was another thought-provoking, defining event. It is an example of how fluid the lines between Orthodox and Conservative were in the 1920s, as well as how undefined the parameters of Orthodoxy were. The proposed merger led to better articulation of the position of Modern Orthodoxy. Philanthropists and business people, who were pragmatists, felt that a union between the two schools, both then embarking on fundraising campaigns, had financial advantages.[71] Another advantage would be to avoid a split along sectarian lines. Those against the merger were obliged to provide convincing arguments regarding why it should not occur. This led to a profound examination of what Modern Orthodoxy stood for. The solution was the idea of "harmonious" education with Jewish studies existing compatibly with non-Jewish studies under the rubric of an Orthodox educational institution.[72]

JTS had been on the brink of bankruptcy in 1921; Cyrus Adler, president of the seminary since 1915, hoped for an enduring arrangement with the Orthodox. Adler requested in 1926 that "steps [be] taken by which the Seminary and Yeshiva could work together for the advancement of Jewish learning." Rabbi Jung was part of the negotiating process for the proposed merger because he had contacts in both camps, many of his devoted congregants were on the board of Yeshiva, and he was a good back room player. Rabbi Jung had worked with Louis Marshall (an active negotiator for JTS and president of the JTS board), on the American Jewish Relief Committee, and on the Cultural

---

70 The Agudath Harabbonim's reaction was extreme; they wished to excommunicate him. That organization, fortified by newcomers to America in the 1940s, did finally excommunicate Kaplan.
71 Gilbert Klaperman, *The Story of Yeshiva University: The First Jewish University in America* (New York: MacMillan Co., 1969), 160.
72 Yeshiva University Archives, General Correspondence, 1926–1927, Box 12, Folders 2–40—letter to Samuel Levy from Cyrus Adler, November 15, 1926.

Dedication of the new building, the main building of Rabbi Isaac Elchanan's Theological Seminary and the Yeshiva College. Courtesy of Yeshiva University Archives

Committee of the Joint Distribution Committee, of which Cyrus Adler was chairman.[73]

In retrospect, the efforts for a merger between JTS and RIETS appear futile. The spokesmen for the Board of Directors of Yeshiva clearly stated from the start that, at the time, they saw no basis for

---

73 Jung, *The Path of a Pioneer*, 171. Louis Marshall was part of the legal team representing Leo Frank, a Jewish pencil factory manager convicted of raping and murdering a 14-year-old girl.

cooperation but had appointed a committee to confer with representatives of the Seminary. Cyrus Adler, in his correspondence, referred to the lack of action on the part of the board of Yeshiva.[74] Yeshiva continued with construction plans during the negotiations, which, in itself, did not show good faith.[75]

Dr. Bernard Revel, president of Yeshiva College, opposed the union because JTS veered from the standards of Orthodoxy and Dr. Kaplan, an "articulate stray from Orthodoxy," was an influential member of JTS. JTS, while offering excuses, allowed him to remain on the JTS faculty.[76] Rabbi Jung had joined the battle to have Kaplan dismissed from JTS.[77] Rabbi Drachman objected to Cyrus Adler allowing Kaplan to continue to "poison the minds of the teachers of the coming generation."[78] On the other hand, Louis Marshall, an outspoken critic of Yeshiva, felt that those affiliated with Yeshiva "were so ultra-Orthodox" that their conditions could not be met.[79]

From the perspective of Revel, JTS and RIETS were very different, but for some lay people at Kehillath Jeshurun on the East Side and The Jewish Center on the West Side, the merger made sense. To the uninformed eye, the schools appeared to be doing the same thing. Though it was known that Yeshiva men knew more Talmud, knowing Talmud was not absolutely necessary to a good American rabbi in the eyes of the laymen. Gurock suggests that the article "Yeshiva College" (by Revel), articulating the goals and purpose of Yeshiva, was a response to why JTS and Yeshiva should not merge.[80]

In that article, Revel articulated the goal of Yeshiva College to provide "harmonious" education not only for the acquisition of knowledge and skill, but also for the development of all the faculties of man,

---

74 Yeshiva University Archives, General Correspondence, 1926–1927, Box 12, Folders 2-40—letter to Mr. Levy from Rabbi Margolies, December 1, 1926; letter to Mr. Levy from Adler, November 15, 1926; letter to Revel from the director of JTS, June 13, 1926.
75 Klaperman, *The Story of Yeshiva University*, 159.
76 Ibid., 130.
77 Gurock and Schacter, *A Modern Heretic and a Traditional Community*, 142–143.
78 Bernard Drachman, *The Unfailing Light: Memoirs of an American Rabbi* (New York: Rabbinical Council of America, 1948), 374.
79 Klaperman, *The Story of Yeshiva University*, 160.
80 Personal interview with Gurock.

Bernard Revel – founding President of Yeshiva University, close friend of Leo Jung. Courtesy of Yeshiva University Archives

Bernard Revel at his desk. Courtesy of Yeshiva University Archives

1. MODERN ORTHODOXY IN THE 1920S

including the spiritual. Its curriculum should not be just for the training of rabbis and teachers; it should teach about Jewish life and culture and it should be for a system of Jewish education in harmony with America. Revel's message was that Yeshiva was not "merely a Theological seminary"; it also graduated doctors, lawyers, businessmen, and rabbis.[81] Revel wrote:

> But the Yeshivah does not exist merely for the training of rabbis and teachers. ...The *yeshiva* looks beyond those fields of service to the general development of Jewish life and culture, to the evolving of a system of Jewish education that will bring harmony into the life of the American Jewish youth and will develop not only his usefulness as a member of his community but his Jewish consciousness and his will to live as a Jew and to advance the cause of Jewry and Judaism; an education through which the human conscience and the Jewish conscience develop harmoniously into the synthesis of a complete Jewish personality, that indicates the guiding laws of life in accordance with the immortal truths of Judaism in harmonious blending with the best thought of the age and the great humanitarian ideals upon which our blessed country is founded.[82]

Proposed Solutions to the Problems

The efforts began to modernize the synagogue, educational institutes, and materials; to strengthen organizations; and to present *halakhah* as compatible with modernity in America.

The Synagogue

The 1920s saw the redevelopment of a number of America's synagogues to become "synagogue centers"; Modern Orthodox synagogues followed suit. Rabbi Jung's Jewish Center Synagogue housed a day school and

---

81 Yeshiva University Archives, General Correspondence, 1926–1927, Box 12, Folders 2–40—press release, "The Yeshiva," on UOJCA stationery.
82 Bernard Revel, "The Yeshiva College," *Jewish Forum* 9, no. 11 (November 1926).

afternoon school. Its programs were pragmatic, well rounded, and varied. In the early 1920s, Jewish Centers proliferated.[83] However, while the majority of synagogues in general were Orthodox, the majority of synagogue centers were Conservative.[84] This is indicative of the fact that the Conservative movement adapted quicker than the Orthodox movement to American conditions, and that the Jewish Center Synagogue was ahead of its time for Orthodoxy.

The Jewish Center Synagogue served as a prototype for hundreds of Orthodox Jewish synagogue centers over the following decades. Synagogues and schools often shared quarters for efficiency but mostly for their shared purpose of perpetuating Judaism.[85] The Jewish Center Synagogue was, as the name indicated, a center for all activities—sports (it had a gymnasium), social, educational, and religious. The synagogue, completed in 1920, had eight stories and was known as "the *shul* with a pool and a school" as well as the "rich man's club."[86] All these varied activities introduced a secular component in addition to its express purpose, which was to develop a sense of camaraderie and a spirit of tradition.

Decorum

Decorum in the synagogue was an example that Orthodoxy could adapt to the modern cultural patterns and remain Orthodox. Americanized, English-speaking Jews perceived the Orthodox service as antiquated, noisy, indecorous, and unaesthetic. The concern for decorum during worship blossomed with the Jewish synagogue centers. Decorum, which can be defined as a proper mode of conduct, mannerism, demeanor, and presentation, was adopted by the Orthodox synagogue in an

---

83 David Kaufman, "'Shul With A Pool': The Synagogue-Center in American Jewish Life, 1875–1925" (PhD diss., Brandeis University, 1994), 474; David Kaufman, *'Shul With A Pool': The Synagogue-Center in American Jewish History* (Hanover, NH: University Press of New England, 1999).
84 Deborah Dash Moore, *At Home in America* (New York: Columbia University Press, 1981), 138.
85 Mel Scult, *Judaism Faces the Twentieth Century: A Biography of Mordecai Kaplan* (Detroit: Wayne State University, 1993), 155.
86 Kaufman, "'Shul With A Pool': The Synagogue-Center in American Jewish Life, 1875–1925," 295.

attempt to meet American needs and to halt the loss of congregants to Conservative and Reform synagogues. Reform Judaism initiated the idea of the quiet, dignified, and orderly service in an attempt to develop a modern form of Judaism. Decorum in the 1920s was also more prevalent in Conservative synagogue services. Rabbi Jung approved of the institutional models of Conservative and Reform, as he restated his position that "every dissenting point of view deserves some gratitude."[87] He did appreciate that Reform stressed an aesthetic Judaism, and that this aspect of Judaism was attractive to American Jews.[88]

The UOJCA (better known as the OU, or the Orthodox Union) endorsed a decorous service and English-language sermons. The UOJCA was established in 1898 for the purpose of strengthening Orthodox Judaism; thus, as Marc Raphael said, self-conscious Orthodoxy began with the UOJCA.[89] It supported Yeshiva College and the Young Israel movement, which promoted the Sabbath, synagogue attendance, charitable work, Zionist and educational interests, and decorum in conducting services.

The hallmark of the Young Israel movement, another Modern Orthodox organization, was also its insistence on decorum. Young Israel, a product of the American scene, was known for its innovations in Orthodoxy, such as sermons in English, congregational singing, and orderly services. Young Israel also demonstrated that it was possible to make the services attractive and inviting without departing from tradition.[90]

In 1915, fifteen young people from the Lower East Side of New York wanted to provide for their own spiritual and social needs. They formed a new organization to conduct a model synagogue under the name "Model Synagogue," but the name soon changed to the Young Israel Synagogue. In 1922, a Council of Young Israel was formed, including several Young Israel organizations that were interested in cooperating to work for Orthodox Judaism "in the American temper."[91]

---

87 Jung, "Modern Trends in American Judaism," 12.
88 Ibid.
89 Marc Lee Raphael, *Profiles in American Judaism* (New York: Harper & Row, 1988), 132.
90 Hyman Goldstein, "History of the Young Israel Movement," *Jewish Forum* 9, no. 12 (December 1926): 531.
91 Gurock, "The Orthodox Synagogue," 529.

The editor of the *Jewish Forum* wrote that "hope for Judaism in America lies in Young Israel," which was seen as the answer to Reform Judaism, a great threat to Orthodoxy.[92] Rabbi Jung said: "Young Israel to me represents the conscious revolt of the loyal Jewish youth both against the negligent Orthodox and the active semi-reformed congregations."[93]

Decorum held an inherent value for Rabbi Jung. It was a pivotal concept, and decorous services would be one thing that would characterize Modern Orthodoxy in contrast to the services of the *shtieblech* (*shtiebel* in singular), the name used to describe the small Eastern European synagogues. Social changes, not religious changes, were needed.

Rabbi Jung felt that the "calamitous situation" in Orthodox synagogues was caused by a lack of decorum and not anything inherent in Orthodoxy itself.[94] He wrote: "The most perfect dish will become repulsive if it served on a musty plate. The most soul stirring melody will fail on a defective instrument."[95] The old tradition that he advocated had to be presented in new garb that was not foreign to American life; the tradition had to be "administered to the student under a true American environment."[96]

Rabbi Jung's Jewish Center Synagogue was designed to maintain decorum, aesthetic appearance, and conduct.[97] Children could not be brought into services because they might be disruptive.[98] Rabbi Jung believed that the physical appearance of both the synagogue and the worshippers should add to the beauty and sanctity of the service. The dress code was formal, as were the services. The clergy and officials

---

92 Editorial, *Jewish Forum* 9, no. 12 (December 1926).
93 Jung, *Living Judaism*, 224; Jung, *Foundations of Judaism*, 18.
94 Jung, "Jew and Jewishness in America," 134.
95 Ibid., 133.
96 Yeshiva University Archives, Harris L. Selig Administration Files, December 2, 1929—press releases, 1925–1926, "The Discovery of Orthodox Judaism in America," 2—personal interview with Rabbi Leo Jung.
97 Personal interview with Rabbi Jacob J. Schacter, November 11, 1996.
98 Ibid.; Rabbi Schacter claimed that Rabbi Jung had said that he did allow children into the synagogue services, but Rabbi Schacter added that Rabbi Jung made provisions too difficult for children to be present.

wore top hats and frock coats during the winter and homburgs in the summer.

Things associated with the *shtiebel* were eliminated. Honors were not to be auctioned off from the pulpit, and there was to be no "swaying" while praying as this was considered old fashioned, undignified, and un-American. Rabbi Jung gave his sermons in English, not in Yiddish; he spoke to the congregants about things to which they could relate. He wrote: "The Jewish message came in a foreign method, and therefore did not reach the youth. ...Our youth here drift away not because the message is distasteful to them, but because they have never received it."[99] Jenna Weissman Joselit and Jeffrey Gurock have both suggested that the Eastern European rabbi's Yiddish sermon—either idealistic or esoteric—built a chasm between the life of the congregant and the rabbi's sermon, keeping the Orthodox congregants away.[100] There were to be no disorderly, drawn out services, with individuals praying at their own speed and to their own tune. The rising generation needed innovations in practice and up-to-date interpretations of Jewish doctrine.

Modern Education—Another Solution

Jewish education in sympathy with the culture and spirit of Judaism and Americanization was advocated by Modern Orthodox leaders. Rabbi Jung felt that Jewish education was essential for Judaism but also a benefit for true Americanism. He wrote that "whatever else we have contributed to this country, industrial genius, scholarly ability, we shall not have done our full duty to America unless we have contributed our real selves, unadulterated Judaism."[101] Rabbi Drachman felt that the Jew must be a Jew to be a true American and that the man without faith was usually a bad citizen. This was a theme presented to sell the idea of parochial

---

99 Jung, "Jew and Jewishness in America," 134.
100 Jenna Weissman Joselit, "Of Manners, Morals, and Orthodox Judaism: Decorum Within the Orthodox Synagogue," in *Ramaz: School, Community, Scholarship and Orthodoxy*, ed. Jeffry S. Gurock (Hoboken, NJ: Ktav Publishing House, 1989), 24; Gurock, *American Jewish Orthodoxy in Historical Perspective*, 36.
101 Jung, *Foundations of Judaism*, 100.

schools, or "day schools."[102] Rabbi Berlin, president of Mizrachi, commented that in America, however, the question in connection with Jewish education is not only of different departments of knowledge but directly one of Americanism; Rabbi Drachman echoed this sentiment.[103] Modern Orthodox proponents defined this as "harmonious" studies, and it was another issue that separated Modern Orthodoxy from other Orthodox groups.

The Role of Young Israel

Rabbi Judah L. Magnes, a well-known community leader ordained at the Hebrew Union College, interested in the revival of cultural life among American Jews, and Israel Friedlander, a professor at JTS, organized Friday night lectures in English under the auspices of the Young Israel movement. Though these men did not consider themselves Orthodox, they felt that these Americanized services would have to be Orthodox to be accepted by the downtown society.[104] The Modern Orthodox movement supported Friday night lectures held in the synagogue as a legitimate American activity as long as the lectures did not interfere with the traditional Friday night and Saturday morning worship services. Rabbi Jung was involved in many of the lectures; other guest lecturers included Rabbi Herbert Goldstein, Maurice Farbridge (a well-known Orthodox sociologist), and—later on—Rabbi Joseph Lookstein.[105]

In an age of growing prejudice against Jews in universities, with quotas for Jewish students, and when many did not even have a chance to aspire to go to university, these lectures fulfilled the need for education.[106] Though they were no substitute for university, the lectures satisfied a desire to learn and served as a vehicle to teach about Judaism.

---

102 Bernard Drachman, "The Jewish Educational Problem in America," *Jewish Forum* 3, no. 9 (November 1920)—Rabbi Drachman said that "the ideal American Jew is one who is a complete Jew and a thorough, genuine American"; Isaac Siegel, "The Selfish Immigration Restrictionists," *Jewish Forum* 3, no. 9 (November 1920).
103 Meyer Berlin, "The Educational Problem in America," *Jewish Forum* 3, no.9 (Nov. 1920) 587–589. Rabbi Berlin was the president of the Mizrachi Organization of America at the time.
104 Gurock, "The Orthodox Synagogue," 529.
105 Yeshiva University Archives, Koenigsberg Papers, Box 1, Young Israel Bulletin.
106 Harry Starr, "The Affair at Harvard," *The Menorah Journal* 11, no. 5 (October 1922).

Late Friday night services and lectures were common in Conservative synagogues and especially in Reform temples in this period.

Yeshiva College

The development of RIETS and the founding of Yeshiva College provided a foundation, and were essential, for Modern Orthodoxy in America. Yeshiva College provided an environment for Modern Orthodoxy to develop and thrive. Yeshiva College and RIETS began to change the idea that Modern Orthodoxy was curiously "un-American alienism" and began to define what Modern Orthodoxy stood for.[107]

RIETS, named after Rabbi Isaac Elhanan Spektor of Kovno, was founded in 1897 and reorganized in 1908, following a student demonstration that began the process of redefinition of RIETS as an institution of religious and secular education. The institution absorbed the Etz Hayyim *yeshiva* in 1915. In 1921, RIETS opened its new expanded headquarters on East Broadway.[108] It was a critical turning point for Orthodox Judaism, and though Rabbi Jung came to New York in 1922, he hailed the new location and expansion of RIETS as trailblazing for the new era. He wrote that "great is the task before us"; he recognized that this event was "an indication of some rearousal" of American Judaism.[109] RIETS was perceived as a "new vessel in which to preserve and recreate on American soil the old, rich vintage of Judaism."[110] The teachers, students, and rabbis of RIETS would be the interpreters, creators, and initiators of Jewish thought and Jewish values in America.[111] A pivotal issue for Modern Orthodox education was a combined school where both Jewish and general subjects are taught, as mentioned, in sympathy with the culture of Judaism and Americanism. Yeshiva College, launched in 1924, was founded as an adjunct to RIETS. It was the first college of liberal arts and sciences under Jewish auspices that

---

107 Jung, *Living Judaism*, 222.
108 Isaac Rosengarten, "A Bulwark of Judaism in America," *Jewish Forum* 4, no. 4 (April 1921): 803.
109 Jung, *Living Judaism*, 221.
110 Klaperman, *The Story of Yeshiva University*, 1.
111 Rosengarten, "A Bulwark of Judaism in America," 804.

became associated with twofold education.[112] European *yeshivot* (plural for *yeshiva*) had been dedicated to rabbinic studies exclusively. Though the curriculum would be the study of liberal arts, the ultimate aim was Revel's idea of a "harmonious education."[113] Traditional Judaism would thus be harmonized with modern thought.[114]

The fundraising for Yeshiva's new campus has been described by Joselit as a "coming of age"; Yeshiva was acting like an American institution ready to compete with other educational institutions.[115] Orthodox Jews were behaving as Americans with resources. Rabbi Jung spent time away from his synagogue, with the approval of his board, serving the institution that he felt was so crucial.[116] Many Yeshiva supporters were also members of the Jewish Center, thus he was well placed to raise funds.[117] Rabbi Jung worked closely with Dr. Revel, Rabbi Herbert Goldstein, Rabbi Moses Sebulun Margolies (the Ramaz), Rabbi de Sola Pool, and other major Orthodox figures in the 1920s in these undertakings.

The Jewish Center Synagogue was the temporary home for the freshman classes of Yeshiva College for several months, until the school was able to move into its own quarters in 1928. Revel wrote to Rabbi Jung that "it is fitting that the center which has taken the initiative—in every phase of harmonious Jewish education—so fully in sympathy with the *yeshiva* ideal" should house the school.[118]

Incorporated into Revel's Yeshiva for the first time was a Teacher's Institute. In 1920, the school opened under the joint auspices of Yeshiva

---

112 Jacob I. Hartstein, "Yeshiva Education in America," in *Israel of Tomorrow*, ed. Leo Jung (New York: Herald Square Press, 1946), 470.
113 Revel, "The Yeshiva College," 477; Aaron Rakeffet-Rothkoff, *Bernard Revel: Builder of American Jewish Orthodoxy* (Philadelphia: Jewish Publication Society of America, 1972), 78–79.
114 Revel, "The Yeshiva College," 479.
115 Joselit, "Of Manners, Morals, and Orthodox Judaism: Decorum Within the Orthodox Synagogue," 54.
116 Yeshiva University Archives, Bernard Revel Papers, Box 3, Folder 5/3-21—letter to Revel from Rabbi Jung, March 26, 1929 (one of many examples of Rabbi Jung's fundraising), and letter to Revel from Rabbi Jung, April 19, 1929 (an example of Rabbi Jung's involvement in administrative functions).
117 Jung, *The Path of A Pioneer*, 88.
118 Yeshiva University Archives, Bernard Revel Papers, Box 3, Folder 5/3-21—letter from Revel to Rabbi Jung, September 13, 1928.

Bidding farewell with Torah scrolls and moving to new headquarters 1928. Courtesy of Yeshiva University Archives

and Mizrachi, providing a course of study leading to Hebrew teachers diplomas, bachelor and masters of religious education degrees.[119] Yeshiva differed from Eastern European *yeshivot* and other types of traditional Orthodox institutions in that it was designed to train rabbis and teachers in "the mould of true Americanism."[120]

Rabbi Jung's Writings—Another Means to Help Modern Orthodoxy Adjust

Just as organizations and educational institutions can be useful tools to educate and influence, so can the pen. Rabbi Jung was one of the first to write about Orthodox Judaism in English to an audience uneducated

---

119 Rakeffet-Rothkoff, *Bernard Revel*, 63; Grinstein, *A Short History of the Jews in the United States*, 79.
120 Revel, "The Yeshiva College," 118.

in Judaism.[121] His writings were guides to his understanding of Jewish law and to living appropriately in America. In his autobiography, Rabbi Jung described the situation when he came to New York in 1922:

> There was almost complete lack of available information about the Jewish solution of modern problems. The rabbinic monthlies and quarterlies too often dealt with praiseworthy but too often out of date problems, a great deal of ingenuity, learning, and hard work concentrating on questions which were far removed from the contemporary scene, while shying away from problems that were uppermost in the minds of men and women of our age. Traditional Judaism was found unrepresented, and that vacuum gave rise to all sorts of unjustified views of our holy Torah.[122]

Rabbi Jung wrote *Foundations of Judaism* in 1923, *Living Judaism* in 1927, and *Toward Sinai* in 1929. These books, largely a collection of his sermons, provide a clear picture of the situation of Orthodoxy in the 1920s and clarify the reasons for the grim situation. Not only were the problems pointed out, but so were the solutions, as he saw them. In 1924, he began the first of many volumes that he edited for the Jewish Library, with *The Essentials of Judaism*. The Jewish Library series enabled its audience to read the writings and sermons of Rabbi Jung and the views of other prominent Modern Orthodox philosophers, rabbis,

---

121 Israel Goldstein, "The Role of the Rabbi in World Jewish Affairs," and Hyman Rabinowitz, "The American Rabbi as Preacher," in *The American Rabbi: A Tribute on the Occasion of the Bicentennial of the United States and the 95th Anniversary of the New York Board of Rabbis*, ed. Gilbert Rosenthal (New York: Ktav Publishing House Inc., 1977), 98. Isaac Leeser (1806-1868) was the first to translate the Bible into English, and his periodical—the "The Occident and American Jewish Advocate," which upheld historical and traditional Judaism—was in English. Many of Leeser's sermons were printed in the English monthly "The Occident"; they dealt with the fundamentals of Judaism, but were unrelated to the issues of the day, which was Rabbi Jung's critique of such sermons. Rabbi Jung's senior confrere, Rabbi Drachman, shared Rabbi Jung's goals; however, his book *The Unfailing Light* was not published until the 1940s.

122 Jung, *The Path of a Pioneer*, 126.

historians, and sociologists. As well, the series updated its audience on current and historical issues in America, Europe, and *Eretz Israel*.

In *Foundations of Judaism*, Rabbi Jung asserts that the material successes of Jews in America come at the expense of moral and spiritual failure, and presents his blueprint for the rehabilitation of Orthodoxy in America, for which he has only praise: "What is America but another effort of God's to let man find himself free from the ballast of past wrongs, free for the glory of self-worked salvation?"[123] The book is a plea to return to Jewish living in the wonderful America where Jews are free to practice their religion and to live in peace.

In *Living Judaism*, he again presents a grim picture of the state of Orthodox Judaism, along with suggestions on how to improve the synagogue, school, and home—three channels by which the Jew can express one's Jewishness. The book also defines what Judaism stands for from the Modern Orthodox perspective; for Rabbi Jung, there is no problem of science versus faith, and both are essential for each other.[124] He defends "chosenness," probably because it was being criticized by Kaplan, and he refers to it as a duty, a task, and a source of pride.[125] *Eretz Israel* is important to Jewish life, to the extent "…that Palestine is the best opportunity for the Jew to attain the ideals for which he was created."[126]

Rabbi Jung wrote many articles for contemporary journals and was on the editorial board of the Orthodox English language journal *Jewish Forum*, which represented the sort of Orthodoxy that he endorsed. That journal was supported by Mizrachi, Young Israel, and UOJCA, and was an important tool in presenting Modern Orthodox philosophy to the public at large.

Strengthening Organizations—Avenues of Influence and Enablers

As Modern Orthodox organizations became stronger and more focused, so did the movement. The goals of Orthodox organizations were to

---

123 Jung, *Foundations of Judaism*, 99.
124 Ibid., *Living Judaism*, 14.
125 Ibid., 156.
126 Ibid., 157.

enhance Jewish life and to retard assimilation while fostering Americanization. This work was vital in the 1920s as denominational competition began for the Eastern European Jews and their children.[127]

An Orthodox community requires certain things, one of which is *kashrut* facilities as observance of the kosher laws is a basic tenet of Judaism. Available kosher products necessitate having properly trained personnel knowledgeable in proper preparation of kosher food and proper facilities for its preparation, as well as personnel capable of enforcing the kosher laws. Conditions in America were more complicated than they had been in Europe; maintaining *kashrut* facilities now required American methods of organization.

Just as proper kosher facilities enable a Jewish community to exist, it is also necessary to establish conditions that enable Sabbath observance. Torn between the demands of earning a living and observing the Sabbath, Jews often had to take the first option. American Orthodox organizations had to involve themselves in activities that ensured economic opportunity for Sabbath observers.

UOJCA

Rabbi Jung was vice president of the UOJCA from 1926 to 1934. In 1920, Rabbi Mendes (like Rabbi Jung) urged the UOJCA to expand its work and unite with others, meaning with Conservative organizations (but not with Reform ones, perceived as a more dangerous threat), to bring Jews back into the fold by providing proper facilities.[128] The Orthodoxy that was espoused by the UOJCA was thus not an "insular Orthodoxy." Rabbi Jung wrote:

> We do not want insular Orthodoxy! We are not divorced from Jewish law! We are not divorced from Jewish life!! And we must not be divorced from the Jewish people! Let our ambition be: To make of this Union the nucleus of a strong, virile, all-embracing Torah-Parliament of American Jewry.[129]

---

127 Wertheimer, ed., *The American Synagogue*, 60.
128 Mendes, "Orthodox Judaism," 33–36.
129 Leo Jung, "The Place of the Union of Orthodox Jewish Congregations in American Israel," *Jewish Forum* 10, no. 12 (December 1927): 608. Also in Jung, *The*

The UOJCA program had to safeguard Orthodoxy, reach out to new recruits, and be involved with "missionary work for Judaism among Jews."[130] Rabbi Jung, while immovable in his own philosophy, was always able to reach out to those not in his camp.[131]

Rabbi Jung felt that the UOJCA must reach out to all Jews, including the old-fashioned rabbi. In its desire to reach English-speaking young people, the UOJCA had alienated the Yiddish-speaking Orthodox rabbis. The Yiddish-speaking, old-style, Eastern European rabbis were becoming a relic of the past according to Rabbi Jung and other UOJCA members. Their role in education and the *kashrut* industry was being reduced, and they were being replaced by English-speaking, more Americanized Orthodox rabbis. Rabbi Jung founded the Rabbonim Aid Society, headquartered at his synagogue, to financially aid the Yiddish-speaking rabbis.[132]

In 1924, the UOJCA decided to become involved with *kashrut* supervision and certification.[133] There was no single body overseeing the *kashrut* industry as a whole; many individuals worked on their own, some of whom were incompetent or dishonest. *Kashrut*, said Rabbi Jung, was a "disheartening spectacle of disorder," and *kashrut* supervision was a disaster. He felt that the lack of *kashrut* enforcement and a lack of kosher facilities was a great handicap for Orthodox Judaism.[134] Recurrent fraud and scandal occurred at the expense of the observant.

Harold P. Gastwirt, in his book, *Fraud, Corruption and Holiness*, provided examples of fraud in this industry for economic gain; the offenders ranged from the Health Department to *shohatim*, butchers, and rabbis. There was price fixing, raising prices before the holidays, and receiving bribes for false kosher certificates, among other offenses.

Rhythm of Life: Sermons, Studies, Addresses (New York: Pardes Publishing House, 1950), 191, and in Jung, *Towards Sinai*, 268.
130 Jung, "The Place of the Union of Orthodox Congregations in American Israel," 608.
131 Ibid.
132 Personal interview with Sadie Silverstein, president of the Rabbonim Aid Society since 1977, Nov. 19, 1997. The organization still exists, but it has outlived its purpose because of social welfare and the dwindling population that it first served, though 35 Hasidic rabbis are still supported.
133 Louis Bernstein, *Challenge and Mission: The Emergence of the English-Speaking Rabbinate* (New York: Shengold Publishers, 1982), 92.
134 Jung, *Living Judaism*, 210.

Gastwirt wrote that American pluralism and voluntarism were the reason for the failures in the *kashrut* industry since people were free to observe as they wished but rules were unenforceable.[135] In Europe, the rabbi of the town, a trusted leader, decided issues concerning *kashrut*. In America, with its separation of church and state, there was no official community or authoritative structure. There was a lack of cooperation among rabbis, and the cost of effective law enforcement from American authorities was prohibitive. The situation was unprecedented; there was thus no tradition to fall back on.

In 1926, Rabbi Jung organized The Rabbinic Council of the UOJCA; he was its president for the following eight years. The Rabbinic Council was to assume the rabbinic functions of the UOJCA, including *kashrut* supervision; the "OU" became its organizational symbol and trademark. For many years, the UOJCA was called a "paper organization," until it came into importance when it developed the *kashrut* certificate department.[136] As the vice president of the UOJCA and organizer of its Rabbinic Council, Rabbi Jung and others began a crusade to fight the corrupt "*kashrut* jungle" and replace it with a reliable system under the OU imprint.[137]

In 1928, Rabbi Jung sent a letter to the UOJCA, which presented a unanimous decision of the Executive Committee of the Rabbinic Council defining its role. The Council was to be the authoritative body with respect to all matters of Jewish law affecting the UOJCA, that all *halakhic* questions were to be submitted to the council, and that they were to be answered exclusively by the Council. All *hekhsherim*, which were formal affirmations that products were kosher, past and present, had to be under the auspices of, or approved by, the Council.[138] The Council,

---

135 Harold P. Gastwirt, *Fraud, Corruption and Holiness: The Controversy Over the Supervision of Jewish Dietary Practice in New York City, 1881–1940* (Port Washington, NY: Kennikat Press, 1974), 189.
136 Grinstein, *A Short History of the Jews in the United States*, 99.
137 Jung, *The Path of a Pioneer*, 51; Yeshiva University Archives, Jung Collection, Box 46, Folder 4, "The Kashrut Jungle" by Leo Jung ("kashrut jungle" is a term that Rabbi Jung used).
138 Yeshiva University Archives, Leo Jung Papers, Box 1, Folder 1—letter to Rabbi B. L. Rosenbloom from Rabbi Jung, president of the Rabbinical Council of America, April 19, 1928.

under the chairmanship of Rabbi Jung, abolished individual *hekhsherim* for its members. This was very important, as it was hoped that the Council would be reputable and could be trusted.

The UOJCA lobbied politically in the area of *kashrut*. Laws were enacted by the state to see that nonkosher food was not misrepresented as kosher by butchers or restaurants. The problem, however, was enforcement and the law enforcers often took bribes. Heavy fines were imposed and culprits were sentenced to jail. This did decrease the number of violations, but the culprits were usually charged only after several warnings, and many continued to disregard the law.[139] Proper kosher facilities would be an issue for a long time to come.

Organizations Facilitating Sabbath Observance

One of the main differences in America was the loss of Saturday as the historical Sabbath. There was a six-day work week in the United States, and it was on Sunday that one did not have to go to work; this denied the Jews religious freedom. Facilitating Sabbath observance was of great importance, as the Orthodox leaders felt that the preservation of the Sabbath was a precondition for the preservation of American Jewry.[140] Jewish groups and individuals paid increasing attention to questions of the Sabbath in the 1920s.[141]

It was the Sabbath Alliance, which had been organized to promote the observance of the Jewish Sabbath and worked in close cooperation with the UOJCA, that took the initiative and was the most active of all the Orthodox groups.

In the 1920s, the Jewish Sabbath movements began focusing on the five-day week for social and economic concerns and supported the

---

139 Gastwirt, *Fraud, Corruption and Holiness*, 129; Bernard M. Patten, "Enforcement of the Jewish Dietary Laws or Kosher Laws," *Jewish Forum* 10, no. 5 (May 1927). Patten was the Commissioner of Public Markets of the City of New York at that point.
140 Mendes, "Orthodox Judaism," 35; Drachman, "Plan for the Organization of a Society for the Promotion of Religious Life," 594.
141 Benjamin Kline Hunnicutt, "The Jewish Sabbath Movement in the Early Twentieth Century," *American Jewish History* 69, no. 2 (December 1979), 196; Yeshiva University Archives, Koenigsberg Papers—letter to Benjamin Koenigsberg from Rabbi Drachman, March 16, 1923 (example of increased attention); Editorial, *Jewish Forum* 9, no. 12 (December 1926): 525.

general labor movement in this demand.¹⁴² It was mainly Orthodox organizations that fought for the five-day week. This effort demonstrated social consciousness and was also a practical way to plead for the traditional Sabbath. Orthodoxy was in the forefront of demands for social, economic, and moral reform, though Reform and Conservative groups also involved themselves with this issue. Only when the Sabbath Alliance began to concentrate on labor reform was it able to make headway. Rabbi Drachman, president of the Sabbath Alliance, supported local unions in large cities launching their campaign for a five-and-a-half-day week.¹⁴³ This was a start, though still not ideal since the half-day had to be a Saturday.

In the 1920s, there was a wave of "blue laws" passed that forbade businesses, under penalty of fine or imprisonment, to operate on Sundays. These blue laws, in many cases, had anti-Semitic overtones, but they did contribute to the widespread nonobservance of the Sabbath. Hence, the Jewish Sabbath Alliance began a national campaign against blue laws, saying that the blue laws violated the philosophy of church and state separation. Jewish groups felt that the blue laws were un-American and repugnant to the fundamental concept of freedom and liberty of conscience.

On the assumption that there was separation of church and state, the Sabbath Alliance promoted the introduction of the Dickstein Bill in the New York legislature in 1919 and 1920.¹⁴⁴ The Sabbath bill, introduced by Samuel Dickstein, a member of the State Assembly of New York, proposed that those who could not work on the Sabbath be allowed to work on Sunday. The bill had no chance to pass in the state legislatures that were passing new blue laws in record numbers, and they had little help from the courts.¹⁴⁵ Hence, the first attempts were blocked. The Dickstein Sabbath bill, though it never passed, demonstrates the effort to secure equal justice and equal opportunity in employment for Sabbath

---

142 Hunnicutt, "The Jewish Sabbath Movement in the Early Twentieth Century," 196.
143 Ibid., 203.
144 Ibid., 201.
145 Ibid., 202.

observers at this time.¹⁴⁶ It is obvious that the Orthodox businessman and worker faced a serious conflict.¹⁴⁷

In 1926, the editorial board of the *Jewish Forum* recommended that all Jewish organizations have Sabbath observance as a fundamental purpose. The UOJCA instituted a Sabbath Committee that included Rabbis Lookstein, Margolies, and Jung.¹⁴⁸ The committee's goal was to educate, to rally loyalty to the Sabbath, and to facilitate employment opportunities for Sabbath observers. The Young Israel movement was active in defending religious rights and sponsored a bureau of employment for Sabbath observers.¹⁴⁹

Rabbi Jung helped eliminate a calendar reform that threatened Sabbath observance. In the late 1920s, a question of calendar reform was presented to the United States Congress that would have made observance of the Sabbath nearly impossible. The fixity of the Sabbath would have been nullified and the Sabbath would move to different days of the week. At the time, this was considered a serious threat. This calendar was proposed for financial reasons and ignored religious concerns.¹⁵⁰ Rabbi Jung was part of the Jewish Sabbath Alliance Committee that was struck to prevent its adoption.¹⁵¹ The threat to the Sabbath in this plan was not completely abandoned until the 1950s.

Approaches to Halakhah

Rabbi Jung did not espouse a hard line against lax observance. His view of *halakhah* was not rigid; he felt that this flexibility was necessary as America society was a "working," as opposed to a "learning," society.¹⁵²

---

146 Hon. Samuel Dickstein, "The Sabbath Bill," *Jewish Forum* 4, no. 4 (April 1921): 784–788.
147 Meyer Kramer, "Is America A Christian Country?," *Tradition* 4, no. 1 (Fall 1961); Krasner, *The Benderly Boys and American Jewish Education*, 240.
148 Yeshiva University Archives, Koenigsberg Papers, Box 11, Folder 5—letter to Koenigsberg.
149 Hyman Goldstein, "History of the Young Israel Movement," 529–532.
150 Samuel Friedman, "The Five Day Week and the Proposed Calendar Reform," *Jewish Forum* 14, no. 9 (September 1931).
151 Yeshiva University Archives, Koenigsberg Papers, Box 11, Folder 5—letter to Koenigsberg from Rabbi Drachman, president of the UOJCA.
152 Jung, *Harvest, Sermons, Addresses, Studies*, 208–210.

Rabbi Jung presented *halakhic* ideas as compatible with modernity; he maintained that Judaism wished control "in such real things of life as honesty in business, ritual food, sexual purity, industrial fairness, and commercial integrity."[153]

Modern Orthodoxy considered that *halakhah* had always been sensitive to the economic, social, geographical, and psychological conditions of the period.[154] Rabbi Jung's role was to draw them back into the fold, to stimulate their will to Jewishness, to educate them, to make them feel comfortable, and to provide attainable goals. Martin Schwarzschild, a former president and member of the synagogue since childhood, recalled: "What was important to him was ethics, morality and human decency." Rabbi Jung never said: "Thou shalt not turn on a light on *Shabbos*."[155]

Rabbi Jung's emphasis was not as much about *mitzvot* because the people to whom he was speaking found it easier to relate to ethics, and he felt that "the Jew puts his ethical ideals above all else."[156] He focused on personal relations and honesty in business, since his synagogue was made up of mostly business people who were suit and cloak manufacturers.

Privatization of religion goes along with separation of religion and state; in the face of anti-Semitism, privatization of Judaism was the rule. This was reflected in the dress code, in which nothing distinguished the Jew from the non-Jew. Few men wore *kippot* (skullcaps) other than in synagogue, and fewer women covered their hair. Men covered their heads with a hat outdoors, as was the fashion of the day; indoors, they were bareheaded except when praying.[157] Rabbi Jung's four daughters were never asked to cover their heads as they were about to marry.[158]

The laws of Judaism had to be presented as compatible with modernity. It had to be demonstrated that Judaism put great emphasis on

---

153 Jung, *Towards Sinai*, 27.
154 Bernard S. Jackson, *Modern Research in Jewish Law* (Leiden and Boston: Brill, 1980), 5.
155 Personal interview with Martin Schwarzschild, November 11, 1996.
156 Jung, *Foundations of Judaism*, 17.
157 Joselit, *New York's Jewish Jews*, 21.
158 Letter from Rosalie Rosenfeld, Rabbi Jung's daughter, October 29, 1997.

bodily health and physical well-being. Rabbi Jung thus felt that it was necessary to point out that modern medical science endorsed the hygienic and eugenic value of Jewish life and of "scrupulous compliance with dietary and marriage laws."[159] He claimed that "Jews never have been taught to know the health-giving, health-preserving properties of Jewish life."[160] Rabbi Drachman also said that Judaism puts "great stress upon bodily health and physical well-being." He felt this was exemplified in the dietary laws.[161]

Rabbi Jung was appealing to an audience that looked over its shoulder for approval from its gentile neighbors. Therefore, he asserted that many Jewish customs were so positive that they had been accepted by the "cultured gentile." Gentile scientists said that the laws of *kashrut* were humane, and their opinions were highly respected.[162]

In keeping with the times, Rabbi Jung, one of the few advocates for the laws of family purity, presented the marriage laws, *taharat hamishpakhah*, as compatible with what was going on in the modern world. Family law was a mission for Rabbi Jung, and he was determined to rescue the Judaic marriage laws from obscurity. These laws, as he stated, were "utterly unknown to the majority of American Jews."[163] He wrote:

> It proclaims the duty to interrupt the love cycle when the menses are expected. It enjoins that it may not be taken up before the bath of immersion has been taken. And this bath of immersion is not legitimate for twelve days. Thus the twelve days of freedom, through separation, are guaranteed to the woman, become self-evident to the man and raise the level and the tone of their married life.[164]

---

159 Jung, *Essentials of Judaism*, 7.
160 Jung, *Rhythm of Life*, 189.
161 Drachman, "Tradition and Modern Thought," *The Sinaist* 3, no. 3 (August 1919): 2.
162 Joselit, "Modern Orthodox Jews and the Ordeal of Civility," *American Jewish History* 74, no. 2 (December 1984): 133.
163 Jung, *Living Judaism*, 22.
164 Leo Jung, "The Jewish Way to Married Happiness," in Jung, *The Rhythm of Life*, 142–143. This article could be found in *The Rhythm of Life* as well as *Jewish Forum*, as seen later.

Rabbi Jung felt that Jewish marital law protected the woman and elevated her and the status of the marriage; the laws provided a sense of holiness and spirituality, therefore kept the marriage on a high level.[165] It was felt that the spiritual benefits and religious reasons of the laws would not alone win adherents, thus he combined modern reasoning with Jewish concepts, which was typical of Modern Orthodox thinkers of that time. According to Jewish law, the ritual bath is more important than a synagogue, but this was not offered as a reason to observe the laws. In America, building a *mikveh* did not carry the same imperative as the establishment of a synagogue, cemetery, or attention to *kashrut*, and the laws of marital purity through the *mikveh* had been neglected.[166] American Jewish women lacked an understanding of the *mikveh*, the ritual bath, which was a religious duty and requirement to fulfill the family laws. This lack of understanding was coupled with great apathy.[167] Therefore, Rabbi Jung pointed out that the laws had health-preserving qualities and were good for romance and the emancipation of women because it gave women control of their own bodies.[168]

The 1920s were an age of female emancipation, with women fighting in the political arena for rights, thus presenting the family law as preserving woman's rights was a good approach. The literature on this subject at this time depicted these laws as preventing promiscuity, suicides, neurosis, divorce, and scandals. They also protected one from the loneliness of the modern world.[169] The marital laws looked after the woman's mental and physiological needs. They were presented as a panacea for everything. Rabbi Jung cited the article of Dr. Mary Stopes, called "Married Love," and Dr. Isaac Macht's article, "Phyto-Pharmacological Study of Menstrual Toxins," both in the *Journal of Pharmacology* in 1924, which underscored the hygienic and eugenic basis of ritual purity. Dr. Stopes wrote that the systematic protection of a woman's physical and mental welfare was

---

165 Ibid., 143.
166 Leo Jung, "The Jewish Way to Married Happiness," *Jewish Forum* 13, no. 1 (January 1930): 157.
167 Karla Goldman, *Beyond the Synagogue Gallery: Finding a Place for Women in American Judaism* (Cambridge, MA and London: Harvard University Press, 2000), 75.
168 Jung, "The Jewish Way to Married Happiness," 156; Jung, *The Rhythm of Life*, 141.
169 Ibid., "The Jewish Way to Married Happiness," *Jewish Forum*, 159.

found in family purity.¹⁷⁰ Science, as well as Torah, was given authority. The article "Ritual Baths," written by a prominent Orthodox rabbi's wife, Mrs. Moses Hyamson, states that "these laws have the approval of scientific experts and the whole hearted support of eminent medical men."¹⁷¹

In the modern world, aesthetics were important. Rabbi Jung wrote about "unsavory, unsanitary, unclean" *mikvaot* (plural of *mikveh*) that alone caused a lack of observance.¹⁷² Rabbi Oscar Fasman quoted Rabbi Jung as saying: "We cannot win women over to the observance of ritual laws if the *mikveh* in the community is a dingy, rundown, and unclean facility."¹⁷³ One of Rabbi Jung's initial projects as a fledgling rabbi in Cleveland had been to build a new *mikveh*, "hygienically and aesthetically on the heights of Judaism."¹⁷⁴ He continued the practice of collecting money from his congregants to support *mikvaot*,¹⁷⁵ and he was responsible for some fifteen aesthetic and modern *mikvaot* in America. He stated in "Rhythm of Life":

> I can remember a number of loathsome places—and I cannot criticize too sharply the carelessness, which made such conditions possible. Coupled with the inability of the rabbis to discuss this all-important subject and with a lack of informed rebellion among women (who should have refused to get married before the community established decent *mikvaot*), the situation prevailed which rendered such hostility on the part of the half informed and uninformed young women more intelligible.¹⁷⁶

In Orthodox circles, there were latent and overt prejudices concerning the role of women. Rabbi Jung held the modern attitude

---

170 Ibid., 157.
171 Moses Hyamson, "Ritual Baths (Mikvaoth)," *Jewish Forum* 10, no. 1 (January 1927): 22.
172 Jung, "The Jewish Way to Married Happiness," *Jewish Forum*, 158.
173 Fasman, "After Fifty Years, an Optimist," 159–174.
174 Jung, *The Path of a Pioneer*, 48.
175 Jewish Center Synagogue, Minutes of Board of Trustees, December 20, 1931.
176 Jung, *The Rhythm of Life*, 144.

that women had a role to play in community affairs, which he fostered, and he was especially defensive in response to slurs about women's intellect and their seclusion from the public arena.[177] The subject was broached in Modern Orthodox circles in the 1920s; this only began the discussion of the role of women and their more active participation.

Another important issue for the welfare and just treatment of Jewish women is *agunot*, women who have been deserted intentionally or unintentionally and whose husbands cannot be found, or women whose husbands will not give them a divorce. The second type of *agunah*, the woman whose husband will not give her a divorce, has remained a terrible problem, for in Jewish law, only the husband can grant a divorce. The American Modern Orthodox leadership tried to take a leading role in solving this important issue. Rabbi Jung recognized that this could be a tremendous contribution to American Judaism, and he acknowledged that the *agunah* problem was one that "interfered with my equanimity"; he felt that the law put women in an unfair, unjust position.[178] The problem is that no authoritative rabbinic body, such as a *Sanhedrin*, is in place to amend the law in any way. It was requested that Rabbi Jung, as head of the Rabbinical Council of the Orthodox Union, write to Rav Avraham Yitzhak Kook, who had been elected the first Ashkenazi Chief Rabbi of Palestine in 1921, urging the convening of a world *Sanhedrin*.[179] It is not known if Rabbi Jung wrote this letter, but it is known that he felt that this would be "one of the tremendous contributions to American Israel."[180] Establishing a *Sanhedrin* was fraught with problems. Without an authority structure in Modern Orthodoxy, it would be difficult to achieve agreement as to which rabbis would sit on this body. The lack of structure was inherent on Orthodoxy as a whole, but especially in Modern Orthodoxy. Also, the decisions of the *Sanhedrin* could not be enforced in America, where religion and government affairs are separated. The situation of *agunot*

---

177 Yeshiva University Archives, Jung Collection, Box 47, Folder 1—"Women as Voters."
178 Jung, *The Path of a Pioneer*, 128.
179 "From the Shearith Israel Archives," *Tradition* 30, no. 1, (1995): 17-18—letter from Rabbi de Sola Pool to Rabbi Jung, April 15, 1930.
180 Jung, *Harvest, Sermons, Addresses, Studies*, 216.

remains problematic and pertinent in Orthodoxy to this day, but the proposal is an example that women's issues were beginning to be broached in the 1920s and that American Modern Orthodox rabbis were beginning to assert themselves.

Another modern *halakhic* dilemma was the issue of *mehitzah* that presented itself many times in the 1920s. A *mehitzah* is a partition in the synagogue that separates the men's area from the women's area. This dilemma was an issue in Modern Orthodoxy and Conservative Judaism at the time; Reform Judaism had completely abolished it in America. Separate seating pitted modernity, Americanization, and women's issues against Jewish legal (*halakhic*) practices.[181] Mixed seating represented local norms; its proponents portrayed it as fostering family togetherness, woman's equality, a modern progressive image, and attracting youth.[182] On the Conservative side, there were congregations that maintained a *mehitzah* and separate seating. In 1921 in the Conservative movement, the question of family pews came up before the Rabbinical Assembly's Committee on Interpretation of Jewish Law. Louis Ginzberg, chair of the committee, felt that seating should be "separate but equal" but that the Jewish custom should be upheld.[183] The Conservative congregational association, called the United Synagogue of America, did not sanction mixed seating. There were also Orthodox congregations without *mehitzot*. The issue fell into a "gray area."

The trend to mixed seating met with opposition from Orthodox groups because they regarded the *mehitzah* as a cardinal principle and a confirmation of preservation of the Orthodox character of the synagogue. However, according to Revel, who represented the Modern Orthodox position, a rabbi could take a pulpit in a non-*mehitzah* synagogue for a limited number of years, as long as he worked to have one installed.[184] This compromise was also a dividing issue for Modern

---

181 Sarna, "The Debate Over Mixed Seating in the American Synagogue," in *The American Synagogue*, ed. Jack Wertheimer, 363.
182 Ibid., 378.
183 Ibid., 380.
184 Rakeffet-Rothkoff, *Bernard Revel*, 227.

Orthodoxy and the Agudath Harabbonim, which remained unresolved for decades. But in the 1920s, this issue was another example of how Modern Orthodoxy had not yet clearly defined itself.

Modern Orthodoxy—Position on Zionism

Support for Zionism was not unanimous in the 1920s among the Jewish people. It would always be problematic in the Orthodox world, but participation within the Zionist movement would be an identifying feature of Modern Orthodoxy. The Orthodox had issues to consider, one of which was bringing redemption before its time. One of the tenets of Judaism is that when the Messiah comes, Israel shall be returned to the Jewish people. How to justify the return of the land through man's efforts and through cooperation with secularists, thus negating the role of the Messiah, was a dilemma for Orthodoxy. Mizrachi, a Modern Orthodox, Zionist organization founded in Vilna in 1902, argued that Jews were permitted, even obliged, to participate in the redemption that was slowly coming.[185] Rabbi Jung, like most Modern Orthodox Jews, did not object to man's efforts to save himself, but rather to the secular emphasis of political Zionism.

Mizrachi and Agudath Israel

Supporters of Zionism organized as the Mizrachi movement. The movement saw Jewish nationalism as an instrument for realizing religious objectives, especially of enhancing the opportunities for the observance of the Torah by a Jewish society living on its own soil. Religious Zionism was brought to America in 1914. The goal of Mizrachi was to regenerate Jewish life in the diaspora and to instill a love for Hebrew and Judaism.[186] In 1920, Rabbi Berlin, president of the Mizrachi Organization of America, said:

> This is the main task of the Mizrachi in this country when it founded the "Beth Hamidrash for Teachers," which is now

---

185 Jeffrey S. Gurock, *The Men and Women of Yeshiva: Higher Education, Orthodoxy, and American Judaism* (New York: Columbia University Press, 1988), 67–68.
186 Ibid., 68.

being conducted by the Mizrachi together with the Rabbi Isaac Elchanan Theological Seminary [RIETS]; namely to train educators to instruct teachers to be able to perceive Judaism as a common whole, indivisible, a Judaism of the past and the future—enabling them to rear an educated, loyal generation of Jews in America.[187]

RIETS had incorporated the Mizrachi's teacher's institute in 1921, signaling a strong Zionist orientation on the part of Modern Orthodoxy's flagship institution.[188] The UOJCA also affirmed that Zionism conflicted with neither religious injunctions nor demands of loyalty to America.[189] This reassurance was necessary since Jews had to be reassured that Zionism would not jeopardize their status in America and would not demand their *aliyah*, or immigration to Israel. American Jews were still adapting to America, and America was their "promised land." For Modern Orthodoxy, Zionism was not only a movement to create a political haven for Jews; it also had a religious connotation.

Mizrachi focused efforts to rebuild a Jewish state and fought for the right of Orthodox Jews to autonomy in cultural and religious affairs within the Zionist movement. However, Mizrachi's role in the development of Israel reflected the role of Modern Orthodoxy itself, as its program was not well organized and it had not established roots in American Orthodox life at that time. Mizrachi had joined the Zionist movement, but was weak. The great masses of Orthodox Jews had not been attracted, although most Modern Orthodox rabbis and organizations supported Mizrachi.[190]

Agudath Israel had been founded in 1912, nearly a decade after Mizrachi, by European Orthodox leaders, heads of *yeshivot*, and

---

187 Berlin, "Jewish Education in America," 587.
188 Shmuel Almog, Jehuda Reinharz, and Anita Shapira, eds., *Zionism and Religion* (Hanover, NH: University Press of New England, 1998), 224.
189 Melvin I. Urofsky, *American Zionism from Herzl to the Holocaust*, 2nd edition (Lincoln, NE: University of Nebraska Press, 1995), 101.
190 Jeffrey S. Gurock, "American Orthodox Organizations in Support of Zionism, 1880–1930," in *Zionism and Religion*, eds. Shmuel Almog, Jehuda Reinharz, and Anita Shapira (Waltham, MA: Brandeis University Press, 1998), 226.

Hasidic *rebbes*, along with some followers of Rabbi Samson Raphael Hirsch. They believed to various degrees that there was no need for a Jewish state, but that if there was to be a Jewish state it must not be run by secular Zionists. It did, however, support religious institutions in Palestine. When Agudath Israel was founded, it was felt that it would represent all Orthodox Jews internationally.[191] This was not to be, especially when anti-Zionism became one of its hallmarks. Rabbi Jung affiliated with both organizations in the 1920s; he was active in Agudath Israel and on the Rabbinic Council of Agudath Israel in America, and he was also a member of Mizrachi. He was a committed lover of *Eretz Israel*, but his support for political Zionism was, at this time, ambiguous.[192] This dual affiliation represented the Modern Orthodox dilemma about Zionism. OUJCA leaders attempted, without success, to unite the two Orthodox movements to reinforce Orthodox cohesion.[193]

The question is how there could be affiliation with both Mizrachi and Agudath Israel, which were philosophically quite different on the issue of Zionism. Clearly, there was an attempt by some Orthodox leaders to misrepresent the differences; in some instances, they did not fully understand the differences themselves.[194] The anti-Zionist philosophy of Agudath Israel was either not discussed or toned down in America. Agudath Israel had proposed cooperation with the Zionist organization based on the notion that religious education should be left to Orthodoxy, while politics and economics could be in the hands of Zionists. For everything other than Jewish law, they would cooperate with all Jews.[195] The Zionist organization would not accept these compromises, but some Modern Orthodox followers could.

---

191 Marc B. Shapiro, *Between the Yeshiva World and Modern Orthodoxy: The Life and Works of Jehiel Jacob Weinberg, 1884–1966* (London and Portland, OR: Littman Library of Jewish Civilization, 1999), 67.
192 Jung, "Agudath Israel, Zionism and a Modus Vivendi," *Jewish Forum* 7, no. 11 (November 1924).
193 Bernstein, *Challenge and Mission*, 63.
194 Jung, "Agudath Israel, Zionism and a Modus Vivendi," 714–716; Almog, Reinharz, and Shapiro, eds., *Zionism and Religion*, 226.
195 Jung, "Agudath Israel, Zionism and a Modus Vivendi," 720.

Rabbi Jung also feared that nationalist Zionism was too powerful, that *Eretz Israel* went beyond a colonizing scheme or refuge. For him, just as modern nationalism (which led to greed and brute force) had failed, so too would "Godless" nationalism in *Eretz Israel* fail.[196] Also, at that time, he liked some Agudath Israel projects. In the 1920s, Agudath Israel adopted educational and economic programs that included work in Palestine, even as it fought Zionism.[197] Agudath Israel was also involved in the sale of land in Palestine to a number of Americans.[198] In defending Agudath Israel, Rabbi Jung pointed to these land sales as an example that Agudath Israel did indeed work for the building up of *Eretz Israel*. He represented Agudath Israel and worked with Dr. Chaim Weizmann on the problem of Agudath Israel's participation in the Jewish Agency. The problem was never solved.[199]

Agudath Israel became more unacceptable over time to the majority of Jews who supported the idea of a Jewish State. It did not want a State of Israel and it would not cooperate with the Jewish Agency. The desire for *Eretz Israel* as a Torah center and the acceptance of a political reality was an obstacle to a unified front.[200] Rabbi Jung's affiliations with Zionism changed over the years; he, like American Jewry, was still feeling his way in the 1920s. By the early 1940s, he quit Agudath Israel over its policy of noncooperation with the Jewish Agency.

Trends and Issues—Conclusion

What Modern Orthodoxy lacked in the 1920s were hard lines and clear concepts. Modern Orthodoxy was making social changes while attempting to keep the *halakhic* tradition intact. A new generation of rabbis was

---

196 Jung, *Foundations of Judaism*, 68; Jung, "Orthodoxy, Reform and Kaplanism," 780.
197 Urofsky, *American Zionism from Herzl to the Holocaust*, 41.
198 Yeshiva University Archives, Koenigsberg Papers, Box 14, Folder 1—letter to Dr. Ehrmann. A copy of letter was sent to Rabbi Jung, dated November 14, 1929. Some of the Americans had defaulted on payments, so that the land reverted to the previous Arab owners. Other Americans had paid in full, but had not yet received their deeds.
199 Ibid., Box 1, Folder 4—letter to Chaim Weizmann from Rabbi Jung, October 31, 1926; Ibid., Box 14, Folder 1.
200 Alan Mittleman, *The Politics of Torah: The Jewish Tradition and the Founding of Agudat Israel* (Albany, NY, State University of New York Press), 53.

emerging with a positive attitude to Americanization. The emphasis was that *halakhah* was relevant and compatible with Americanism and modernity. The ethical, this-worldly aspect of Judaism, congruent with modernity, was stressed; secular undertakings should accompany Torah living. This was reflected in "harmonious" education, the drive for decorum, and the attitude towards Zionism.

The establishment of Yeshiva College helped to define Modern Orthodoxy, as it would begin to establish policy and precedents. With the advent of Yeshiva, differences between Conservative and Orthodox Judaism in the 1920s became clearer and greater.

The Modern Orthodox leadership began to establish and develop institutions and organizations to educate the Jewish population and create the necessities for an Orthodox life. They began to reach out to all Jews, vowing not to practice "insular" Orthodoxy.

Modern Orthodoxy began to develop in the 1920s; those were the formative years of Modern Orthodoxy and much else in American Jewish life. Orthodoxy was beginning to tackle its problems.

2. MODERN ORTHODOXY IN THE 1930S

...

"What a dark place the world has become of late! How full it is of hopes thwarted, expectations disappointed."
(Leo Jung, "Sovietism, Gangsterism, Cynicism")

Introduction

The 1920s was a prosperous period; the American dream and Enlightenment ideals led to newfound freedoms. There was a new approach to American-style Orthodoxy—the leaders talked to the anxieties of the age and the problems of religious life that the modern age presented.[1] The "Roaring Twenties," however, came to an abrupt stop in the 1930s. There were changes in the 1930s that colored all aspects of life. The Depression and the rise of Hitler represented added challenges. The 1930s were troubled times, when physical survival was paramount, thus progress slowed as efforts went into maintaining what had already been achieved. Orthodox organizations were obliged to postpone the development of new facilities as there was no money. They did concentrate on new types of programs, however, and groundwork in educational and organizational activities continued. This chapter will demonstrate that, despite all this, seeds for progress in Orthodoxy were planted that only germinated in later decades.

Very important was the foundation of the Rabbinical Council of America (RCA). This organization helped to define, defend, and represent Modern Orthodoxy and what it stood for, and in doing so, added prestige to Modern Orthodoxy.

---

1 Matthew S. Hadstrom, *The Rise of Liberal Religion* (Oxford and New York: Oxford University Press, 2013), 36.

Rabbi Jung had emphasized that Judaism was a religion of social justice; this emphasis grew in importance during the 1930s. His "this-worldly approach" and ability to participate in the secular world became an important defining point for Modern Orthodoxy in the 1930s. His philosophy of "cooperation without compromise" and of respecting differences was equated by him with true Americanism.[2] Modern Orthodoxy was brought into the realm of social activism, which was necessary for its survival.

Necessity made Rabbi Jung's role and the role of other Modern Orthodox leaders more pragmatic. Modern Orthodox leaders began to be more involved in Jewish and non-Jewish community activities. Modern Orthodoxy thus attempted to function in both the sacred and the secular sphere. This was important, as it enabled them to present and implement the ideas of Modern Orthodoxy and to make demands to render the observance of *kashrut* and the Sabbath possible. Yet, Rabbi Jung's message that the secular approach of modernity was imperfect and that science had its limitations was beginning to be heard.

Rabbi Jung used every tool available to reach out to the community at large. His example demonstrated the expanded role that American rabbis had to assume. Rabbi Jung tried to save Jews and Judaism; he worked from his synagogue pulpit and boardroom, in organizations created for the rescue of Jews, educational activities, and Zionist efforts. He helped to bring European Jewish scholars to America, where their influence would be felt in the future; he used his pulpit and his writings to stress the virtues of Modern Orthodoxy. By the end of the 1930s, American Modern Orthodox rabbis were beginning to have more influence, and Modern Orthodoxy was beginning to show more self-confidence.

The State of Orthodoxy

Lack of Religious Fervor

In 1931, the Union of Orthodox Jewish Congregations of America (UOJCA; otherwise known as the Orthodox Union, or the OU)

---

2   Leo Jung, "Jewry Today," *Jewish Forum* 19, no. 7 (September 1936): 202.

identified a spiritual depression in American life.³ As the vice-president of the UOJCA, Rabbi Jung joined in its effort to combat anti-religious activities. Rabbi William Weiss, the president of the UOJCA, called on the community to "combat the spirit of religious indifference which had accompanied the economic depression."⁴ Most Jews, however, ignored efforts to attract them to religious institutions.

There was so little support for Orthodoxy that, in 1935, the OU willingly joined with its Reform and Conservative rivals in a "back to the synagogue" endeavor, which met with limited success.⁵ This project was intended to stimulate interest in synagogue and congregational membership; it was an example of the weakness of the religious community and its affiliations.⁶ Modern Orthodoxy was not alone in fighting for a religious life. If it had been stronger, this project would not have been necessary.

Rabbi Jung convened a special committee to see that the practice of opening Jewish theaters on Rosh Hashana, the Jewish New Year, be stopped.⁷ Yiddish theater was an important pastime for Eastern European Jews, evoking nostalgia while expressing values and attitudes, and opening on Rosh Hashana purposely demonstrated an anti-religious position. Rabbi Jung received support in this effort from various Jewish organizations, including Mizrachi, the American Jewish Committee, B'nai Brith, The New York Board of Jewish Ministers, and the American Jewish Congress.⁸ He met with success in this endeavor; a general rule resulted that the Yiddish theater would remain closed on Rosh Hashana.⁹ It was a small victory, as Rabbi Jung was able to convince the

---

3   Beth Wenger, *New York Jews and the Great Depression* (New Haven: Yale University Press, 1996), 184.
4   Saul Bernstein, *The Orthodox Story: A Centenary Portrayal* (Northvale, NJ and Jerusalem: Jason Aronson Inc., 1997), 109.
5   Jeffrey S. Gurock, "The Orthodox Synagogue," in *American Jewish Orthodoxy in Historical Perspective*, ed. Jeffrey S. Gurock (New York: Ktav Publishing House Inc., 1996), 96.
6   Ibid., 245; Wenger, *New York Jews and the Great Depression*, 178.
7   Yeshiva University Archives, Jung Collection, Box 20, Folder 10—letter to Rabbi Jung from Rabbi William Weiss, president of UOJCA, December 27, 1936.
8   Ibid.—letter to Rabbi Jung from Stephen Wise, December 3, 1936, and letter to Rabbi Jung from Cyrus Adler, December 4, 1936.
9   Ibid.—letter to Mr. Reubin Guskin from Rabbi Jung, July 30, 1937.

non-Orthodox to cooperate, and religious values were upheld, strengthening Jewish life in America and eliminating a source of embarrassment to Jews on the American scene.

Emphasizing Social Issues

Mainstream American religious movements began to emphasize social issues.[10] Rabbi Jung echoed this message. He wrote:

> There are people who would like to confine religion to the dietary laws, the Sabbath, Jewish education and the laws of family purity, which of course are basic. They look with misgivings, however, upon any sermon on social justice and would advise the rabbi not to mix in politics. They have never arrived at an appreciation of the function of religion.[11]

Rabbi Jung believed that ensuring social justice was a function of religion and that the clergy should "mix into politics." He wrote:

> Religion, as the Jewish tradition sees it, has to do with every aspect of life and with every class of every age, sex, occupation. Judaism is a social religion, interested in the poor, the laborer, the woman, the alien, the man in the dock.[12]

Rabbi Jung reiterated throughout his career that the purpose of the Torah teachings was to bring "justice, righteousness, and freedom."[13] He wrote in his synagogue bulletin: "...but its major purpose [the *mitzvot* or laws] is to make us conscious of our social responsibility..."[14]

---

10 Edwin Scott Gaustad, *A Religious History of America* (New York: Harper & Row Publishers, 1966), 334–340. Also discussed in Martin Marty, "The Church Against the World: The Recovery of Protest and Realism," in *Righteous Empire: The Protestant Experience in America*, ed. Martin Marty (New York: Dial Press, 1970).
11 Leo Jung, "Judaism and Economic Freedom," *Jewish Forum* 18, no. 9 (June 1935): 119.
12 Leo Jung, *Between Man and Man* (New York: Jewish Educational Press, 1976), 6. First published under the title *Human Relations in Jewish Law* (New York: Jewish Educational Press, 1967).
13 Jung, "Judaism and Economic Freedom," 119.
14 Jung, "Things Without Measure and Other Editorials," *The Jewish Center Bulletin*, 1937, 12.

Torah laws prevented exploitation and oppression; Rabbi Jung pointed out that business ethics and morals were taught in the Torah: "... honesty in business is no achievement; it is a minimum contribution to social welfare as demanded by Jewish law."[15] So many rabbinic sermons dealt with this theme that, in one synagogue, a congregant jokingly remarked: "How about some social justice for the congregation by preaching on a different subject?"[16] Modern Orthodoxy thus attempted to function in both sacred and secular spheres.

Modern Orthodoxy Involved in Social Issues

During the 1930s, Rabbi Jung participated "in an utterly new kind of work," as Orthodoxy in the United States became involved in "every form of charitable activity."[17] He emphasized religious leadership and the synagogue's leadership in communal affairs. Rabbi Jung had to stop himself from total involvement in social service so as not to neglect "teaching and preaching, [and] on developing his knowledge of both Jewish law and modern disciplines."[18] During the 1920s, he had concentrated on the conventional roles of teaching, preaching, writing, visiting the sick, and comforting the mourners, but in the 1930s, this was not enough. The rabbis and teachers in Europe, those who could teach about Judaism and their pupils, had to be rescued from danger. He became very active on the Cultural Committee of the Joint Distribution Committee (JDC), with which he had been associated since 1926. The JDC was established in 1914 in a merger of three relief committees— the American Jewish Relief Committee, the Central Relief Committee, and the People's Relief Committee, as an organization for the civil protection of Jewish people all over the world. Its work included relief and reconstruction in places where this was necessary, and it was the largest and most important organization of its kind. In addition to

---

15 Yeshiva University Archives, Jung Collection, Box 48, Folder 4 (published articles)—Jung, "Orthodox Judaism," 2.
16 Mendel Lewittes, "The Semi-Centennial of the Jewish Theological Seminary," *Jewish Forum* 20, no. 8 (August 1937): 135.
17 Wenger, *New York Jews and the Great Depression*, 195.
18 Leo Jung, *The Path of a Pioneer: Autobiography of Leo Jung*, Jewish Library, Second Series, vol. 8 (London and New York: Soncino Press, 1980), 138.

rescue and relief activities, the JDC acted as a funding source for several groups, including the maintenance of certain German Jewish Children's Associations (GJCA). It built up social welfare institutions and trained local populations to run them.

From 1933 to 1935, its program abroad was seen "as the greatest single effort on the part of the Jewish people of one country for the welfare of the Jews of other countries, recorded in Jewish history."[19] The JDC took on new importance because of the situation in Nazi Germany. It became the representative agency for Jews in the United States and Canada in the fight to rescue Jews in Europe,[20] and it inaugurated the beginning of a major role for American Jewry in world Jewish affairs. Rabbi Jung's involvement raised the profile of Modern Orthodoxy, and he saw to it that Orthodox concerns were addressed.

The Cultural Committee's raison d'être was to meet societal-religious needs.[21] One of many examples of this is when Rabbi Jung took exception to the small amount allotted to Orthodox institutions in Poland in 1935, as against grants for Yiddishist and *Tarbut* schools in Poland.[22] Dr. Cyrus Adler, chair of the Cultural Committee, was also unhappy that decisions were left with the European directors, and felt that they should be made in New York. It can be seen that American Jewry was beginning to take on a more responsible role in world Jewish affairs. Proportionately very small amounts were being allocated to cultural-religious activities as physical needs were being given primary consideration. Rabbi Jung repeatedly pleaded with American Jews to endorse the cultural activities of the JDC:

> Physical relief is impossible with spiritual decadence... I call my people in this country... to make their contributions

---

19 Maurice J. Karpf, "Community Organization in the United States," *American Jewish Year Book*, 39 (1937–1938): 120.
20 Joseph Hyman, "25 Years of American Aid to Jews Overseas: A Record of the JDC," *American Jewish Year Book*, 41 (1939–1940): 177.
21 Joint Distribution Committee (JDC) Archives, File 92, 33/44—"Requirements for Cultural Religious Institutes," August 19, 1940; Ibid., File 89, 33/44—"Rabbi Leo Jung Demands Support For The Security of the Spiritual and Cultural Institutions," February 6, 1935.
22 Ibid., File 89, 33/44—minutes of meeting, May 8, 1935.

towards the survival of Judaism; that the Cultural Committee of the Jewish Joint Distribution Committee revive its essential work; that every shade of Jewish religious opinion...unite in a single effort to provide sustenance for the institutes of Jewish learning both here and abroad.[23]

By 1940, the Cultural Committee gave assistance to more than 100 school organizations, *yeshivot,* and other institutes of learning in Eastern Europe, Palestine, and South America.[24] Rabbi Jung worked with Louis Marshall (a renowned lawyer and the head of the American Jewish Committee), New York Governor Herbert Lehman, and Adler (the president of Jewish Theological Seminary [JTS]). It is another example of Modern Orthodox involvement with the community at large. The Cultural Committee members throughout the 1930s also included the Orthodox presence of Rabbi Herbert Goldstein and Morris Engelman, active committee member of the cultural and religious Central Relief Committee and originator of the plan for American relief for Jews who suffered in the war.[25] Rabbi Jung later reminisced, as follows:

> The cultural work of the JDC embraces the whole horizon of Jewish education, the flowering of the Jewish spirit; *yeshivoth* in Europe and Israel, schools for infants, children, adolescents, and adults, the promotion of Jewish literature, and the encouragement of spiritual life in all the countries of our people's migration. The whole panorama of a life-enriching, life-endorsing program has been a task, both taxing and inspiring, which has challenged my heart and mind, my energies and steadfastness for over forty years. For twenty-six years, it has

---

23 Ibid.—"Rabbi Leo Jung Demands Support for the Security of the Spiritual and Cultural Institutions."
24 Ibid., File 92, 33/44—"Requirements for Cultural-Religious Institutions," August 19, 1940.
25 Bernstein, *The Orthodox Story*, 119. For information on Morris Engelman: Yeshiva University Archives, Mendel Gottesman Library—"Records of Central Relief Committee: Morris Engelman, 1872-1948."

been my privilege to head the cultural-religious committee and to see the moral and spiritual rehabilitations of our people...[26]

Rabbi Jung's efforts to save European Jewry as well as its *yeshivot* began in the 1930s. He traveled the world on behalf of the JDC and acquired an understanding of the situation of world Jewry. In the 1930s, he went to Poland under the auspices of the JDC.[27] The Agudath Harabbonim and many other Jewish organizations sent appeals to President Hoover to help Jews in Poland.[28] However, it was the JDC rather than the UOJCA that was most effective in this area.[29]

After Kristallnacht, on November 11, 1938, when the intentions of Hitler and German anti-Semitism became clearer, many European Jews sought avenues of rescue for their children. The German Jewish Children's Aid Group would only place the children in the type of religious homes that they came from, thus Orthodox children encountered particular problems because there was an inadequate number of observant homes available in the United States. It became an unwritten policy to avoid bringing Orthodox children to America.[30] This lack of Orthodox homes was another sign of American Orthodoxy's weakness. Rabbi Jung was instrumental in getting at least a few Orthodox children to America during the 1930s. According to Judith Tydor Baumel, who researched the rescue of children at this time, "he was a one-man dynamo, the only Orthodox rabbi on record to attempt to locate observant homes."[31] Homes for some of these children were found in Rochester, Chicago, and a few in Boston, but not in New York. One major problem was that the government did not allow homes to have more than two children to a bedroom and Orthodox homes tended to have many children.[32] Though there was a lack of money, the main issue

---

26 Jung, *The Path of a Pioneer*, 81.
27 Ibid., 150.
28 Harry Schneiderman, "Review of the Year 5692," *American Jewish Year Book* 34 (1932–1933): 26.
29 Judith Tydor Baumel, *Unfulfilled Promise: Rescue and Resettlement of Jewish Refugee Children in the United States, 1934–1945* (Juneau, AK: Denali Press, 1990), 147.
30 Ibid., 105.
31 Ibid., 147; email from Baumel to Maxine Jacobson, September 24, 1997.
32 Email from Baumel to Jacobson, September 8, 1997.

2. MODERN ORTHODOXY IN THE 1930S

was lack of space. Few Orthodox children were rescued, and some were placed in non-Orthodox homes. Some of these children became assimilated; parents reclaimed others after the war. Rabbi Jung found no homes in his own congregation. This is significant; perhaps his congregants did not meet the standards for Orthodox homes, though it is not clear who set the standards. Rabbi Jung did not write about this disappointing situation.

Rabbi Jung, in his role with the JDC, received varied requests, each demonstrating once more a new leadership role for American Orthodoxy. A letter from the first Chief Rabbi of Spain explained the plight of Jews there. In 1934, after 442 years, Spain opened its doors to Jews forced from their homes in Germany and Central Europe who sought refuge there. These refugees had no established community to assist them, thus they looked to American Jews.[33]

Letters also arrived from Germany. According to the scholar and author, Marc B. Shapiro, when Hermann Goering demanded of Jewish leaders in Berlin, in 1933, that they contact newspapers outside Germany to deny that there were anti-Semitic German assaults on the Jews, Rabbi Ezra Munk (an important Orthodox rabbi in Berlin) chose to write to Rabbi Jung requesting that he contact all newspapers declaring that atrocities against the Jews were false.[34] This letter, we can assume, was written under duress; it was felt that external pressure was damaging. Rabbi Jung was involved in rescuing Jews, thus he had to know that this letter brought false information; he did not follow up on the request. Another letter, on behalf of German Jewry to the American JDC, explained that, since 1935, the supply of kosher food had been cut; American Jewish assistance was again requested.[35] Rabbi Jung and Adler, as JDC members, tried to respond to the German Jewish community's request to provide kosher food, which was unavailable because of Nazi decrees

---

33 Jung, *The Path of a Pioneer*, 226.
34 Marc B. Shapiro, *Between the Yeshiva World and Modern Orthodoxy: The Life and Works of Jehiel Jacob Weinberg, 1884–1966* (London and Portland, OR: Littman Library of Jewish Civilization, 1999), 209.
35 Ibid., 227; Yeshiva University Archives, Jung Collection, Box 9, Folder 3—to the Joint Distribution Committee from Reichszentraie fur Schachtangelegenheiten (Jewish organization representing all the Jewish organizations), September 30, 1936.

against ritual slaughter. They tried to see if frozen food could be sent, but that was found to be unacceptable, as it would not be edible upon arrival. They looked into the option of sending salted or pickled meat. However, they were not successful because, according to Rabbi Jung, wholesale butchers "are unwilling to give something for nothing," and there were "no funds available for the purpose of supplying kosher meat for Jewish institutions in Germany."[36]

Rabbi Jung was constantly in touch with American government officials urging that consideration be given to individual applications for immigration visas.[37] Some German Jewish refugees escaped from Germany and did come to America, where Rabbi Jung urged his synagogue to welcome them.[38] That he had to urge the congregation, which was made up mostly of Eastern European Jews, to welcome these refugees suggests that the pattern with the orphans was being repeated. Strained relationships between German Jews and Eastern European Jews had a history going back to Europe; as Shapiro wrote, the relationship was never marked by mutual respect or understanding.[39] However, Rabbi Jung had studied in Germany and was part of the German Orthodox world, thus he could understand them. The German Jewish refugees who came to America created an Orthodox subcommunity in Washington Heights, snidely called "the Fourth Reich" by other Jews.[40] Their cool welcome might be one factor that kept the Orthodox German refugee community autonomous and separate from other Jewish and Orthodox groups.

New Influences

It was difficult to get into America in the 1930s, but with the help of Jewish agencies and individual Jews, immigrants did come. These new

---

36 Yeshiva University Archives, Jung Collection, Box 9, Folder 3—letter to Rabbi Ezra Munk from Rabbi Jung, January 27, 1937. See all correspondence between Rabbi Munk and Rabbi Jung in Box 9, Folder 3.
37 Ibid., Box 40, Folder 3—letter from Robert F. Wagner, Chairman of U.S. Committee on Banking and Currency, September 20, 1939.
38 Jewish Center Synagogue Archives—minutes of Board of Trustees meeting, Jewish Center Synagogue, November 12, 1936.
39 Shapiro, *Between the Yeshiva World and Modern Orthodoxy*, 54.
40 Wenger, *New York Jews and the Great Depression*, 94.

immigrants would influence Modern Orthodoxy in the future. New immigrants came with religious backgrounds, devoted to tradition. Included in their number were a significant percentage of traditional Orthodox and Hasidic groups, the spiritual and intellectual elite. Earlier immigrants had come seeking a better financial future, often with the desire to throw off the yoke of their earlier religious life. This time, however, efforts to build a Torah life were more successful than before.

Yeshiva College and Rabbi Jung were involved in a frantic race to bring students, rabbis, and professionals to the United States in the face of threats to the lives and welfare of European Jews.[41] At Rabbi Jung's request, Dr. Bernard Revel prepared the necessary nonquota admissions papers for various rabbis.[42] Refugees augmented the Yeshiva student body and recent arrivals joined the staff.[43] Though Yeshiva College was under tremendous financial strain, it provided refuge, shelter, instruction, and scholarships. Yeshiva also established refugee grants.[44]

A new influence was Rabbi Moses Soloveitchik. Reb Moshe, as he was known, became an integral part of the Yeshiva scene. After the death of Rabbi Solomon Polatchek, the Rabbi Isaac Elchanan Theological Seminary (RIETS) offered his position as *rosh yeshiva* (head of the *yeshiva*) to Rabbi Moses Soloveitchik, who came to America in 1929.[45] The new *rosh yeshiva* brought prestige to American Orthodoxy and to Yeshiva; his family had been leading Talmudic scholars.[46] His background was not Modern Orthodox, but his daughter, Shulamit

---

41 Aaron Rakeffet-Rothkoff, *Bernard Revel: Builder of American Jewish Orthodoxy* (Philadelphia: Jewish Publication Society of America, 1972), 200.
42 Yeshiva University Archives, Revel Papers, Box 3, Folder 5/3-21—letter to Rabbi Jung from Dr. Revel, February 28, 1930; letter to Dr. Revel from Rabbi Jung, October 25, 1932. Rabbi Jung arranged for two men from Bombay to receive free board and lodging from Yeshiva; this is but one example.
43 Yeshiva University Archives, "Yeshiva Establishes Refugee Grants," *The Synthesis* (RIETS and Yeshiva College newspaper; April 1939): 1.
44 Ibid.
45 Aaron Rakeffet-Rothkoff, "The Semi-Centennial of Yeshiva and Yeshiva College," in *Ramaz: School, Community, Scholarship and Orthodoxy*, ed. Jeffrey S. Gurock (Hoboken, NJ: Ktav Publishing House, 1989), 6.
46 Yeshiva University Archives, "Our Rosh Yeshiva Rabbi Moses Soloveitchik," *Hazedek* (publication of Student Organization of Yeshiva University) 8, no. 4 (March 31, 1940): 2.

Meiselman, confirmed that he had adopted a new approach to secular education: "he now maintained a new philosophy that in this changing world both religious and general education were necessary if one was to have an effective influence on Jewish young people"—provided that it did not conflict with tradition.[47] His son, Rabbi Joseph B. Soloveitchik, had attended the University of Berlin where he received a PhD, thus his view of education had probably changed even while in Europe. Rabbi Moses Soloveitchik joined Dr. Revel and Benjamin Aranowitz to form the Yeshiva ordination board during the 1930s.[48] In 1932, Rabbi Joseph B. Soloveitchik was brought to the United States by the Hebrew Theological College.[49] He later became the mentor, par excellence, for Modern Orthodox rabbis and lay people.

In his travels for the Cultural Committee of the JDC, Rabbi Jung encountered the good work of Lubavitch Hasidim, whom he grew to admire. Lubavitch Hasidim had originally come from the town of Lubavitch (Lyubavichi), which is in the Smolensk Oblast (region) in Russia (next to the border with Belarus), but by the twentieth century had spread far beyond its place of origin. It may not be a coincidence that Lubavitch refugees first settled near Rabbi Jung's Jewish Center Synagogue, and the Upper West Side of Manhattan became an area of Hasidic settlement. Rabbi Joseph Isaac Schneersohn, head of the Lubavitch movement (also known as Habad), and descendent of the founder of the movement, delivered his first American address at the Jewish Center Synagogue. Every year after that, the Jewish Center raised money for Habad. Rabbi Jung reminisced in his autobiography:

> Thereafter every year, a *Malavah Malkah* (after-Sabbath night dinner) helped to ease financial problems of his [Rabbi Joseph Schneerson's] organization. Its *yeshiva* received part of my annual Hanukkah Appeal funds.[50]

---

47 Shulamit Soloveitchik Meiselman, *The Soloveitchik Heritage: A Daughter's Memoirs* (Hoboken, NJ: Ktav Publishing House Inc., 1995), 214.
48 Rakeffet-Rothkoff, "The Semi-Centennial of Yeshiva and Yeshiva College," 7.
49 Oscar Fasman, "After Fifty Years, an Optimist," *American Jewish History* 69, no. 2 (December 1979): 160.
50 Jung, *The Path of a Pioneer*, 125.

Rabbi Jung tried to modernize Orthodoxy, yet he gave them a platform where their message could be heard—a message heard could in some way influence. As Rabbi Jung had taken out of Reform and Reconstructionist Judaism what he liked, he could appreciate the enthusiasm and devotion of the Lubavitch. Even if unintentional, this was an important influence on the congregation.

Many new *yeshivot* began in the 1930s. They did not wish to Americanize, as did the Modern Orthodox, whom they opposed.[51] The graduates of these *yeshivot* would, over the course of decades, come to influence Modern Orthodoxy as they would teach in Modern Orthodox institutions, be hired as professionals in Modern Orthodox synagogues, and be an example to Orthodox Jews of an appealing devotion and fervor.[52]

New Look at Modernity

Rabbi Jung cited the examples of the spiritual failures of modernity as confirmation that Orthodoxy had been correct in its uncompromising stand for the observance of Torah laws. He believed that modernity had not brought about a life of justice, righteousness, equality, or happiness.[53] The Orthodox message was that people had been woefully deceived by the promises of modernity and that the compromises of Reform Judaism and Mordecai Kaplan, as well as Conservative Judaism, had accomplished nothing.[54] People had assimilated at the expense of religious observance, believing that it would bring about equality, but the 1930s brought social discrimination and political calamity.

In the eyes of the Orthodox, other Jewish groups had made concessions to the society at large with the idea that this would erase anti-Semitism. In Rabbi Jung's opinion, the Reform movement

---

51 Jeffrey S. Gurock, "The Orthodox Synagogue," in *The American Synagogue: A Sanctuary Transformed*, ed. Jack Wertheimer (Cambridge, UK, and New York: Cambridge University Press, 1987), 64.
52 William Helmreich, "Old Wine in New Bottles: Advanced Yeshivot in the United States," *American Jewish History* 69, no. 2 (December 1979): 243 and 251.
53 Leo Jung, "The Way Up," *Jewish Forum* 16, vol. 10 (October 1933): 103.
54 Leo Jung, "Modern Trends in American Judaism" (New York: Mizrachi Jubilee Publication, 1936), 8. Available at the Jewish Center Synagogue Archives.

(a product of modernity) had encouraged assimilation, and he lamented the result:

> None have tried harder than a certain section of German Jewry to escape Jewishness. They eliminated every reference to Zion from their prayer book. Hebrew became almost forbidden to them. ... In no country did Jewry contribute to the glory of the fatherland as fully, successfully and abidingly as in Germany. ... They denied their names, their parents, their grandparents. ... There were no assimilationists like the German Jewish self-haters.[55]

None had been assimilated more than German Jews, yet Rabbi Jung pointed out that they could not escape the consequences of being Jewish.[56] He claimed that "un-Jewish Jews denying Judaism" still existed everywhere; yet they were not being admitted into gentile society.[57] The rise of Hitler prompted new anti-Semitism in the United States, which caused Jews to feel not quite so at home in America.

Rabbi Jung wrote that the world was in moral turmoil; Russia's godless society, the rise of Hitler, and gangsterism in America pointed to the fallibility of modernity.[58] Rabbi Jung said that the youth had drifted away from the synagogue, "not because the synagogue had been too Jewish, but because it had not been Jewish enough."[59]

In the 1920s, it was popular to evaluate all phenomena through the lens of science; it was difficult for a religious individual to justify one's

---

55 Jung, "The Way Up," 103-104.
56 Ibid.; Yeshiva University Archives, Revel Papers, Box 3/5—letter from Revel to Mr. Salasky in Dallas, October 27, 1936. Professor Einstein's acceptance speech on receiving an honourary degree reads: "If German Jewry had institutions like Yeshiva College, their fate would not have been so tragic as they would have been fortified and sustained spiritually."
57 Jung, "The Way Up," 104.
58 Leo Jung, "Sovietism, Gangsterism, Cynicism: The Challenges of Today," *Jewish Forum* 14, no. 9 (September 1931): 303-307.
59 Yeshiva University Archives, Saphire Papers, Box 14, Folder 30/2-55—Jung, "Some Aspects of Judaism," 10. Also in Leo Jung, ed., *Judaism in a Changing World*, Jewish Library, First Series, vol. 4 (Oxford, England, and New York: Oxford University Press, 1939).

2. MODERN ORTHODOXY IN THE 1930S

position in that atmosphere. It was especially difficult for Modern Orthodoxy, which was perceived incorrectly by the Reform and Conservative movements as being in opposition to the world of science, though the consistent goal of Yeshiva College and Modern Orthodoxy had been to promote harmony between Judaism and science.[60] Earlier claims that religion had retarded the influence of science were challenged. Rabbi Jung included in his Jewish Library series the article by Moses Isaacs that recognized the limitations of science.[61] Rabbi Jung said that "science has become aware of its limitations."[62] In May 1938, the RIETS newspaper wrote that "the most eminent scientists of today have learned not to scoff at religion."[63]

The concept that science had its limitations was echoed by Conservative and Reform rabbis as religion gained more respect.[64] Orthodox Rabbi Mendel Lewittes lauded the 1937 conference of the JTS held to celebrate its 50th anniversary, because it emphasized the "inadequacies of science without faith."[65]

For Rabbi Jung, the more comfortable people were with science, the more confident they could be that science and religion did not threaten each other. In fact, archaeology was "proving that biblical tradition is right" and renewing interest in biblical studies and religion.[66] For the first time, instead of weakening religion, science was furnishing it with new strength.

---

60 David Macht, "Torah and Science Twenty-Five Years Ago and Now," *Jewish Forum* 14, no. 9 (September 1931): 322.
61 Moses Isaacs, "The Challenge of Science," in *Judaism in a Changing World*, ed. Leo Jung, Jewish Library, Second Series, vol. 4 (London and New York: The Soncino Press, 1971).
62 Jung, Introduction, in ed. Jung, *Judaism in a Changing World*, 1971 edition, x.
63 Yeshiva University Archives, "Macht Treats Medical Aspect of Purity Laws," *Hazedek* 6, no. 1 (May 11, 1938): 1.
64 Israel H. Weisfeld, Introduction, and Louis Finkelstein, Forward, in *The Message of Israel: Twenty-four Religious Essays and Sermons by Outstanding Orthodox, Conservative and Reform Rabbis*, ed. Israel H. Weisfeld (New York: Bloch Publishing Co., 1936); Isaac Klein, "The Ten Commandments in a Changing World," in Weisfeld, ed., *The Message of Israel*, XII–XIII; Louis I. Newman, "Profit Motive and Prophet Motif," in Weisfeld, ed., *The Message of Israel*, 88 and 98.
65 Lewittes, "The Semi-Centennial of the Jewish Theological Seminary," 137.
66 Macht, "Torah and Science Twenty-Five Years Ago and Now," 327—quoting *New York Times*, February 15, 1931.

Modern Orthodox Image

Decorum in the synagogue continued to be an important issue for Modern Orthodoxy; it was associated with Americanism and a positive image. The seeds of decorous synagogue behavior that had been planted in the 1920s were cultivated throughout the 1930s. The main area of achievement in this area was improvement in the conduct of the services. The Jewish Center had "blazed a new trail combining conformity to the *Din Torah* [laws of Torah] with modernity of method," and the Jewish Center Synagogue continued to be a model because of its emphasis on congregational singing and on the beauty of its service.[67] Modern Orthodoxy's most representative organization, the UOJCA, continued to emphasize decorum and dignity, and it associated Judaism "with high aesthetic values."[68]

Yet, at the end of the 1930s, a student wrote in one of the RIETS newspapers that "others have introduced so much decorum that its atmosphere is like a fascist military review."[69] There was a call for a "synagogue laboratory" to determine proper length of service, of sermon, type of decorum, and duration of singing. We thus see discontent with decorum from a rabbinical student. This discontent would be shared by others in the Modern Orthodox movement over the decades to come. The wheels of change are slow.

In terms of self-image, it was important to appear to be Americanized, thus the American Modern Orthodox Jew presented himself in the American fashion of the era. Most of the rabbis of the RCA and the UOJCA representing Modern Orthodoxy were clean shaven.[70] Rabbi Joseph B. Soloveitchik, who became the mentor of Modern Orthodoxy, did not have a beard in the 1930s.[71] This was even more true of Orthodox laymen. Traditional Orthodox and Hasidic rabbis all had beards, symbolizing that for them, Americanization was undesirable. Rabbi

---

67 Jewish Center Synagogue Archives—Jung, "Things Without Measure and Other Essentials," *Jewish Center Bulletin* (1937): 15.
68 Ibid.
69 Yeshiva University Archives—B. Finkelstein, "Let's Try It," *Hazedek* (November 2, 1938): 2.
70 Fasman, "After Fifty Years, an Optimist," 161.
71 Personal interview with Norman Lamm, January 16, 2003.

Jung came to America in 1920 with a beard and always had one; his beard, however, was neatly and stylishly trimmed. He was a man with his foot in both worlds, religious and modern.

Changes in Synagogue Outlook and Activities

During the Depression, synagogues became even more concerned with practical and secular issues. Synagogues, like all other institutions, were preoccupied with financial difficulties while their raison d'être of furthering religion was neglected. Integrating the secular and the sacred kept the synagogues afloat during periods of economic hardship and religious apathy.[72] Lectures were given at Rabbi Jung's synagogue on "Basic Concepts of the Jewish Religion"; there were classes on "Maimonides' Philosophy" as well as advertisements saying to "keep trim at the Center gym."[73] As with Modern Orthodoxy itself, this pull for synagogue involvement in both the sacred and secular caused tension. The Upper West Side, the "gilded ghetto" where Jung's synagogue was located, lost approximately 10,000 residents early in the Depression, but its population did increase late in the decade. The ten synagogues in the area, many of them large and ornate, which were supported largely by Eastern European garment manufacturers, suffered somewhat during the Depression, but not as much as synagogues in other areas.[74]

Financial support decreased to the point that merger discussions were again held between the Jewish Center Synagogue and the Society for the Advancement of Judaism, Kaplan's synagogue. Additional families and combined resources would alleviate the financial problems. This proposed merger was an interesting phenomenon, given the anger and bitterness on the part of both rabbis.[75] The merger proposal was

---

72 Wenger, *New York Jews and the Great Depression*, 205.
73 Jewish Center Synagogue Archives—*Jewish Center Bulletin*, December 22, 1939—various advertisements.
74 Wenger, *New York Jews and the Great Depression*, 94.
75 Personal interview with Rabbi Jacob J. Schacter, November 11, 1996. The minutes of the discussion of this merger were missing from the Jewish Center Synagogue records, a physical reminder of how anything to do with Kaplan was ripped out of the records. Clearly, the later board of the Jewish Center did not want this fact known. Rabbi Schacter claimed to have found the record in the minutes of the Society for the Advancement of Judaism, Kaplan's synagogue. He believes that it

not unique to Rabbi Jung's and Kaplan's synagogues; smaller institutions were even more affected. Rabbi Nachum H. Ebin, president of the Rabbinical Association of RIETS, pointed out the need for centralization and advocated merging small *yeshivot* and synagogues. The Depression also reduced the need for new rabbis; in order to reduce the number of rabbis in need of a position by keeping them in school, plans to increase the rabbinical course of study at RIETS by one year were discussed, but never implemented.[76]

American Zionism

Zionism in the 1930s was still not a key issue for the American Jewish community.[77] The Orthodox movements, Mizrachi and Agudath Israel, became more involved with Palestine. There was rising anti-Semitism in America, which made it easier to spread the Zionist doctrine. European Jews were being forced out of their countries and had no place to go, as they were refused entry to other countries. Palestine was seen as a haven for oppressed Jews in Europe, and the problem was relocation, not temporary relief. Great Britain did not stand behind the Balfour Declaration, which gave recognition to Palestine as a Jewish homeland, and legal immigration to Palestine was restricted in 1939 with "The White Paper."[78] However, the American Jewish community's position remained generally non-Zionist during the 1930s. Only after 1940, when it became clear that no other solution to Hitler's persecution was possible, did it favor a Jewish homeland for oppressed Jews.[79]

Rabbi Jung's efforts to see the Jewish homeland restored became more urgent. He visited Palestine in 1933 to raise the American Jewish consciousness and support for some of its institutions.

---

is deliberately buried somewhere. Also, there is a letter from Rosalie Rosenfeld (Rabbi Jung's daughter) to Maxine Jacobson dated October 29, 1997. Rosenfeld said that "nothing was ever mentioned about a proposed merger of the Jewish Center and Kaplan's 'synagogue.'"

76 Schneiderman, "Review of the Year 5692," 33.
77 Melvin I. Urofsky, *American Zionism from Herzl to the Holocaust* (Garden City, NY: Anchor Press and Doubleday, 1975), 422.
78 Tamar de Sola Pool, "Palestine in the Post-War World," in *Israel of Tomorrow*, ed. Leo Jung, Jewish Library, First Series, vol. 5 (New York: Herald Square Press, 1946), 329.
79 Hyman B. Grinstein, *A Short History of the Jews in the United States*, ed. Leo Jung, Jewish Library, Second Series, vol. 7 (London and New York: Soncino Press, 1980), 175.

Rabbi Jung and other Orthodox leaders continued to confront the dilemma of their dual attachment to Agudath Israel and Mizrachi because, as discussed in the previous chapters, each organization had a different philosophy regarding Zionism. Rabbi Jung continued his involvement with Agudath Israel and befriended Jacob Rosenheim, head of Agudath Israel.[80] He also aligned himself with Mizrachi. In 1940, Rabbi Eliezer Silver and Rabbi Joseph Soloveitchik became co-presidents of Agudath Israel. They worked to raise money for settlements in *Eretz Israel* (the Land of Israel) for refugees from Nazi persecution. Following the Holocaust, Rabbi Soloveitchik left Agudath Israel and joined Mizrachi. In 1946, Rabbi Silver became honorary president of Mizrachi. According to Aaron Rakeffet-Rothkoff, Rabbi Silver—while always committed to Agudath Israel—was also a "fellow companion of the Mizrachi movement." Rabbi Silver attended many Mizrachi conventions and conferences, and wanted to see a merger of the two movements.[81] Rabbi Jung felt that supporting both was supporting Orthodox unity; his call for unity was for the most part unheeded:

> Let Agudath [Israel] and Mizrachi adhere, as loyally as they can, to their separate ideologies. But they must learn to agree to disagree on platforms and to join forces in work. For while we rejoice each in fidelity to one's principle, those in our camp opposing the Jewish religion are forging on with amazing success.[82]

Rabbi Jung emphasized that in all matters touching on the abolition of the White Paper and of the laws restricting land purchase, as well as unlimited immigration, Agudath Israel stood with the others.[83]

---

80 Jung, "Jacob Rosenheim, the Man and his Work," *Jewish Forum* 14, no. 3 (March 1931): 81.
81 Rakeffet-Rothkoff, *The Silver Era in American Jewish Orthodoxy: Rabbi Eliezer Silver and His Generation* (New York: Yeshiva University Press; Jerusalem: Feldheim Publishers, 1981), 156–157.
82 Jung, "Jewry Today," 200.
83 Leo Jung, "Palestine Today," *Jewish Forum* 30, no. 10 (September 1947): 221; Yeshiva University Archives, Jung Collection, Box 48, Folder 5 (published articles)—first page of article.

He could support their educational projects, as well as their Jewish rescue programs. He had seen some of their projects first hand and was also involved with some of their colonization projects.

Both Mizrachi and Agudath Israel's projects won favor in Orthodox circles. Agudath Israel worked to save *yeshivot* in Europe. Mizrachi established The Mizrachi Land Development Corporation for colonization by American religious Jews in Palestine, and in 1936, it founded a colony in Palestine for Orthodox laborers and middle class Jews.[84] Seeds were being planted by Orthodox organizations; not only was *Eretz Israel* a refuge, but also a place for enriching religious life.

Rabbi Jung supported *yeshivot* in Palestine that were non-Zionist, though he did not share their ideology. Rabbi Jung continued to blur the differences between Agudath Israel and Mizrachi in the 1930s. His dilemma would continue to plague many Modern Orthodox Jews caught between emotionalism and dedication to the religious aspect, and to the practicality and necessity of a Jewish homeland.

Identification with *Eretz Israel* was something that, in the 1930s, was not taken for granted.[85] However, one positive sign was that Jewish educators seized on Zionism as a tool for Jewish renewal, and Zionism became somewhat of a morale booster.[86]

Education

In the 1930s, a lack of funding added to the problems that Jewish education faced with incapable teachers, a lack of status, and a lack of a suitable curriculum.[87] The majority of homes did not reinforce what was taught in the schools.[88] This lack of commitment to Jewish education, coupled with dwindling financial resources, obliged Modern Orthodoxy to broaden its base and develop an effective outreach program. Orthodox leaders, including Rabbi Jung, had to focus efforts

---

84 Yeshiva University Archives, Jung Collection, Box 1, Folder 2—letter from Dr. Isaac Breuer to Rabbi Jung, June 30, 1937.
85 Jung, *The Path of a Pioneer*, 124.
86 Wenger, *New York Jews and the Great Depression*, 193.
87 Karpf, "Community Organization in the United States," 75–76.
88 Isaac Breuer, "Judaism and the World Order," in *Judaism in a Changing World*, 1939 edition, ed. Jung, 57.

on fundraising and building public awareness of the need for Jewish education. He also had to work to keep Yeshiva College viable through the Depression.[89]

The Modern Orthodox apologia for Jewish education in the 1920s was that Jewish education facilitated true Americanization, adjustment, and "harmonization." During the 1930s, Rabbi Jung and others presented it also as a weapon against anti-Semitism.[90] There would be stronger Jewish commitment as well as a more self-assured and self-confident defense against anti-Semitism with a better understanding of Judaism. Rabbi Jung wrote that "for our self-defense, our children must receive a Jewish education, academic, social, and crowned by the pattern of Jewish communal enterprise that will give them self-knowledge and a sense of historic importance."[91] In 1938, at the annual Jewish Education Society dinner, New York Governor Herbert Lehman stated that the best way to combat anti-Semitism was to know and to show that Jewish education and Jewish ethical principles led to good citizenship.[92] Rabbi David de Sola Pool wrote that anti-Semitism shocked "even indifferent Jews into realization of their need for Jewish knowledge if only in defencse of their own respect and raison d'être."[93]

Yeshiva College

Modern Orthodoxy still had to defend and define itself. During the 1930s, the Agudath Harabbonim, still well represented at Yeshiva, had conflicts with Dr. Revel.[94] Revel tried to show respect while maintaining his assertive Modern Orthodox position. The antagonism of the Agudath Harabbonim was contained until Revel's death because they

---

89 Joseph T. Shipley, "Ten Years a College," *Jewish Forum* 21, no. 11 (December 1938): 205.
90 Leo Jung, "The Soncino Press of London," *Jewish Forum* 19, no. 9 (November 1936): 261.
91 Jung, "News Years Program," in *Crumbs and Character: Sermons, Addresses, and Essays*, ed. Leo Jung (New York: The Night and Day Press, 1942), 155.
92 Harry Schneiderman, "Review of the Year 5698—United States," *American Jewish Year Book* 40 (1938–1939): 147.
93 David de Sola Pool, "The Challenge to Jewish Education," in *Judaism in a Changing World*, 1939 edition, ed. Jung, 64.
94 Jeffrey S. Gurock, *The Men and Women of Yeshiva: Higher Education, Orthodoxy, and American Judaism* (New York: Columbia University Press, 1988), 122.

respected him, his Yeshiva training, and Talmudic expertise, as well as the fact that he tried to deal with them fairly and with consideration. Revel had to explain, defend, and justify his position when confronted by the Agudath Harabbonim. This dialogue and debate may have helped lead to a clearer definition of Modern Orthodoxy.[95]

Yeshiva College expansion halted during the Depression. Students were "starving in their unkempt, deteriorating dormitories."[96] Staff members were not receiving salaries; Rabbi Jung, in July 1932, had not been paid since December 1931.[97] The faculty remained because of loyalty and probably because jobs elsewhere were difficult to find. During the summer of 1931, the financial situation was so bad that it was unclear whether Yeshiva College would reopen.[98] By 1934, Yeshiva reported an increased enrollment and the Depression had eased, but things remained difficult. However, only in 1937 could the Alumni Quarterly, one of the school newspapers, "report that teachers were being paid on time."[99]

Yeshiva had to make a major effort to reach the masses as leaders looked beyond Orthodox circles to sustain their institutions. Rabbi Jung, considered one of the spokesmen for American Modern Orthodoxy and for Yeshiva, was appointed in 1931 to the faculty as professor of Ethics for both the Yeshiva proper and Yeshiva College.[100] Rabbi Jung was good at public relations, which was what Yeshiva needed. He instilled in his synagogue members, "the Center family" (as he referred to them), the need to support and work for Yeshiva; many of the members did join Rabbi Jung in this effort.[101] When Revel was

---

95 Ibid., 127.
96 Ibid., 124.
97 Yeshiva University Archives, Revel Papers, Box 3, Folder 5/3-21—letter to Revel from Rabbi Jung, July 29, 1932.
98 Aaron Rakeffet-Rothkoff, "The Semi-Centennial Celebrations of Yeshiva and Yeshiva College," in *Ramaz: School, Community, Scholarship and Orthodoxy*, ed. Jeffrey S. Gurock (Hoboken, NJ: Ktav Publishing House, 1989), 9.
99 Yeshiva University Archives—"Here and There," (by E.L.), 2, and *The Alumni Quarterly* (March 1937): 2.
100 Jung, *The Path of a Pioneer*, 106; Yeshiva University Archives, Revel Papers, Box 3, Folder 5/3-21—letter to Rabbi Jung from President of the Faculty, January 4, 1931.
101 Jewish Center Synagogue Archives—*Jewish Center Bulletin* 9, no. 8 (December 22, 1939).

unable to attend functions (his health was an issue from the mid-1930s on), Rabbi Jung was often asked to replace him.[102]

In 1936, Professor Albert Einstein agreed to lend his name to the college and work on its behalf in conjunction with Rabbi Jung.[103] The Orthodox institutions needed to seek help beyond their own community, and they would always continue to do so. That they needed plugs from the non-Orthodox shows that they felt the Orthodox appeal was limited. It also shows that they were true to their philosophy of being "non-insular." Einstein, who was not Orthodox, appreciated the uniqueness of the institution and was one of its ardent champions. Einstein said that "Yeshiva College was vital for the survival of American Israel."[104] Revel wrote a letter of introduction to prospective donors along with a personally addressed letter from Einstein; then Rabbi Jung and Dr. Samuel Sar, the registrar of Yeshiva, were sent to speak. The by-products of these trips were far reaching; they paved the way for better understanding of the ideals and needs of Yeshiva College and therefore of Modern Orthodoxy.

In 1934, Einstein received a Doctor of Humane Letters from Yeshiva. Revel admired the great Torah scholars of the time and succeeded in having some teach at Yeshiva, but he equally appreciated modern scientists attached to Yeshiva. Torah scholars and scientists harmonized the value of religion and science. Rabbi Jung remarked that, though Einstein had little theology and less Torah-true Judaism, Revel could "square it with his *weltanschauung* to offer him an honorary degree."[105]

Parochial Schools

In the 1930s, most Orthodox synagogues maintained their interest and commitment to their schools, though the schools were not always

---

102 Yeshiva University Archives, Revel Papers, Box 3, Folder 5/3-21—letters to Rabbi Jung from Revel, March 24, 1937 and January 13, 1935.
103 Ibid.—letter to Rabbi Jung from Revel, April 21, 1937.
104 Ibid., Box 5, Folder 5/1-27—letter to Oscar Fasman from Revel, October 30, 1936; Leo Jung, "Bernard Revel," *American Jewish Year Book* 43 (1941–1942): 424. Also in Jung, ed., *Crumbs and Character*.
105 Jung, "Bernard Revel," in *Crumbs and Character*, ed. Jung, 313. Or Jung, "Bernard Revel," *American Jewish Year Book*, 424.

successful. Almost every synagogue had afternoon schools or Sunday schools, and a handful had launched Jewish day schools.[106] The Jewish Center Day School was unsuccessful, however, and its curriculum did not meet with Rabbi Jung's approval. Rabbi Jung wrote:

> There was a day school at the Center, in control of a lay pedagogue, to whom its leadership was entrusted and with whom I could not agree on either curriculum or division of authority. Established before its time and looked upon as fanciful luxury by many important Centerites, it was an expensive and inherently unsuccessful enterprise.[107]

In 1932, the Jewish Center Synagogue plans for a Hebrew afternoon school were rejected because the board feared it would undermine support for the existing day school, The Jewish Center Talmud Torah.[108] Afternoon schools were more prevalent than day schools, thus it was unusual for a congregation to make this decision.[109] The Jewish Center had a Sunday school for members' children that was abolished in 1935.[110] The synagogue did go on to have an afternoon school. The principal of the afternoon school was Dr. Joseph Kaminetsky, who became executive director of Manhattan Day School, which evolved from The Jewish Center Day School, and then director of the Torah Umesorah parochial schools.[111]

In light of the fact that Rabbi Jung did not build a successful day school, we can really appreciate the accomplishment of Rabbi Joseph Lookstein at the neighboring synagogue, Kehillath Jeshurun, which was able to establish a day school, called Ramaz, in 1937. Like the

---

106 Schneiderman, "Review of the Year 5698—United States," 72–73.
107 Jung, *The Path of a Pioneer*, 72.
108 Jewish Center Synagogue Archives—minutes of Board of Trustees meeting, October 19, 1932.
109 Karpf, "Community Organization in the United States," 72–74.
110 Jewish Center Synagogue Archives—minutes of Board of Trustees meeting, June 12, 1935.
111 Betzalel Kahn, Torah Umesorah, and Mordecai Plaut, "Dr. Joseph Kaminetsky zt"l," *Dei'ah ve-Dibur: Information and Insight* (1999): accessed August 12, 2015, http://www.chareidi.org/archives5759/tzav/kamintzk.htm.

congregants of the Jewish Center Synagogue, Rabbi Lookstein's congregants supported Jewish education and the idea of the school, but few sent their children there. The school attracted, to a large extent, children from the Americanized affluent class who were not observant.[112] It was the most Americanized of the *yeshivot*. Mixed dances were held; there was vacation at Christmas time and the precedent continued in Modern Orthodox day schools.

Ramaz is an example of Jewish education being taken out of the *eissheder* and the social atmosphere of Eastern European Jewish ghettos. This was a significant change from the 1920s. Ramaz was a great accomplishment in a decade in which some synagogues, because of lack of money, had hired untrained volunteers to teach in their schools and in a decade in which there was significant anti-Semitism.[113] The supply of modern teachers increased; the old type of *melamed* was rapidly disappearing.

The UOJCA had developed a million-dollar Jewish education program to be coordinated by the National Orthodox Board of Education. The fund supported Yeshiva College, the Hebrew Theological College in Chicago, and other Modern Orthodox schools of higher learning, which were not specifically mentioned. They included, as well, subsidies for schools that were not in big cities.[114] Among those recruited to raise funds and spread the message were Rabbis Moses Zebulun Margolies (the Ramaz), Dr. Henry Pereira Mendes, Bernard Drachman, Phillip Klein, Herbert Goldstein, Lookstein, William Weiss, and Jung. The effort was not successful.[115] Parochial schools continued to attract only a small fraction of the Jewish population.

The publication "A Model Program for the Talmud Torah," by Rabbi Jung and Kaminetzky, which was an outcome of the million-dollar

---

112 Personal interview with Martin Schwarzschild, November 11, 1996.
113 Jeffrey S. Gurock, "The Ramaz Version of American Orthodoxy," in Gurock, ed., *Ramaz*, 49; personal interview with Sadie Silverstein, November 19, 1997. A long-time member of the Jewish Center Synagogue, Silverstein said that she and only a few other members sent their children to Ramaz.
114 Gurock, "The Ramaz Version of American Orthodoxy," in Gurock, ed., *Ramaz*, 41.
115 Schneiderman, "Review of the Year 5698—United States," 140–141.

campaign, was used by many of the schools.[116] Talmud Torahs had come into being at the turn of the century with the great wave of Eastern European Jewish immigration. The Talmud Torahs began as an afterschool program with a curriculum based on teaching the Hebrew language, the Pentateuch, the Prophets, Jewish history, Jewish prayer, and Jewish religious practice. In the mid-1920s, congregational schools multiplied; the Depression strengthened the trend. The growth of the congregational schools and the growth of the all-day schools, though small, did not bode well for the Talmud Torah.[117] The curriculum, classroom procedures, texts, and grading of pupils needed revitalization.[118] Rabbi Jung believed that without a uniform model curriculum, the schools would flounder.[119] As chairman of the Publications Committee of the UOJCA, Rabbi Jung spent seven years surveying and analyzing methods of Jewish education that would be appropriate for the hundreds of Orthodox Talmud Torahs across the United States, and prepared uniform textbooks for them.[120] The final manuscript was completed in 1941.

The aim of his curriculum was "to build ... bonds ... between the child and the Jewish past, present ... particularly the American scene ... and future."[121] Rabbi Jung's curriculum for Talmud Torahs included "*Ivrit be-Ivrit,*" which meant that the Hebrew language was used to teach Hebrew and Jewish subjects. All the earmarks of Modern Orthodoxy were included in the curriculum: positive exposure to the religious and secular world, aesthetic presentation, Zionism, reaching out to all Jews and even non-Jews, and the use of Hebrew as a living language.

Rabbi Jung's publications and work to establish uniform textbooks for parochial schools helped to educate and Americanize the standards

---

116 Bernstein, *The Orthodox Story*, 110.
117 Ibid., 95.
118 Morris B. Benathen, "The Role of Talmud Torah in Jewish Education in America," Leo Jung, Ed., *Israel of Tomorrow*, The Jewish Library Series. 5, NY: Herald Square Press, 483–484.
119 Ibid., 488.
120 Yeshiva University Archives, Koenigsberg Papers, Box 9, Folder 2—letter from Rabbi Jung to William Weiss, December 19, 1940, announcing the conference to be held in Jung's study for the purpose of getting reaction regarding a proposed uniform model curriculum.
121 Ibid.

of Jewish education. Adult education, and the realization that education was a community responsibility, increased.[122]

By the end of the 1930s, the number of Talmud Torah buildings increased, and registration in Jewish religious schools grew, but at the beginning of the 1930s, they were "gasping for breath."[123]

Hebrew in the Curriculum

The rebirth of Hebrew in Palestine had repercussions in America. There were new opportunities to learn Hebrew. This was important for the Orthodox movement, because the Orthodox services were conducted in Hebrew. This revival of Hebrew had a positive effect on Judaism and Modern Orthodoxy in particular, though the forces behind Hebrew classes were not always Orthodox.

Young Israel advanced the cause of Hebrew.[124] Modern Orthodoxy embraced this program, as it was eager to adopt Hebrew as a living language. This differentiated Modern Orthodoxy from the traditional Orthodox groups that regarded Hebrew exclusively as a holy language. The traditional Orthodox groups continued to use Yiddish in their educational institutions and to use Hebrew only as a language of prayer, as they felt it demeaned the holy language to use it in conversation. Hebrew was presented by Rabbi Jung as a unifying force; it is additional evidence of his cooperation with the non-Orthodox. For Rabbi Jung, Hebrew was a protection against assimilation, and it was a means of Jewish identity and authenticity. For him, it inculcated religious-national values. Knowledge of modern Hebrew facilitated knowledge of the ancient texts and prayer books; it was a link to the past and the future. Rabbi Jung stated:

> The disappearance of the Hebrew prayer from our life would mean the breaking down of one more barrier between

---

122 Ibid.—meeting notices from William Weiss, president of UOJCA, October 2, 1939, November 20, 1940, and December 19, 1940. The draft of the curriculum is available in the Koenigsberg Papers, Box 9, Folder 2.
123 Isaac Rosengarten, "Organizing Orthodox Jewry in America," *Jewish Forum* 16, no. 3 (March 1933): 8; Schneiderman, "Review of the Year 5698—United States," 147.
124 Harry Bluestone, "Program of Young Israel," *Jewish Forum* 16, no. 9 (September 1933): 206.

assimilation and us. Hence Hebrew is not alone the only means of genuine expression but because it is in Hebrew that our historical and religious associations are presented... that the unity of Jewry everywhere is maintained, that the fervor of earlier worship and that the strength of our hereditary trust in God is continued.[125]

The context of this quotation shows how important Hebrew in prayer was for Rabbi Jung. However, from the curriculum that he prepared for the Talmud Torah schools in the late 1930s, it is evident that Hebrew as a living language was also very important to him and that knowledge of Hebrew in prayer facilitated the knowledge of Hebrew as a living language, and vice-versa.

Requests for Hebrew instruction at the College of the City of New York were rejected in the 1920s.[126] In the 1930s, those who petitioned were able to convince the educators of the cultural values of Hebrew. Some universities (i.e., New York University, City College of New York, Hunter, Queens, Fordham, and St. John's), public high schools, and night high schools began to give credits for Hebrew courses, teaching Hebrew as a modern language spoken in Palestine, not an ancient one. Hebrew clubs sprung up, promoted by the Bureau of Jewish Education.[127]

Educational Outreach Publications and Radio

Throughout the 1930s, Jewish leaders and other religious leaders relied on radio as one avenue to sell religion and the synagogue, as they realized that vast audiences could be reached and ideas disseminated. This was a use of modern techniques in the modern age to sell religion, and Modern Orthodoxy was involved in this endeavor. The radio was used to inform the unaffiliated Jews and non-Jews, and the UOJCA

---

125 Yeshiva University Archives, Jung Collection, Box 44, Folder 3—Jung, "Yissgadal Veyisskadash," 2.
126 Mordecai H. Lewittes, "Hebrew Enters New York High Schools," *The Menorah Journal*, volume and issue unknown (Spring 1938): page number(s) unknown.
127 Ibid., 235.

broadcasted its message.[128] Rabbi Jung was the Modern Orthodox representative on the radio in the 1930s and 1940s. His high-profile position brought positive exposure and prestige to Modern Orthodoxy.

Rabbi Jung's radio broadcasts were also an aspect of his interfaith activities; he felt that better understanding would bring about better relations, and that it would lessen anti-Semitism.

The Depression had coalesced extremists and reactionary movements: Father Coughlin, a Catholic priest, used the radio to express anti-Semitic propaganda. Father Coughlin, in particular, had a large audience—having someone like Rabbi Jung on the radio to counter the racism by presenting the proper facts was very important for the Jewish population.[129]

The JTS also produced a number of radio broadcasts in conjunction with local stations or national networks.[130] Rabbi Jung spoke on the radio for both Orthodoxy and for the JDC. On behalf of the Cultural Committee of the JDC, he requested donations from his audience and explained the work of the JDC, constantly reminding his listeners that the needs for physical and spiritual relief were urgent.[131] The situation for the Jewish people was, per Rabbi Jung, "bleak and getting bleaker."[132] At the Jewish New Year in 1937, Rabbi Jung made a radio plea to help JDC in a time of cruelty.[133]

The more traditional outreach tool was publications. Modern Orthodox involvement in publications became greater in the 1930s. Several Orthodox organizations published textbooks and educational material in English. In 1933, the UOJCA introduced a bimonthly periodical, the *Orthodox Union*, which published organizational news and

---

128 Bernstein, *The Orthodox Story*, 109.
129 Albert I. Slomovitz, *The Fighting Rabbis: A History of Jewish Military Chaplains, 1860–1945* (Ann Arbor, MI: UMI Dissertation Services, 1996), 198.
130 Jeffrey Shandler and Elihu Katz, "Broadcasting American Judaism: The Radio and Television Department of the Jewish Theological Seminary," in *Tradition Renewed: A History of the Jewish Theological Seminary of America*, ed. Jack Wertheimer, vol. 2 (New York: Jewish Theological Seminary, 1997), 366.
131 Jung, *The Path of a Pioneer*, 175.
132 Jung, "Jewry Today," 200.
133 Yeshiva University Archives, Jung Collection, Box 1—script from Rabbi Jung's address on the Columbia Broadcasting System (CBS) network station WABC.

informative articles. Rabbi Jung contributed articles to this journal.[134] The National Council of Torah Education of Mizrachi was established in 1939 for the purpose of publishing Jewish material.[135]

Jewish literature had to reach the American Jewish public; to do so, it had to be translated into English. Rabbi Jung wrote:

> A Jewish community comes of age when an attempt has been made to make available for the average Jew the classics of Jewish literature, not only the Bible, but, especially Rabbinics.[136]

This began to happen in the 1930s. Rabbi Jung hailed the Soncino Press of London, which he felt was destined to play an important role in the history of English-speaking Jewry. A major achievement of the Soncino Press was the publication of the English translation of an annotated text of the Babylonian Talmud, with all the volumes completed by the early 1940s. The editions provided introductions, appendices, and indexes. Rabbi Jung stated: "No more will the Talmud be a closed book to Jew or non-Jew." He was a participant in the Soncino English translation of the Talmud, translating Tractates *Arakhin* and *Yoma* with introductions and notes.[137] The Soncino Press also published an English translation of the *Zohar*. Rabbi Jung wrote that the "Talmud and Zohar together reveal more of the Jew and Judaism than anything else from the pen of any commentator, however learned and persuasive."[138] In addition, the Soncino Press published a collection of studies by Jewish scholars in the *Moses Maimonides VII Centenary Volume* (1936).[139]

Jung's praise of the Soncino Press, which was (and still is) an Orthodox publication, can also be construed as criticism of the

---

134 Editorial, *Jewish Forum* 16, no. 9 (September 1933): 43.
135 Grinstein, *A Short History of the Jews in the United States*, 113.
136 Jung, "The Soncino Press of London," 261.
137 Yeshiva University Archives, Public Relations Files, Honorary Degrees, 1947–1968— citation by Dr. Samuel Belkin in conferring degree upon Rabbi Jung.
138 Jung, "The Soncino Press of London," 261.
139 Ibid., 262.

American Jewish Publication Society, which in 1917 began to publish the Hebrew classics.[140] In 1920, the series was renamed the Schiff Library of Jewish Classics when Jacob Schiff, its main supporter, died.[141] No Orthodox Jews were active either in Jewish Publication Society (JPS) projects or on the JPS board. Rabbi Jung critically pointed out that JPS policy was to stay clear of controversial issues that they felt would offend the Christian or modern mind.[142] Defending the Jewish image was their basic issue. If it was felt that a classic did not place the Jew in a good light or that it could possibly be a cause of anti-Semitism, it was rejected. It is likely that they did not publish the *Zohar*, a medieval book of mysticism, for these reasons and because of their rationalist bent. This was a characteristic of the day, and not unique to JPS. Rabbi Jung pointed out that the Soncino Press had published a thesis on the history of anti-Semitism; this type of literature had been rejected by the JPS.[143] The JPS was involved with things that Rabbi Jung was philosophically opposed to, thus he could appreciate all the more the need for the Soncino Press. Though the JPS did publish a translation of a portion of the Talmud, it was edited by the Reform scholar Henry Malter, who employed a scientific approach.[144] They also published volumes of *The Book of Principles*, by Joseph Albo.[145] The final volume, Moses Hayyim Luzzatto's ethical treatise—*Mesillat Yesharim*—was translated by Kaplan. The introduction reflected Kaplan's philosophy, which was that the classics should be studied since they were a mirror to a given time and period.[146] Rabbi Jung's dislike of this philosophy, which contravened Orthodox principles, was well known.

Yet, Rabbi Jung appreciated that the JPS did try to awaken interest in the Jewish classics, which had been previously unknown to English readers.

---

140 Email from Nachum Shapiro to Jacobson, June 17, 2002: "Soncino Press always was and is an Orthodox publication."
141 Jonathan D. Sarna, *JPS: The Americanization of Jewish Culture, 1888–1988* (Philadelphia, New York, and Jerusalem: The Jewish Publication Society, 1989, 122.
142 Ibid., 143.
143 Jung, "The Soncino Press of London," 263.
144 Sarna, *JPS*, 154.
145 Ibid., 156.
146 Ibid., 158.

The JPS wanted to teach about Jewish heritage, publishing works of general literary interest such as poetry and ethics. He also praised the JPS for publishing the translation of the Hebrew Bible, the belles-lettres volumes, and—through the Schiff classics—Hebrew texts of importance.[147] In 1941, the JPS appointed Dr. Samuel Belkin, Rabbi Oscar Fasman, Rabbi Lookstein, and Rabbi de Sola Pool to its board in response to Orthodox criticism and the demand to be represented.[148] This was an example of Modern Orthodoxy's expanding influence. Orthodox leaders were present at the JPS for the first time; perhaps that is because Rabbi Jung's criticism was heard.

Since Orthodoxy was not well represented in the Jewish-American publication world, Rabbi Jung's Jewish Library series and his other works played an important role. Among some of Rabbi Jung's own publications in the 1930s were *Judaism in a Changing World* and *Woman*.[149] The essays in *Judaism in a Changing World* dealt with the outlook and the significance of traditional Judaism, as did all the volumes of the Jewish Library up to this date.

This volume explored the challenges Judaism faced during the 1930s in a world that was becoming imbued with the spirit of science, industrialization, and democratic unrest. Some of the challenges were for Judaism to survive in a foreign environment, to erase evil, to be saved from a world lacking moral and spiritual values, to resolve the conflict between religion and science, and to provide a proper Jewish education in a non-Jewish environment. Modern dilemmas faced in the home—along with economic and social difficulties resulting from migration, mixed marriages, urbanization, and birth control—were other issues discussed. The solutions proposed by Rabbi Jung all derived from Torah-true living.

Judaism was explained using the categories of modern thought. Jewish theology, Jewish sociology, and psychological analysis of Judaism were presented.[150] The perception that Judaism was particularistic,

---

147 Jung, "The Soncino Press of London," 261.
148 Sarna, *JPS*, 139.
149 Jung, ed., *Judaism in a Changing World*, 1939 edition; Leo Jung, *Woman*, Jewish Library, First Series, vol. 3 (New York, 1934).
150 Jung, ed., *Judaism in a Changing World*, 1939 edition. See articles by H. Raphael Gold and Maurice Farbridge.

separatist, or clannish had to be dispelled.[151] Judaism was not static and unresponsive to changing conditions and the advancement of knowledge. It was a religion of full life integrating the intellectual and emotional, which was one reason it survived.[152]

The third volume of Rabbi Jung's Jewish Library was devoted to women. He edited the book *Woman*, which highlighted the noble work of Jewish women in various endeavors through time. *Woman* contains articles about powerful, active, contributing women in the religious life of Israel, in economic life, in community and organizational work, and in political life. In his introduction, he wrote that:

> The Jewish woman looms large in the heart of family and nation. The noblest term in the Hebrew vocabulary is *rachmanut*, usually translated as mercy but meaning literally, other love, the only genuinely unselfish devotion.[153]

The book dispels the misapprehension that women had limited knowledge, or that they always held inferior positions in traditional Jewish life. Nina H. Adlerblum, Rabbi Jung's good friend and biographer, wrote:

> This volume has no doubt been projected by the editor less as an account of the achievements of Jewish women than as a stimulus to further development on their part.[154]

This type of book was a stimulus to women's further development. This attitude also is a mark of Modern Orthodoxy. Rabbi Jung seemed to be aware of contemporary issues, but in his writings at this time, there is no evidence that he dealt with inequities in synagogue rituals.

---

151 H. Raphael Gold, "A Psychological Approach to the Torah," in ed. Jung, *Judaism in a Changing World*, 1939 edition, 106.
152 Ibid., 141.
153 Leo Jung, "Introduction," in *Woman*, ed. Leo Jung, Jewish Library, Second Series, vol. 3 (London and New York: Soncino Press, 1970), xi.
154 Nima H. Adlerblum, "The Elan Vital of the Jewish Woman," in *Woman*, ed. Jung, 143.

Organizational Activity—Issues of Concern

Disorganization

Lack of organizational skills and unity were still important issues. The *Jewish Forum* discussed the "chaotic conditions of religious life," as branches of Modern Orthodoxy still acted independently.[155] Rabbi Goldstein, a colleague of Rabbi Jung, wrote in the *Jewish Tribune*:

> These organizations (referring to Orthodox organizations) at best have only nibbled at the various problems confronting them. The reason ... is largely due to the fact that not one of these organizations really represents the whole Orthodox Jewry. Either they represent only the Yiddish- or the English-speaking element or the older or the younger alone.[156]

At the UOJCA convention of January 29, 1933, chairman Isaac Rosengarten criticized the organization for not representing Orthodoxy across America and for not including representatives from Mizrachi, Young Israel, and others.[157] Though the UOJCA conducted educational activities through its central organization, prepared textbooks, and stimulated synagogue brotherhoods and sisterhoods, it was criticized for not embracing enough of America's 3,000 to 5,000 Orthodox congregations, which had little connection with each other. Rabbi Jung felt that the more representative an organization became, the more the organization could develop public opinion, "which alone in this country takes the place of the well-knit *kehilla* in European countries."[158]

Sabbath Observance

There was still resolve on the part of Orthodox organizations to invoke rights as American citizens and to ensure proper conditions for Sabbath

---

155 Editorial, *Jewish Forum* 14, no. 9 (September 1931): 291 and 302.
156 Herbert S. Goldstein, "A Clarion Call for Harmony," *Jewish Tribune* (August 1930): 4.
157 Rosengarten, "Organizing Orthodox Jewry in America," 8. Rosengarten was the editor of the *Jewish Forum* and the chairman of the UOJCA conference. This is his speech delivered before the convention of the UOJCA, January 29, 1933.
158 Ibid.

observers. Rabbi Jung was active in UOJCA and the Jewish Sabbath Alliance, of which Rabbi Bernard Drachman was still president.[159] Isaac Rosengarten wrote that the raison d'être of the UOJCA was "its work on behalf of Judaism proper," and that the UOJCA's principle goal should be a systematic effort to ensure Sabbath observance to enable stores to close on the Sabbath, and to ensure that Sabbath observers were hired and not penalized.[160]

There was some praiseworthy activity in this area. The Jewish Sabbath Alliance made strenuous efforts to obtain for the Sabbath observer an equal chance to earn a living and obtain opportunity for the free development of religion. A larger number of organizations were involved in this area than ever before; among them were the American Jewish Congress, Young Israel, the UOJCA, other rabbinical bodies, and the newly formed District Sabbath Councils from several sections of the city (under the auspices of the UOJCA).

These organizations supported the Hofstadter-Moffat Sabbath Bill, which was presented in 1931 to the New York legislature. Besides including rights for Sabbath observers to earn a living, this bill also included a prohibition against holding examinations on the Jewish Sabbath or other Jewish holy days.[161] The bill was not passed, but it fostered more awareness, involvement, and cooperation in this direction. Since the Dickstein Sabbath bill in the 1920s, some progress had been made.

In 1933, a large symposium, "Sabbath Recovery in Jewish Life," took place in order to organize for Sabbath preservation and to enable people to earn a living without penalty. Rabbi Jung, as president of the Rabbinical Council of the UOJCA, was a presenter. He urged the organizations and synagogues "to absorb the great masses of Jewish working men and women now, for the first time, able to observe the Sabbath without economic loss and in full accord with Jewish law and custom."[162] When the New York–Brooklyn Jewish Federation insisted that an

---

159 Editorial, *Jewish Forum* 14, no. 3 (March 1931): 67.
160 Rosengarten, "Organizing Orthodox Jewry in America," 9–10.
161 Editorial, *Jewish Forum* 14, no. 3 (March 1931): 67.
162 "Sabbath Recovery in Jewish Life," Symposium, *Jewish Forum* 16, no. 12 (December 1933): 127–129.

employee come to work on the Sabbath before their major fundraising event, Rabbi Jung fought for the Sabbath-observing employee.[163] It was abhorrent to him that a Jewish organization would do such a thing.

Because of the Orthodox concern to maintain and encourage Sabbath observance, the Young Israel Employment Bureau (organized in 1925) expanded its activities during the Depression as Orthodox synagogues initiated successful efforts to help Jews find jobs that would not require Sabbath work.[164] The Board of Education in New York City sanctioned a Bureau of Vocational Guidance for Sabbath observers.

Advent of the Rabbinical Council of America (RCA)

The advent of the RCA in 1935 brought a sense of unity and prestige to Modern Orthodoxy and garnered additional respect for its rabbinate from the public and other religious leaders. The role of the rabbi became more visible as the affiliated rabbis took an active role in the Jewish community at large through the RCA. The RCA was truly representative of Modern Orthodoxy, because it recognized American differences as well as recognizing that accommodation and adjustment to American culture was necessary. Rabbis Jacob M. Charlap, Judah Damesek, and Herbert Goldstein were elected co-presidents, while Rabbi Drachman, Solomon Reichman, and Bernard Rosenbloom became vice-presidents. Rabbi Jung became treasurer, and Rabbi Lookstein was financial secretary. This organization of Orthodox rabbis evolved out of what had been the Rabbinical Council of the UOJCA, of which Leo Jung had been president from 1926 to 1934.[165] Though the RCA was allied to the UOJCA, it operated independently.[166]

---

163 Yeshiva University Archives, Jung Collection, Box 40, Folder 2—letter to Rabbi Jung from an observant employee, October 10, 1934. There are many letters to and from Judge Joseph Proskauer and Rabbi Jung on issues of the federation respecting observant Jews.
164 Wenger, *New York Jews and The Great Depression*, 188; Harry Bluestone, "Program of Young Israel," 205.
165 Louis Bernstein, *Challenge and Mission: The Emergence of the English-Speaking Rabbinate* (New York: Shengold Publishers, 1982), 92.
166 S. Bernstein, *The Orthodox Story*, 112.

The conflict between the RCA and the older European rabbis of the Agudath Harabbonim continued, and helped define the RCA. Their philosophies differed on the issues that clearly defined Modern Orthodoxy, such as attitude to secular education, cooperation with other Jewish and non-Jewish groups, and the use of Hebrew. The Agudath Harabbonim perceived the RCA to be a competitor when the RCA involved itself in the area of *kashrut*, but this was not a new issue.[167] It is in the area of *kashrut* that there was endless controversy that detracted from the Agudath Harabbonim's reputation.[168]

RCA became a member of the Synagogue Council of America, an amalgamation of Conservative and Reform rabbinical organizations that dealt with matters of concern to all Jews. This was not acceptable to the Agudath Harabbonim, which felt that rabbis should not serve in congregations with mixed seating. While the decision to accept a job in synagogues without a *mehitzah* was tactical and problematic, their cooperation with other Jewish groups was part of the philosophy.

In 1939 to 1940, Rabbi Jacob Agus, then still affiliated with Orthodox Judaism, took a pulpit at a synagogue in Chicago without a *mehitzah* that allowed mixed seating on certain occasions. According to Rabbi Agus's son, Robert E. Agus, Dr. Revel recommended that Rabbi Agus accept the position in order to try to change the situation. Rabbi Lookstein visited the synagogue and preached there in 1940 or 1941, and the RCA allowed this. Rabbi Jung asked Rabbi Agus, then helping Rabbi Jung with the teaching of Talmud and lectures, to research the question of *mehitzah* so that a definite position could be taken. The intent was to send a *she'elah*, which is a *halakhic* question, to the *roshei yeshivot* in Europe about the *mehitzah* itself. Due to the unsettled environment of the mid-1930s, it was not sent.[169] The issue of *mehitzah* was not only a dividing line between Modern Orthodoxy and the Agudath Harabbonim; it became a dividing line between the Orthodox and Conservative movements in the late 1940s and early 1950s, and it was

---

167 L. Bernstein, *Challenge and Mission*, 96.
168 Ibid.; Rakeffet-Rothkoff, *The Silver Era in American Jewish Orthodoxy*, 99 and 133.
169 Email from Robert Agus to Jacobson, April 3, 1998.

only clarified in the early 1950s. The Conservative movement maintained that the *mehitzah* was not an essential requirement.

Differences also existed in the area of ordination. The Agudath Harabbonim recognized only their members as qualified rabbis, recognizing only those granted *Yadin Yadin* (the more advanced type of *semikhah*, or rabbinic ordination) and not the *Yoreh Yoreh*, or regular, type of *semikhah* that RIETS granted to its rabbis.[170] The Agudath Harabbonim resented that RIETS ordained its own rabbis and that individual rabbis did not give *semikhah*, as was the European custom.[171] The problem remained of rabbis not being properly accredited, and Rabbi Jung was vigilant in scrutinizing the ethical behavior of rabbis, some of whom took money and improperly facilitated divorces or who gave *hekhsherim* to unqualified recipients.[172]

In 1939, the Agudath Harabbonim tried to persuade the RCA to disband and become an alumni association of RIETS. This incident provoked the merger of the two groups, the RCA and the Alumni Association of RIETS.[173] Rabbi Jung was on the committee to effect this merger, which he always wanted because it contributed to a united front for the Modern Orthodox rabbinate in America.[174]

Involvement in Kashrut

Rabbi Jung was in the forefront of organizing properly supervised kosher facilities, which expanded in the 1930s. An increased independent and qualified number of inspectors were needed for proper coverage throughout the state.[175] Proper enforcement remained the

---

170 Gurock, *The Men and Women of Yeshiva*, 13.
171 Louis Bernstein, "Generational Conflict in American Orthodoxy," *American Jewish History* 69, no. 2 (December 1979): 228.
172 Yeshiva University Archives, Jung Collection, Box 1, Folder 1—letter to Rabbi Jung from Rabbi S. Gerstenfeld, denying charges that he received $100 to facilitate a divorce, and letter from Rabbi S. A. Pardes denying that he gave a *hekhsher* to a non-Jew; Jung, *The Path of a Pioneer*, 51–52.
173 L. Bernstein, *Challenge and Mission*, 13–14.
174 Ibid., 11–12.
175 Harry Schneiderman, "Review of the Year 5695," *American Jewish Year Book* 37 (1935–1936): 164; Yeshiva University Archives, Koenigsberg Papers, Box 11, Folder 1—letter, August 1, 1933, from Benjamin Koenigsberg to unknown (headed: My Dear…); Yeshiva University Archives, Koenigsberg Papers, Box 11, Folder

main issue because of lack of a proper inspection system.[176] The editor of the *Jewish Forum* wrote that unity in the *kashrut* endeavor was possible, and that "credit … [would be] due to the determined stand of Rabbi Leo Jung."[177]

In 1935, when the RCA was established, the concept of communal supervision of *kashrut* rather than individual endorsement continued. The OU symbol represented the UOJCA *kashrut* standards, which were managed by the UOJCA. In the early years of the RCA, *kashrut* was a major item on the agenda of every executive meeting.

In the 1930s, much effort went into making an advisory board for the Kosher Law of the State of New York a reality. The goal of this board was to give guidance and assistance to the implementers of the New York State Kosher Law and to see that the Kosher Law was enforced like any other law on the statute books. A *kashrut* association of rabbis and laymen would have jurisdiction over all matters pertaining to proper supervision. The state allowed for an Orthodox interpretation of the law, and *kashrut* supervision was to be taken out of the hands of those who had personally benefited. Rabbi Jung credited the eventual improvement in the *kashrut* industry to the Advisory Board.[178]

A bill to enforce the Kosher Law and establish a permanent advisory board on Kosher Law enforcement in the New York Department of Agriculture was introduced by Senator Mahoney, but it was not passed in the state legislature of New York in the 1930s. Rabbi Jung headed the advisory board for this endeavor.[179] In the 1930s, the Board worked in an unofficial capacity, but in 1940, it became a Statutory Official Board in the Department of Agriculture and Markets, on which Rabbi Jung served as chairman for 30 years.[180] Rabbi Jung pointed out

---

2—Samuel Rottenberg, "Kosher Food and the Struggle for Community Supervision."
176 Harold P. Gastwirt, *Fraud, Corruption and Holiness: The Controversy Over the Supervision of Jewish Dietary Practice in New York City, 1881–1940* (Port Washington, NY: Kennikat Press, 1974), 188.
177 Editorial, *Jewish Forum* 17, no. 5 (May 1934): 159.
178 L. Bernstein, *Challenge and Mission*, 93.
179 Jung, *The Path of a Pioneer*, 249.
180 Yeshiva University Archives, Jung Collection, Box 40, Folder 1—letter to Rabbi Jung from Max Yellen, May 19, 1939, and letter to Governor Lehman from Rabbi

that the fact that New York State and the Jewish community worked together in this endeavor represented "an utterly unique, truly American achievement."[181]

Rabbi Jung talked about *kashrut* the same way that he talked about Sabbath employment: in universal terms, that it was a democratic right in a country based on religious freedom and equality of all citizens:

> ...Whereas *kashrut* enforcement may appear a purely Jewish consideration, the principle behind the various bills touches upon righteousness and the promotion of justice which are treasures of interdenominational thought.[182]

An example of the expanded role of *kashrut* supervision is Rabbi Jung's involvement with kosher facilities aboard ships. Two steamships—called the "Palazzo D'Italia," and the "U.S. Lines Company"—on the suggestion of Rabbi Jung provided kosher facilities on some of their ships. Louis Bernstein wrote that when the Italian line, a major trans-Atlantic steamship company, asked the UOJCA to assume the responsibility for *kashrut* on its ships, it was a major breakthrough. The arrangement continued until Mussolini joined the Axis.[183]

Kashrut observance was ignored by national Jewish organizations; as the lack of kosher facilities was a deterrent to Orthodox involvement, it was an important issue.[184] Rabbi Jung wrote to the president of the Federation of Jewish Charities:

> For principles which I know you understand, I steadfastly refuse to attend any dinner to which Orthodox Jews are invited

---

Jung, May 29, 1938; Gastwirt, *Fraud, Corruption and Holiness*, 133.
181 Jung, *The Path of a Pioneer*, 248.
182 Yeshiva University Archives, Jung Collection, Box 40, Folder 1—letter to Senator Mahoney from Rabbi Jung, May 1, 1941.
183 L. Bernstein, *Challenge and Mission*, 93.
184 Yeshiva University Archives, Jung Collection, Box 41, Folder 1—correspondence between Rabbi Jung and Judge Proskauer, president of the Federation of Jewish Charities, September 20, 1934, September 23, 1934, and October 26, 1936.

unless it is prepared and served in accord with the Jewish dietary laws. I should be very glad to place at your disposal free of charge a *mashgiach* or supervisor and I hope you will see your way to remove this stumbling block to Jewish unity from the only sectarian non-kosher dinner of Federation.[185]

As the RCA's self-confidence increased, this trend continued to be challenged.[186] In December 1939, the RCA wrote to Hadassah and the Federation of Jewish Philanthropies protesting their non-kosher dinners.[187] Rabbi Jung was uncompromising on this issue. Providing special meals or special tables was unacceptable because Rabbi Jung felt that the Torah-true Jew must not be excluded or isolated from any of the community's activities.

Women

Women's roles outside the home continued to evolve in this decade. Social and economic needs were so great that women were needed in the workforce and in the volunteer force; their role thus began to expand. Rabbi Jung's attitude toward women corresponded with his philosophy of harmonizing Judaism with the ongoing changes of the times.[188] Rabbi Jung believed that women had the same need and right to fulfillment as men, though he never addressed feminism as a movement. His four daughters, with his encouragement, went to college and worked after marriage.[189] This attitude separated Modern Orthodoxy from traditional Orthodoxy and defined his type of Orthodoxy.

Rabbi Jung was chairman of the American Beth Jacob Committee, founded to support schools for European Orthodox Jewish girls

---

185 Yeshiva University Archives, Jung Collection, Box 41, Folder 1 (Autobiography—Photocopied Letters)—letter to Judge Proskauer, September 20, 1934; Jung, *Path of a Pioneer*, 254.
186 L. Bernstein, *Challenge and Mission*, 93.
187 Ibid., 94.
188 Jung, Introduction, in *Woman*, ed. Jung, xi.
189 Letter from Rosalie Rosenfeld to Maxine Jacobson, October 29, 1997.

formed in 1927. It was one of Jung's favorite projects, fostered and nurtured by Agudath Israel.[190] The movement was founded by Sarah Schenirer, with the help of some leading Western European Jews, to provide an education for girls. Traditionally, more emphasis was placed on Jewish education for boys, because it was understood that they needed to receive grounding in Jewish sources. Many traditional Orthodox Jews thought that it was unnecessary, and even wrong in some cases, for girls to receive an education. To have a women's school of learning was revolutionary; it needed the support of Orthodox trailblazers such as Rabbi Jung. Mid-nineteenth-century German Orthodoxy had recognized the changing status and role of women, and began to stress women's education. Rabbis Samson Raphael Hirsch and Ezriel Hildesheimer both were concerned with women's education.[191]

For Rabbi Jung, the Beth Jacob type of school was the "feminine counterpart of Yeshiva" and a much needed institution that "provided a curriculum for her education and a challenge for her moral and mental energies."[192] Rabbi Jung brought the message to America.[193] It was a women's movement with only a few men on the committee, including Cyrus Adler, Judge Otto A. Rosalsky, and Rabbi Jung.[194] Girls in America were increasingly entering Jewish schools, but there were no Beth Jacob schools in the United States during the 1930s.[195]

---

190 Monty Noam Penkower, *The Holocaust and Israel Reborn: From Catastrophe to Sovereignty* (Champaign-Urbana, IL: University of Illinois Press, 1994), 239.
191 Shapiro, *Between the Yeshiva World and Modern Orthodoxy*, 210.
192 Jung, *The Path of a Pioneer*, 149.
193 Jung, "Jewry Today," 200; Jung, Introduction, in *Woman*, ed. Jung, xi; Yeshiva University Archives, Jung Collection, Box 48, Folder 3 (published articles)—Jung, "The Renaissance of East European Womanhood," whole article (the article appeared in the First Series of the Jewish Library, vol. 3—*The Jewish Woman*.)
194 Yeshiva University Archives, Jung Collection, Box 48, Folder 3 (published articles)—Jung, "The Renaissance of East European Womanhood," last page of article.
195 Judah Pilch, "Beth Jacob Schools," *Encyclopaedia Judaica* (Jerusalem: Keter Publishing House Jerusalem Ltd., 1974), vol. 16, 1260; Mrs. Herbert [Rebecca] Goldstein, "Orthodox Women's Organization of America," *Jewish Forum* 17, no. 4 (April 1934): 111.

In April 1934, the *Jewish Forum* dedicated an issue to the Jewish woman and her "proper place in the life of the coming generation." The articles demonstrated the expanded and important work in which the women were involved, which at this point was largely organizational.[196] Mizrachi Women's organizational work was new; the organization grew rapidly because of awakening interest in Palestine. It sponsored a technical school and cultural center for girls in Jerusalem.[197] The Union of Orthodox Jewish Congregations of America Women's Organization in 1930 established a Hebrew Teacher Training School for girls.[198] The Ladies Auxiliary of Yeshiva College played an important role in supporting the refugees' program.[199]

The problem of the *agunah* (the deserted wife, or wife not given a divorce) remained on the agenda. What was new was a proposal from the Conservative movement. In December 1937, Dr. Louis Epstein, reporting for the Committee on Jewish Law (part of the Conservative movement's Rabbinical Assembly of America), recommended the adoption of a resolution to solve the problem of the *agunah*, by permitting a dissolution of the marriage.[200] This attempt to modify divorce laws was declared illegal by the UOJCA convention that followed the Conservative Rabbinic Assembly convention.[201] The Orthodox rabbis felt that the Conservative solution did not follow the *halakhah*. Orthodox women in future decades would confront this unsolved problem that remains a dilemma for Orthodoxy.

Conclusion

Modern Orthodox leaders were busy laying the groundwork in education and in organizational activity that would lead to successes in the decades to follow. The advent of the RCA was very important, as it

---

196 Editorial, *Jewish Forum* 17, no. 4 (April 1934): 97.
197 Miriam Ginsberg, "The Mozart's Women's Organization of America," *Jewish Forum* 17, no. 4 (April 1934): 110.
198 R. Goldstein, "Orthodox Women's Organization of America," 111.
199 Yeshiva University Archives—"Women Grant 136 Aid Scholarships," *Hazedek*, November 15, 1939, 1.
200 Schneiderman, "Review of the Year 5698—United States," 143.
201 Schneiderman, "Review of the Year 5695," 164.

helped define what Modern Orthodoxy stood for, it helped unify Modern Orthodoxy to some extent, and it added prestige to the Modern Orthodox rabbinate. The trend to social activism meant that Modern Orthodox leaders, with their expanded role, were reaching a wider audience as they functioned in both the modern and religious world. Concepts of Torah were applied to everyday life. Rabbi Jung, as a social activist, began his efforts to save Jews, while continuing to teach about Judaism and work to make Orthodoxy viable and attractive in America.

3. MODERN ORTHODOXY IN THE 1940S

• • •

*"Watchman, what of the night—I see the dawn,
but it is still night."*
(Isaiah 21:11-12)

Introduction

Modern Orthodoxy became more important in the 1940s; it became more active, better known, and more influential. In that decade, Modern Orthodoxy took on a more expanded, visible, and leading role; its image improved. There was an interest and demand for more Jewish knowledge on the part of the layman, and the clergy began to demand more observance from their congregants. Clearer policies served to broaden the gap between the Orthodox and Conservative movements.[1]

Orthodox leaders took an active role in the war effort, which gave them experience in various activities and provided another avenue to get their message across. There was a realization that it was important to have an Orthodox presence in relief agencies and political affairs. World War II resulted in a call for societal changes, leading to a more important role for religion. Modern Orthodoxy took a leading role in the search for deeper values and the call for justice and rights for minority groups.

---

1   Jonathan D. Sarna, "The Debate Over Mixed Seating in the American Synagogue," in *The American Synagogue: A Sanctuary Transformed*, ed. Jack Wertheimer (Cambridge, UK, and New York: Cambridge University Press, 1987), 380.

In the 1940s, Modern Orthodoxy began to be associated with active participation in its own organizations, as well as organizations and community activities that involved the welfare of all Jews, although it began this participation in the 1930s. But in the 1940s, this was exemplified by their war effort and their attitude toward Zionism. Zionism took on new importance, and was supported by Modern Orthodoxy without reservations. *Eretz Israel* (the Land of Israel) was looked upon as a sign that Jews were equals in the world.

There were new leaders at Yeshiva; the Modern Orthodox had to take up the new responsibility and try to fill the gap of the loss of Talmudic leadership in Europe. Yeshiva expanded into a full university in 1945. The reputation of Modern Orthodoxy and its rabbis was greatly enhanced for all Jewish people and in the community at large.

Resistance to Americanization by Jews broadened after the war. By the mid-1940s, American Jews were ready to analyze and to critique political happenings when necessary; they became less fearful of diversity. The general Jewish community matured; many Jews in America were no longer immigrants, and therefore, Americanization was no longer so prominent a theme. *The Commentator*, the Yeshiva College newspaper, observed that first-generation American Jews could not write their own history. The second generation was not interested, as they wanted to forget and escape from their Jewish past, which included a foreign language spoken in the home, their religion, and their childhood struggles; "the principle of the third generation" is that "what the son wishes to forget, the grandson wishes to remember."[2] In the 1940s, the third generation was more interested in its history and religion. This was good for Orthodoxy.

There was an increase in the sale of general- religion books, which was a sign of a general-religious revival, the beginning of a return to religion.[3] Rabbi Jung's books and writings reflected the new interest in

---

2 Yeshiva University Archives—Alexander Brody, "Grinstein Authors Volume on Early Jewish Community," *The Commentator* 22, no. 3 (November 29, 1945): 2; Yeshiva University Archives—Brody, "American Jewish History Viewed From New Outlook." *The Commentator* 24, no. 3 (November 21, 1946): 4.

3 Matthew S. Hadstrom, *The Rise of Liberal Religion* (Oxford and New York: Oxford University Press, 2013), 120.

Jewish roots and religion, and he exuded confidence in his critique of society and in his suggestions for a greater future. He edited his fifth volume for the Jewish Library series, *Israel of Tomorrow*, which deals with many of the problems, achievements, and dilemmas that confronted Jews in the past and that they had to face in the present. It served as a guide towards a deeper understanding of the Jewish background in Europe and America.[4] Rabbi Jung's influential articles in the 1940s espoused the benefits of religion and advocated a major role for religion. The articles all articulated the same thing—the Modern Orthodox philosophy that religion was a rational phenomenon and that humans had a great role to play in their own destiny.[5]

Rabbi Jung's educational endeavors continued. He helped Yeshiva through trying times, he was on various boards, and he continued to raise funds on their behalf. Rabbi Jung became very involved in the war effort in his role as Jewish chaplain. He received the Selective Service Medal in 1949 for his devoted voluntary work; also, in 1949, he received an invitation from the Pentagon to tour areas of the Far East.[6]

He continued his work with the American Jewish Joint Distribution Committee (JDC). When Cyrus Adler died in 1940, Rabbi Jung took over his duties, but only became the official chair of the Cultural Committee in 1943. He remained the chair of the JDC Cultural Committee until 1978; this was the longest chairmanship in JDC history.[7] He also continued as the chair of American Beth Jacob.

---

4   Yeshiva University Archives—"Professor L. Jung Edits New Publication on Jewish Problems," *The Commentator* 23, no. 6 (May 9, 1946): 1.
5   Yeshiva University Archives, Leo Jung Collection, Box 46, Folder 4—Leo Jung, "Judaism and The New World Order," 11; Ibid., Box 48, Folder 5 (published articles)—"The Problems of Sovereignty and Minorities." Also in the *American Journal of Economics and Sociology* 4, no. 4 (July 1945): 515–528; in Jung, *Israel of Tomorrow*, ed. Jung, Jewish Library, First Series, vol. 5 (New York: Herald Square Press, 1946); Yeshiva University Archives, Jung Collection, Box 44, Folder 1—Jung, "Social Engineering"; *Jewish Forum* 29, no. 10 (October 1946).
6   Yeshiva University Archives, Jung Collection, Folder 42, Box 1—letter from Rabbi Jung to the Honorable John Foster Dulles, Secretary of State, February 9, 1956; Ibid., Folder 40, Box 7—autobiographical letters, photocopy of the Congress of the United States, the Selective Service Medal.
7   Joint Distribution Committee Archives, File 93, 1933-44—letter to Rabbi Jung from Paul Baerwald, March 10, 1943.

After the war, he traveled extensively in Palestine for various organizations.[8] He began his work with the American Fund for Palestine in the 1940s.[9]

Rabbi Jung also continued his efforts in the area of *kashrut*. He was the chairman of the Advisory Board for the Kosher Law Enforcement Bureau of New York, and he was also the chairman of the Committee of Rabbis to supervise *kashrut* at Beth Israel Hospital.[10]

The War Effort

The Role of the Modern Orthodox Chaplain and its Significance

The Orthodox chaplain played a great role in World War II, which was very significant for the development of Modern Orthodoxy. Louis Bernstein, in *Challenge and Mission*, points out that Orthodoxy took more of a leading role during the period of the war and that it has become an important component of American life since World War II.[11] Bernstein wrote that the role of Orthodoxy was enhanced on the American scene by the contributions that the Rabbinical Council of America (RCA) made in the area of military chaplaincy.[12] The participation on the part of the Orthodox meant that there were, when possible, Jewish programs and provisions of the Orthodox standard. They were there to solve military-religious problems, to guide, and to influence. The role of the rabbi enhanced Orthodoxy's image, and in a world of anti-Semitism, image building was important. According to Bernstein, the

---

8 Yeshiva University Archives—"Dr. Jung Says Gentile World Needs Judaism," *The Commentator* 26, no. 5 (January 1, 1948): 1.
9 Yeshiva University Archives, Leo Jung Collection, Box 44, Folder 3—Jung, "Palestine Today," third page of article (no page numbers). Article also in *Jewish Forum* 30, no. 9 (September 1947) and *Jewish Forum* 30, no. 10 (October 1947). Address delivered at a reception for Rabbi Jung by the American Fund for the Palestine Institute, Essex House, NY, June 4, 1947.
10 Yeshiva University Archives, Leo Jung Collection, Box 44, Folder 2—letter from Nathan Ratcoff, M.D., to Rabbi Jung, November 30, 1942, and letter to Senator Walter Mahoney from Rabbi Jung, May 1, 1941.
11 Louis Bernstein, *Challenge and Mission: The Emergence of the English-Speaking Rabbinate* (New York: Shengold Publishers, 1982), 9.
12 Ibid., 256.

rabbi took Torah learning out to the masses serving in the armed forces, an example of a successful outreach program.

Most, but certainly not all, of the Orthodox clergy were from the Rabbi Isaac Elchanan Theological Seminary (RIETS), thus were Modern Orthodox. However, this meant that the perspectives of Yeshiva College were presented. Rabbi Sidney Hoenig, a graduate of RIETS and chaplain in the armed forces, explained why. It was required by the armed forces that chaplains have a secular education as well as a religious education. The rabbis from RIETS had both a secular and religious education, which allowed them to become military chaplains.[13] Also, having to work with other denominations was a prerequisite, which was a problem for many traditional Orthodox rabbis who would not work with Conservative or Reform rabbis. These traditional Orthodox groups resented and criticized the perspectives of the Jewish Welfare Board (JWB), which had brought together the three official rabbinic groups and Yeshiva for their philosophy of education and outreach to other Jewish groups.[14] Orthodox, Conservative, and Reform rabbis worked together on issues of mutual concern. Because of what Modern Orthodoxy stood for, they were able to participate.

The chaplains impacted directly on the lives of servicemen; therefore, an Orthodox presence was very important. Dr. Samuel Belkin, the president of Yeshiva College, asked Rabbi Joseph B. Soloveitchik if he would write a *responsum* on the role, if any, of an Orthodox military chaplain. Rabbi Soloveitchik headed the *Halakhic* Committee of the RCA, and by the 1940s, he had been recognized as a rabbinic genius and master of Jewish law. Rabbi Soloveitchik's responses influenced the religious practices of Modern Orthodox Jews. He felt that it was not only permissible for, but a duty of, every Orthodox rabbi to enlist in the armed forces for the purpose of rendering spiritual guidance.[15] When the JWB requested that more clergy enlist, among those who

---

13 Sidney B. Hoenig, "The Orthodox Rabbi as a Military Chaplain," *Tradition* 16, no. 2 (Fall 1976): 39.
14 Ibid., 39–40, 43.
15 Albert I. Slomovitz, *The Fighting Rabbis: A History of Jewish Military Chaplains, 1860–1945* (Ann Arbor, MI: UMI Dissertation Services, 1996), 78.

signed the request of December 16, 1941, were Rabbis Joseph Lookstein (the president of the RCA), Saul Silber (the president of the Hebrew Theological College of Chicago), William Weiss (the president of the UOJCA), and David de Sola Pool, the chairman of CANRA (Committee for Army and Navy Religious Activities; also known as the Chaplain's Committee).[16] There were twenty-six Jewish chaplains in World War I in the American forces; none were Orthodox.[17] More Orthodox applications than Reform ones were received for World War II.[18] This is certainly one example of Rabbi Soloveitchik's influence in unifying Modern Orthodoxy. In 1942, the three official rabbinic bodies—the Reform Central Conference of American Rabbis (CCAR), the Conservative Rabbinical Assembly (RA), and the RCA—were brought together by Frank Weil, president of the JWB, to form the CANRA within the JWB. It should be noted that, in 1942, the RCA merged with the alumni of Hebrew Theological College, but the RCA name was retained.[19] Rabbi Jung was an executive member of the JWB, and he toured army camps representing the JWB.[20]

Chaplains were chosen by their respective organizations to be members of the CANRA, and Rabbi Jung was chosen to be a chaplain by the RCA. Within the CANRA, representatives from the RCA decided all Orthodox matters.[21] Other Orthodox rabbis active in the CANRA were Rabbis Herbert S. Goldstein, Lookstein, and de Sola Pool. The CANRA impacted greatly on the lives of service personnel.

One of the most active of the subcommittees of the CANRA in the 1940s was the Responsa Committee. Rabbi Jung acted as the Orthodox representative, and a Reform rabbi (Dr. Solomon B. Freehof) served as the chairman. Rabbis on the Responsa Committee were to answer

---

16 Phillip S. Bernstein, *Rabbis at War: The CANRA Story* (Waltham, MA: American Jewish Historical Society, 1971), 55–56.
17 Hoenig, "The Orthodox Rabbi as a Military Chaplain," 38; L. Bernstein, *Challenge and Mission*, 239.
18 Hoenig, "The Orthodox Rabbi as a Military Chaplain," 40.
19 L. Bernstein, *Challenge and Mission*, 14–15.
20 Yeshiva University Archives, Jung Collection, Folder 1, Box 5—letter from Congregation Ramath Orah, January 28, 1945.
21 Hoenig, "The Orthodox Rabbi as a Military Chaplain," 41; Slomovitz, *The Fighting Rabbis*, 202–203.

Jewish legal questions from Jewish chaplains and servicemen as well as from the government. Their task was not easy; they had to deal with war emergency conditions, and they had to operate on a tri-rabbinic level. However, there was harmony—they published "War Responsa," which attested to this successful cooperation.[22] The presence of a Modern Orthodox rabbi, in this case Rabbi Jung, ensured that the Modern Orthodox view was heard and respected.

Modern Orthodox rabbis such as Rabbis Jung, Goldstein, and Lookstein played an important role in CANRA seminar programs that took place in the Chaplain School at Harvard University.[23] The fact that Modern Orthodox rabbis lectured at Harvard, even if it was the Chaplain School, was an example of successful outreach, of getting their message out to a broader audience, and of image building.

The CANRA devoted much attention to publications.[24] Material on Jewish rites, holidays, *kashrut*, sermons, and guides to biblical readings were made available. These publications were an important source of information for the Jewish soldier, as well as giving the soldier a sense of Jewish history, and a sense of belonging. Rabbi de Sola Pool revised an edition of the JWB prayer book in 1941 that also contained a separate Reform service, unlike the previously accepted 1917 edition that was for all Jewish denominations. This prayer book catered more to the Orthodox than the one before, which is evidence of Orthodox successful participation. Also, the Chaplaincy Committee later produced an abridged *mahzor*, the prayer book used for the Jewish New Year and Yom Kippur (the High Holidays) for all the Jewish denominations.[25] Rabbi Jung represented the Orthodox rabbinate to prepare this prayer book to be used by all servicemen. According to Hoenig, there were still complaints by some Orthodox chaplains about pages missing in this edition; these chaplains continued to use the previous editions.[26]

---

22 Hoenig, "The Orthodox Rabbi as a Military Chaplain," 42.
23 Ibid., 43.
24 Ibid., 44–45.
25 Ibid., 42–43.
26 Ibid., 43.

The duties of the Jewish chaplain were many. The rabbi was an educator, a recreational organizer, a source of kosher food, a personal counsellor, and a spokesman for the Jewish soldier. He arranged for furloughs to be granted to Jewish soldiers for the High Holidays and for Passover. Chaplains conducted Passover seders and other holiday services, and provided Jewish texts, kosher food, and Passover packages.[27] Rabbi Jung lectured to soldiers; his mail—with requests for summaries of his lectures and questions—shows appreciation on the part of the soldiers.[28]

There was concern that Jews would be accused of disloyalty to America. In 1944, Rabbi Jung received a letter from Rabbi de Sola Pool dealing with the fact that there was embarrassment on the part of Jewish servicemen regarding a line in the *Haggadah*, the text read at the Passover seder. The line cited was: "This year we are here, next year may we be in the Land of Israel." Rabbi de Sola Pool wrote: "The point is important enough to justify making a new plate of page nineteen for any reprint of the *Haggadah* that the JWB may make..." and he requested that the "embarrassing words" be deleted,[29] as follows:

> I suggest that the embarrassing words be paraphrased in a little doggerel, since no literal or even free translation can avoid the possibility of misinterpretation, and an explanatory footnote would be out of place and unsatisfactory. A note would call attention to the difficulty and *qui s'excuse s'accuse*.[30]

There was still fear of showing dual loyalties to America and the Jewish homeland; the approach was still somewhat timid, and the feeling was still one of vulnerability. That attitude would change in the postwar years.

---

27 Yeshiva University Archives—"Chaplain Siegel Speaks at Edison," *The Commentator* 20, no. 6 (January 18, 1945): 1.
28 Yeshiva University Archives, Jung Collection, Box 1, Folder 7—letter from Aryeh Lev of the National Welfare Board requesting summary of "Divrai Torah," December 8, 1949.
29 Yeshiva University Archives, Jung Collection, Box 1, Folder 4—letter from Rabbi de Sola Pool to Rabbi Jung, September 7, 1944.
30 Ibid.

There was prejudice regarding the untrue stereotype of Jewish nonparticipation in the army that had anti-Semitic overtones. Rabbis dealt with these issues as well.[31] The JWB issued a news released with detailed information about Jewish participation and the percentages of Jewish servicemen. Rabbi Jung sent out many copies of this news release to those needing clarification.[32]

The stereotype of Jewish non-participation continued; to combat this and other forms of anti-Semitism and to promote and present the Modern Orthodox point of view of Judaism, the Yeshiva College alumni went on radio every Sunday at 6:00 PM with their program called "The Jewish Tradition." The program, which began in January 1945 and was on station WLIB, had been initiated by Rabbi Jung.[33] The program dealt with the role of the clergy in the war effort; it certainly raised the image of the rabbi in both the Jewish and non-Jewish community.

Orthodox Organizational Involvement

The great concern for saving Jews in a war-torn world became more intense in the 1940s, and most organizations became involved in the war effort. Rabbi Jung continued his efforts for the JDC and, in 1943, became the chairman of its Cultural Religious Committee. As the chairman, Rabbi Jung traveled to many parts of the world to check on how funds were distributed and used by religious and cultural institutions that the JDC supported. Through the JDC, in addition to his cultural activities, Rabbi Jung also saw to it that basic needs for such things as kosher food, blankets, beds, and books were met as material aid continued to take on great importance.[34] Thousands of books that had been saved from destruction during the war were brought to America. The Cultural Committee of the JDC, of which Rabbi Jung

---

31 Slomovitz, *The Fighting Rabbis*, 180 and 196.
32 Yeshiva University Archives, Jung Collection, Box 40, Folder 7—letter to Rev. Father J. Elliot Ross, March 16, 1944.
33 Yeshiva University Archives—"Y.C. Alumni Takes to Air," *The Commentator* 20, no. 6 (January 18, 1945): 1.
34 Yeshiva University Archives, Jung Collection, Box 1, Folder 6—letter from Rabbi Jung to Haym Gitler (Poalei Agudath Israel), August 1946.

had served as the chairman, had saved many of these books. After the war, the Yeshiva library received the Morris Friedman Collection of rare books dating back to the sixteenth and seventeenth centuries, which had been obtained through Rabbi Jung.[35] More educational material of high quality would become available in America; America would not be the Jewish "wasteland" it once was.

Rabbi Jung collected more than 1,200 affidavits that led to the rescue of over 9,000 Jews.[36] He wrote in his autobiography: "To answer the cry for deliverance from Hitler's hell, I determined on a campaign of obtaining affidavits."[37]

In April 1943, Rabbi Jung was also sent to Bermuda to plead the case of the Jewish people who were "walking through the valley of the shadow of death." This turned out to be a most frustrating and demoralizing experience.[38] The Bermuda Conference was an Anglo-American Conference, held from April 19 to April 30 of that year, to discuss helping refugees. Official delegates of the American and British governments were there. However, the Bermuda Conference dealt exclusively with those who had already reached neutral territory and totally failed to address the plight of Jews under Nazi occupation.[39] Jews demanded that Allied governments rescue the victims of Nazi persecution; however, the delegates were unwilling to refer to Jews as the Nazis' main victims. Furthermore, Britain refused to abandon its White Paper policy, which limited Jewish immigration to Palestine and clearly demonstrated that the British did not want a Jewish state. Instead, the White Paper proposed the impractical idea of opening camps in North America as

---

35 Yeshiva University Archives, Jung Collection, Box 1, Folder 5—correspondence with Bernard Turk, October 28, 1945, and November 21, 1945.
36 Yeshiva University Archives, Public Relations Files (Leo Jung)—Milton R. Konvitz, "Leo Jung—Rabbi for All Jews," 39. Also in *Midstream* 39, no. 6 (August/September 1993).
37 Leo Jung, *The Path of a Pioneer: The Autobiography of Leo Jung*, Jewish Library, Second Series, vol. 8 (London and New York: Soncino Press, 1980), 140.
38 Yeshiva University Archives, Jung Collection, Box 1, Folder 4—letter to the Honorable Sol Bloom from Rabbi Jung, April 14, 1943.
39 Efraim Zuroff, *The Response of Orthodox Jewry in the United States to the Holocaust: The Activities of the Vaad Ha-Hatzala Rescue Committee, 1939–1945* (New York: The Michael Sharf Publications Trust of Yeshiva University Press; Hoboken, NJ: Ktav Publishing House Inc., 2000), 245.

havens for these refugees. The conference did not save a single Jew from the Holocaust.[40]

Rabbi Jung's participation in the JDC was another example of how the Modern Orthodox leadership functioned, as was demonstrated in the last chapter. However, the Agudath Harabbonim (the Union of Orthodox Rabbis of the United States and Canada) found it difficult to accept the leadership of the JDC, which included non-Orthodox Jews, who they felt could not appreciate their worldview. In 1939, it founded the *Vaad Hahatzala* to preserve Torah scholarship and the sages who represented it.[41] The Agudath Harabbonim would not join the United Jewish Appeal (UJA).[42] The relationship of the *Vaad Hahatzala* with the JDC and Modern Orthodoxy was problematic, exemplifying the conflict of Modern Orthodoxy and traditional Orthodoxy. The establishment of the *Vaad Hahatzala* was symbolic of the disunity in the Orthodox community. The leadership of the Modern Orthodox was once again at odds with the leadership of the Agudath Harabbonim and their norms.

The JDC, as well as several Orthodox organizations, were skeptical about a separate relief-and-rescue organization for refugee rabbis and their *yeshivot*. These organizations felt that the establishment of a new fundraising agency was not justified as it overlapped with the work of the JDC, which bore the major burden of overseas Jewish relief-and-rescue work and fundraising efforts, and it drained needed resources from the UJA, which funded the JDC.[43] The *Vaad Hahatzala* worked in the same countries as the JDC—in Asiatic Russia and Shanghai, to name two.[44] Both organizations sent funds for the maintenance of Orthodox refugees in Japan. The JDC had allocated funds for the

---

40 Aaron Rakeffet-Rothkoff, *The Silver Era in American Jewish Orthodoxy: Rabbi Eliezer Silver and His Generation* (New York: Yeshiva University Press; Jerusalem: Feldheim Publishers, 1981), 218.
41 Zuroff, *The Response of Orthodox Jewry in the United States to the Holocaust*, foreword (page number unknown), 33, and 38.
42 Ibid., 33.
43 Ibid., 65, 131, and 255; JDC Archives, File 93, 1933-44—minutes of JDC Meeting, February 16, 1944.
44 JDC Archives, File 362—letter to Harry Dickstein from Joseph Hyman, executive vice-chairman of the JDC, August 31, 1944.

transportation of Polish refugees via the Far East, half of which were earmarked for rabbis and *yeshivot*.[45]

Until late in the war, the *Vaad Hahatzala* had focused exclusively on rescuing rabbis and *yeshiva* students, which led to bitter, ongoing debates with the rest of the Jewish community, as the *Vaad Hahatzala*'s work gave preferential treatment to one group at the expense of other Jews.[46] However, the JDC could accept the *Vaad Hahatzala* if they limited themselves to just that, even if in that field the JDC had also contributed greatly to religious institutions, rabbis, and *yeshiva* students, and even if they felt that they themselves had more experience and were better equipped to spend intelligently and effectively for rescue relief and rehabilitation. The executive vice-chairman of the JDC, Joseph Hyman, wrote:

> If the *Vaad Hahatzala* were to limit itself to that type of aid [for *yeshivot* and rabbinical groups], it would be more understandable... Nevertheless, what has happened is that the *Vaad Hahatzala* has announced that it has become a general rescue and relief organization not merely for *yeshivot* and rabbinical groups but for others as well. It has claimed to be the primary organization in the field of rescue.[47]

The JDC felt that the *Vaad Hahatzala* had embarrassed and prejudiced the interests of the JDC. Friction and accusations were not new; the JDC accused the *Vaad Hahatzala* of making statements unfavorable to the JDC before.[48] The JDC found itself in a position in which it had to answer to the UJA, which disliked the competitive campaign.[49] The

---

45 Zuroff, *The Response of Orthodox Jewry in the United States to the Holocaust*, 132 and 252; Rakeffet-Rothkoff, *The Silver Era in American Jewish Orthodoxy*, 201.
46 Zuroff, Introduction, *The Response of Orthodox Jewry in the United States to the Holocaust*, xvii.
47 JDC Archives, File 362, 1933-44—letter to Dickstein from Hyman, August 31, 1944.
48 JDC Archives, File 361, 1933-44—letter to Rabbi Wohlgelernter, chairman of *Vaad Hahatzala* Committee of RCA, from Hyman, November 16, 1943, 2.
49 JDC Archives, File 361, 1933-44—letter to Hyman from Henry Montor, the executive vice-chair of the UJA, May 14, 1943.

3. MODERN ORTHODOXY IN THE 1940S

Vaad Hahatzala also had to face the Council of Jewish Federations and Welfare Funds, which put out a bulletin (dated June 1944) questioning the relationship between the two organizations and calling upon the *Vaad Hahatzala* to coordinate its efforts with the JDC.[50] The two groups did come to some arrangement to coordinate efforts in order to prevent the spectacle of competitive fundraising and divisiveness. The *Vaad Hahatzala* claimed that it preferred its original task to work only for *yeshivot* and Torah institutions and that it would leave the work of relief and reconstruction to other groups. It made requests of the JDC, one of which was that some Orthodox Jewish Europeans be hired by the JDC.[51] Rabbi Jung shared the *Vaad Hahatzala*'s goal of supporting *yeshivot* and Torah scholars, but he worked to convince local agencies to transfer funds to *yeshivot* and Torah scholars through the JDC.[52] Also, Rabbi Jung had assured Rabbi Isaac Herzog, the Chief Rabbi of Palestine, that the JDC would always be mindful of religious requirements as irreligious influences were making their mark in European communities.[53]

The *Vaad Hahatzala* did have Modern Orthodox supporters, such as Rabbis Herbert Goldstein, Joseph Konvitz, and Jacob Levinson of the RCA.[54] In 1945, some *yeshiva* students and faculty participated in a campaign to raise money for the *Vaad Hahatzala*. Though Rabbi Jung was an outstanding fundraiser, his name was not on the list for this endeavor, as the JDC was seen as a competitor and he was involved with the JDC.[55] However, it should be noted that Rabbi Jung had a very good relationship with Rabbi Aaron Kotler, who came to America

---

50 JDC Archives, File 362—letter to Dickstein from Hyman, August 31, 1944.
51 JDC Archives, File 93, 1933-44—letter to Rabbi Jung from Jacob Rosenheim, head of Agudath Israel, December 26, 1944.
52 Jung, *The Path of a Pioneer*, 172.
53 JDC Archives, File 93—cable to Rabbi Herzog from Rabbi Jung, December 9, 1944.
54 Rakeffet-Rothkoff, *The Silver Era in American Jewish Orthodoxy*, 189 and 200-201; Zuroff, *The Response of Orthodox Jewry in the United States to the Holocaust*, 119 and 126.
55 Yeshiva University Archives—"Vaad Hahatzalah Achieves Record Goal of Raising $25,000," *The Commentator* 20, no. 6 (January 18, 1945): 1.

in 1941 and became an active leader in the *Vaad Hahatzala*.[56] The fact that Modern Orthodox leaders gave their support to the *Vaad Hahatzala*, and therefore to more right-wing factions of Orthodoxy, is an example of Modern Orthodoxy being influenced by this group.

It should be noted that, by 1942, when the Final Solution became public knowledge, the attention of all Orthodox organizations went to rescuing the Jewish people.[57] Young Israel, the UOJCA, and the RCA supported the *Vaad Hahatzala*'s efforts in this direction. Yeshiva College was also involved in many ways from rescue to rehabilitation.[58] The Agudath Harabbonim and the Modern Orthodox groups worked together for the purpose of rescue, though they still differed ideologically.

The RCA was involved in saving Jewish lives, and involved in world politics as well.[59] It also became active in the JDC in projects overseas in an effort to solve the problem of refugee rabbis. Israel Klaven of the RCA met with Rabbi Jung to see if the organization that Rabbi and Mrs. Jung had begun in the 1920s to deal with rabbis in need of aid, the Rabbonim Aid Society, run independently by women from Rabbi Jung's synagogue, could help. The Rabbonim Aid Society and the Jewish Center were only too willing. The synagogue held dinners in the 1940s to raise money, and certain donors gave to this cause on a regular basis. They raised money and helped rabbis in need right up until the 1990s.[60]

Rabbi Jung's Response to World War II

Through his refugee work, Rabbi Jung became intimately acquainted with the social ills of the time. For him, World War II was an example of rampant "social infection," meaning lack of moral values. Rabbi Jung

---

56 Personal interview with Norman Lamm, January 16, 2003. Lamm commented on the good relationship with Rabbi Kotler. Also found in the Jung Collection was friendly correspondence between Rabbis Kotler and Jung.
57 Zuroff, *The Response of Orthodox Jewry in the United States to the Holocaust*, 126.
58 Yeshiva University Archives—"Vaad Hahatzalah Achieves Record Goal of Raising $25,000," 1.
59 L. Bernstein, *Challenge and Mission*, 162.
60 Personal interview with Sadie Silverstein (president of the Rabbonim Aid Society since 1977, member of the Jewish Center Synagogue since the early 1940s), November 19, 1997.

discussed the dangers of indifference and intolerance and the meaning or significance of World War II in his articles—"God in Crisis," "Social Engineering," "Judaism and The New World Order: The Problems of Sovereignty and of Minorities," "Religion in the American Dream," and "American Religion: Its Opportunity and Responsibility." Most of Rabbi Jung's writings and radio addresses were peppered with the same message in the 1940s. The problems were the failure of modernity, the existence of national sovereignty, and the failure of organized religion to create liberty and equality for individuals. There had been no cooperation between social groups, nations, and religious groups. Rabbi Jung repeatedly presented this critique, since he felt that it was important to restore the importance of religion in society. Values had to be explored and the political and spiritual systems had to be re-examined. Jung wrote: "…Ruthless self-criticism for a useful blueprint of the future must be a sine qua non for achievement."[61]

Modernity had not seen a role for religion and had ignored religious principles that were seen as outdated.[62] Modern philosophy could not infuse ethical and moral ways into society, and had failed to work out a system of social justice.[63] Rabbi Jung felt that the main value in society was materialism and that the tragedy of society was that it lacked spiritual values.[64] Though there was talk of this in the 1930s, there was no question of its truth in the 1940s.

National interests prevented nations from helping other nations.[65] Organized religion had failed in its role to prevent evil and to give

---

61 Yeshiva University Archives, Jung Collection, Box 23, Folder 2—Jung, "Program for 5701," *B'nai Brith Messenger* with the *Jewish Community Press* (September 27, 1940): 24.
62 Yeshiva University Archives, Jung Collection, Box 44, Folder 1—Jung, "American Religion: Its Opportunity and Responsibility," on "Message of Israel," WJZ (radio station), June 17, 1945, 2.
63 Leo Jung, "Jewish Foundations of the New World Order," in *Israel of Tomorrow*, ed. Leo Jung, 4.
64 Yeshiva University Archives, Jung Collection, Box 1, Folder 5—"American Religion: Its Opportunities and Responsibilities," on "Message of Israel," WJZ (radio station), June 17, 1945; Yeshiva University Archives, Jung Collection, Box 46, Folder 4—"Religion in the American Dream," on Mutual's Radio Chapel Station WOR, May 6, 1945.
65 Jung, "Jewish Foundations of the New World Order," 12.

moral guidance, and it had been intolerant.⁶⁶ Rabbi Jung specifically targeted Christianity and expressed his disappointment with the failure of Christendom to rise for the saving of Jews: "Hitler couldn't have accomplished what he did if there wasn't a wrong attitude towards fellow humans."⁶⁷ It was a time when people had forgotten to be "their brother's keeper." Anti-Semitism was undemocratic and un-American, and it lacked religious values. Intolerance undermined the spiritual foundations and moral basis of all religions. Whenever persecution and poverty were permitted, everyone suffered. Rabbi Jung wrote:

> Organized religion has often been undermined by its own inconsistent attitude, by frequent disregard of its own standards in its approach to other creeds, to treat one's neighbour with respect is not only in accordance with the principles of every religion, but it is essential for one's own survival.⁶⁸

Rabbi Jung called for a more important, expanded, and influential role for religion in society. He felt that religions should work together to ensure equal rights of the individual and of the group, as well as to secure peace, social justice, and social interdependence. He was part of the climate of interfaith dialogue, the desire to find common ground, which flourished in the 1940s.⁶⁹ Rabbi Jung's articles were read, and his message was heard on his radio program. There are about 50 requests for copies of his message from non-Jewish sources; one comes from the National Conference of Christians and Jews, Inc.: "Copies for distribution to clergy leaders…"⁷⁰ He stressed social interdependence, or "social engineering," which meant cooperation, mutuality, and concern with everyone's welfare on the part of social groups, nations, and religious groups. In fact, for Rabbi Jung, democracy implied the right to be

---

66 Ibid., 8.
67 Jung, "Rome and Jerusalem," in *Crumbs and Character: Sermons, Addresses, and Essays*, ed. Leo Jung (New York: The Night and Day Press, 1942), 219.
68 Leo Jung, "The Challenges of Today," in *Crumbs and Character*, ed. Leo Jung, 259.
69 Hadstrom, *The Rise of Liberal Religion*, 163.
70 Yeshiva University Archives, Jung Collection, Box 1, Folder 5.

different.[71] The majority must look out for the minorities and the underprivileged:[72]

> The whole texture of our divine book expresses the conviction that the culture of a nation must be gauged not by its attitude towards majorities, but precisely by its attitude towards minorities, towards those who politically, socially, and financially are without adequate support."[73]

Before publishing his manuscript, "Jewish Foundations of the New World Order," Rabbi Jung had asked Salo W. Baron, world-renowned historian and professor at Columbia University, to read it and to make suggestions. Baron noted that Rabbi Jung had failed to address one important issue: How to "wrestle with one major difficulty; what sanctions can religion put behind its demands today." The secular society and modern state had to stay clear of religious influences.[74] Baron, of course, had touched on the key dilemma of what religions faced in America. However, Baron felt that even though religion lacked power of enforcement, it was important to express this dilemma, and it was important to bring to the public what religion had to say.

The article that Baron critiqued appeared in the *American Journal of Economics and Sociology*. The journal's editor, Mr. Will Lissner, wanted the part of the article deleted in which Rabbi Jung expresses disappointment at the failure of Christendom to rise to save Israel. Rabbi Jung requested that it be put in a note rather than completely omitted.[75] The reference was ultimately omitted, but the article does discuss the duties

---

71 Yeshiva University Archives, Jung Collection, Box 46, Folder 4—"Religion in the American Dream," on Mutual's Radio Chapel Station WOR, May 6, 1945.
72 Leo Jung, "Judaism and the New World Order," *American Journal of Economics and Sociology* 4, no. 4 (July 1945): 519. Also at Yeshiva University Archives, Jung Collection, Box 48, Folder 5 (published articles).
73 Jung, "The Rights of Majorities," in *Crumbs and Character*, 229.
74 Yeshiva University Archives, Jung Collection, Box 16, Folder 2—letter from Salo Baron to Rabbi Jung, October 29, 1943.
75 Yeshiva University Archives, Jung Collection, Box 16, Folder 2—letter to the editor (Mr. Will Lissner) from Rabbi Jung, October 11, 1944.

of the religious majorities. This incident is an example of the limits of freedom of expression on this subject, even in "friendly" places.

Rabbi Jung tried to put his suggestions into concrete action. During the war, he hoped that each denomination could rally the faithful around its own flag to work with other groups for the promotion of universal peace and happiness.[76] He planned this project with Pearl Buck, a well-known author; the suggestion had come through a pamphlet that Buck had written, called "Can the Church Lead?" Rabbi Jung wanted a statement of "common conviction" made by representative, clerical, and lay leaders of all religions emphasizing, in the name of God, "an unlimited and dynamic insistence on the dignity of the individual, on interdependence of ideals of religion and human security."[77] He tried to engage world religious leaders of different faiths, such as Rev. Dr. Harry Emerson Fosdick (a Baptist minister), the Dalai Lama in Tibet, and the rector of Al Azhar University in Cairo, as well as every prominent leader of the various faiths, to work together in a leadership role to champion the cause of universal justice. He pleaded:

> God must be re-introduced to the common people not as a special possession of separate classes of groups, not with His holy name made almost shabby with overmuch indiscriminate use at mass meetings, but as the Supreme Court before whom no specious argument, however learned or brilliant, has any chance.[78]

Rev. Fosdick, one of the leaders of religion in the English-speaking world, shared with Rabbi Jung certain modern approaches to religion. Fosdick had written a petition that was printed in the *New York Times* on May 26, 1933, protesting the plight of Jews in Germany and

---

76 Yeshiva University Archives, Jung Collection, Box 46, Folder 4—letter to Rev. Dr. Harry Emerson Fosdick, February 12, 1943; Yeshiva University Archives, Jung Collection, Box 1, Folder 4. "American Religion: Its Opportunity and Responsibility," on "Message of Israel," WJZ (radio station), June 17, 1945, 2.

77 Yeshiva University Archives, Jung Collection, Box 1, Folder 4—letter to Fosdick, February 12, 1943.

78 Yeshiva University Archives, Jung Collection, Box 48, Folder 5 (published articles)—Jung, "The Problems of Sovereignty and of Minorities," *American Journal of Economics and Sociology* 4, no. 4 (July 1945): 516.

religious and racial prejudice in America. However, Fosdick was unenthusiastic about the project, as he felt that to include all religions, the statement would have to be too general and that the generalities included would render the petition hardly worth signing.[79] Fosdick's years as an activist fighting fundamentalists had given him good insight.[80] The project ended in failure and Rev. Fosdick had been correct; a universal statement could not be agreed upon.[81]

Other Modern Orthodox rabbis made the plea that democracy meant the right to be different. This was in Isaac Breuer's article "Judaism and The World of Tomorrow," which appears in Jung's *Israel of Tomorrow*. Breuer wrote that World War II represented aggression, along with the attempt of the strong to exploit the weak, and called for self-determination of all people and respect for minority rights.[82] Rabbi William Weiss, national president of the UOJCA, wrote that democracy and the people of America were on trial; that the Bill of Rights guaranteed freedom of religion, worship, speech, and assembly; and that "manifestation of anti-Semitism in this country is un-American conduct."[83] Rabbi Weiss, too, pointed out that in preaching bigotry and hatred, the church had failed the people. Modern Orthodox leaders were assertive and fearless in their condemnation.

The Effects of the Modern Orthodox Presence in the War Effort and Trends Coming Out of World War II

Upsurge of Jewish Religious Life During and After the War Years: Upsurge in Status of Religion and its Institutions

Rabbi Jung's efforts, as well as those of the other Modern Orthodox leaders, contributed to the more prominent role that religion would

---

79 Yeshiva University Archives, Jung Collection, Box 1, Folder 4—letter to Rabbi Jung from Fosdick, February 18, 1943.
80 William Jennings Bryan had attacked Fosdick (cf. the Scopes Trial), and this controversy made him a world figure. Jennings Bryan fought fundamentalism and was a liberal activist.
81 Jung, *The Path of a Pioneer*, 210.
82 Isaac Breuer, "Judaism and the World of Tomorrow," in *Israel of Tomorrow*, ed. Leo Jung, 88.
83 Yeshiva University Archives, Jung Collection, Box 44, Folder 4—Rabbi William Weiss, "Democracy on Trial."

play. In the 1940s, the course of secularism did begin to change, and the role of religion began to be elevated. In 1949, Carlos Romulo (president of the United Nations General Assembly and guest speaker at a Yeshiva University dinner), discussed the interrelationship between faith and freedom in general and Jewish tradition and American freedom in particular.[84] Romulo echoed Rabbi Jung's message that it was necessary for the various religious faiths to unite and cooperate if democracy was to survive. Romulo asserted that the vital task of religion was the promotion of health, welfare, and peace; this was Rabbi Jung's theme in the 1940s.

World War II demonstrated that modernity and pure secularism had serious flaws. While all agreed that there was a return to religion, different explanations by Modern Orthodox thinkers were given for the return, and perhaps all the reasons were correct. Norman Lamm felt that it was due to the post-war fear of communism.[85] Rabbi Jung felt that the new influx of observant Orthodox Jews from Eastern Europe was responsible for the return to religion:

> We have learned to value their positive contributions to Jewish life in our country. The unquestioning loyalty to Torah-true Judaism of a great number, and their eager sacrifice to the promotion of its cause, have proved a considerable stimulus to religious life in America and have added to the fighting strength of the Lord's Army in our state.[86]

In 1944, Samuel Belkin (the president of Yeshiva College) reported that new Orthodox congregations were springing up all over America and that there had been a reawakening of a long dormant interest in Judaism, not only in civilian life but in the armed forces. Belkin felt that the war experience had led to more interest in Jewish life, more

---

84 Yeshiva University Archives—"General Romulo Emphasizes Bond Between Faith and Freedom," *The Commentator* 30, no. 5 (December 19, 1949): 1.
85 Yeshiva University Archives—"Symposium Studies Jewry in America," *The Commentator* 29, no. 5 (May 12, 1949): 4.
86 Yeshiva University Archives, Jung Collection, Box 1, Folder 5—letter to Siegmund Hanover from Rabbi Jung, November 2, 1945.

group consciousness, and more awareness and care for the past.[87] The challenge was to bring Judaism to the thousands of soldiers returning home who were more favorably disposed to Judaism than ever.

As demonstrated, Modern Orthodox Jews took on a greater leading role during the period of the war. Many servicemen rediscovered Judaism through the chaplains they had met; given that many were Orthodox, Orthodoxy had an influence. Modern Orthodox clergy were there to see that religious conditions had been met and that servicemen received educational material satisfactory to the Orthodox view. The Orthodox presence maintained, and in some cases awakened, the servicemen to religious experience and knowledge. It also gave the soldiers a feeling of identity, belonging, and equality. The rabbi became a positive model.

Also, the soldiers had met Jews in other lands, and some saw Palestine and/or concentration camps; their experiences made them rethink their Jewish commitment. The religious, moral, and psychological needs of the servicemen had been met at a very vulnerable time in their lives. The clergy had to be alert to having proper literature and answers; this kept them alert and more knowledgeable regarding both religious and secular issues. Hence, both the clergy and the laypeople became better educated. The challenge was to maintain and advance this learning, and to sustain the "manifestation of foxhole religion."[88]

Rabbi Emanuel Rackman—a chaplain in the American Army Air Force, a graduate of RIETS, and the rabbi of Manhattan's Fifth Avenue Synagogue—did not see a religious revival among the soldiers. On the other hand, he saw a "resurgence of a strong feeling of kinship with one's Jewish co-religionists," a desire to be restored to a certain pride in their spiritual heritage, and more interest in Jewish history books and in learning Hebrew in order to more fully participate in religious services.[89] However, Rabbi Rackman suggested that Jewish identity,

---

87 Yeshiva University Archives—"Congregations on the Increase," *Yeshiva and Yeshiva College News* 2, no. 2 (December 1944): 2.
88 Ibid.
89 Yeshiva University Archives, Box 19, Folder 4—Emanuel Rackman, "A Chaplain Speaks," *News and Views* 1, no. 6 (May 1944): 3.

pride, and appetite for Jewish education was a prelude to religious observance, and that the war left people with nostalgia for deeper values.[90]

Image (Change)

A story about image building is the story of the Beth Jacob girls. As chairman of the American Beth Jacob Committee, Rabbi Jung was involved with the promulgating in America of the tragic but heroic story of the Beth Jacob "Martyrs" in America. It was the story, in Poland, of 93 Beth Jacob girls (14 to 22 years old) and their teacher who preferred death to being forced into prostitution at the hands of the enemy, thus committed suicide. This represents an image change for Jewish people in modern times, a change away from being passive and inactive, though Zionists had also projected this image. It is the first occasion in modern times that the Orthodox group was depicted in this role. The eyes of Americans were on the plight and virtue of the Orthodox in America. While the story was eloquent testimony to Jews (and to Jewish women in particular) in a heroic role, it also brought attention to the Beth Jacob schools and their goals, which would aid Rabbi Jung in his work on behalf of Beth Jacob.

Due to Rabbi Jung's efforts, the story appeared in the *New York Times* on January 8, 1943, under the title, "The Martyrs of Warsaw." It should be noted that Jacob Rosenheim, president of the Agudath Israel World Organization, who had sent the document to Rabbi Jung detailing the event, felt that the *New York Times* would not publish such a Jewish document, probably because he felt that it would not lend its sympathies in that direction.[91] That the *New York Times* did publish it perhaps demonstrated a changing attitude, or perhaps it was felt that the heroic story would be interesting and appealing. Rabbi Jung showed great respect for this type of martyrdom. He wrote that:

> This document tells a story true to the noblest pattern of Jewish martyrdom. It is unmatched in simplicity and sublimity,

---

90 Ibid.
91 Yeshiva University Archives, Jung Collection, Box 40, Folder 7—letter to Rabbi Jung from Jacob Rosenheim, January 5, 1943.

a living testimony of Beth Jacob's service to Israel, indeed to all believers in the Universal Father of man.[92]

The story received an interdenominational sympathetic reaction. But Judith Tydor Baumel (a historian, writer, and child survivor of the Holocaust) in her research, found evidence that some people, as early as the 1940s, were questioning the story.[93] However, Rabbi Jung indeed believed the story to be true:

> I do not think that any doubt has ever arisen about the authenticity of the document. I had the document in my own hands. I can give you a talk about the authenticity... It was not addressed to me but I believe it is genuine. I have never heard any doubt about its authenticity.[94]

However, the fact that its authenticity was discussed at a JDC Cultural Committee meeting, in 1950, showed that the authenticity needed defense. Baumel referred to the story as a new type of genre, the heroic Orthodox story, which lent prestige and good image at a time when it was needed and very important. However, she pointed out that it was not seen that way at the time.[95]

Cooperation with Other Jewish Groups

The relationship between Orthodox Jews and other Jewish groups was an important issue. Working well with Reform and Conservative clergy and with non-Jewish chaplains was an experience with, to use Rabbi Jung's expression, "cooperation without compromise."[96] Rabbi Soloveitchik acknowledged the importance of unity and peace in joint social and polit-

---

92 Yeshiva University Archives, Jung Collection, Box 40, Folder 7. "Foreword" written by Rabbi Jung attached to "The Martyrs of Warsaw" and sent to the *New York Times* on American Beth Jacob Committee Inc. stationery. The story appeared in the *New York Times* on January 8, 1943.
93 Email from Judith Tydor Baumel to Maxine Jacobson, October 9, 1997.
94 JDC Archives, File 3390—minutes of meeting of Cultural Committee, March 21, 1950.
95 Email from Baumel to Maxine Jacobson, October 9, 1997. Baumel and Rabbi Jacob J. Schacter wrote "The Ninety-three Bais Yaakov Girls of Cracow: History or Typology?"
96 Leo Jung, "Jewry Today," *Jewish Forum* 19, no. 7 (September 1936): 202.

ical matters.[97] When Rabbi Jung joined the JDC in 1926, he was a pioneer in Orthodox circles, as he worked with all denominations; he proved to be a good model. He wrote:

> We must resign ourselves to the fact of three American Jewish denominations. This is one more handicap, but it need not negate our efforts to prevent us from working for the common weal."[98]

The chaplaincy role also provided a model for American Jewish religious life in the postwar era. The wartime role created a sense of interfaith rabbinic fellowship, which spilled over into other areas of communal life, such as the New York Board of Rabbis and the Synagogue Council of America.[99] This cooperation carried on into the 1950s and 1960s.[100] It meant that Modern Orthodoxy was present in all aspects of Jewish communal life. Traditional Orthodox Jews continued to disapprove of this cooperation.

Accent on Renaissance and the Future—New Role for American Jewry

The onslaught overseas left American Jewry as the sustaining force for Jews throughout the world.[101] America had to take on a new responsibility. The center of Judaism was transferred to America because of the tragedy. Rabbi Jung remarked:

> ...The Jewish community is adolescent in this young country, and as the result of the world's chaos, has obligations of maturity suddenly thrust upon it, both as a section of the great

---

97 Yeshiva University Archives—"Rabbi Soloveitchik's Address," *The Commentator* 25, no. 3 (March 20, 1947): 4.
98 Leo Jung, "Program for 5701," *The Modern View* (1940): 43. Also in the *B'nai Brith Messenger* with the *Jewish Community Press* (September 27, 1940), 25.
99 Gilbert Kollin, "The Impact of the Military Chaplaincy on the American Rabbinate," in *The American Rabbi: A Tribute on the Occasion of the Bicentennial of the U.S., and the Ninety-fifth Birthday of the New York Board of Rabbis*, ed. Gilbert Rosenthal (New York: Ktav Publication House, 1977), 24.
100 Kollin, "The Impact of the Military Chaplaincy on the American Rabbinate," 34.
101 Yeshiva University Archives—"Celebrities To Attend 13th Annual Affair at Hotel Astor," *Yeshiva College Quarterly* 4, no. 5 (December 1941): 2.

American community and as a group with its own cultural and spiritual heritage."[102]

In Orthodox circles, an event of some importance was the transfer, in April 1941, of the world executive center of Agudath Israel from London to New York. This transfer reflected the increased importance of the American community in Jewish affairs. At the Agudath Israel convention that year, Rabbi Eliezer Silver was reelected president. Rabbi Silver called for the transfer of a number of famous Jewish religious academies from Germany and Soviet-occupied territories to the United States. He called for a chain of Orthodox schools in America and for a wider campaign for education.[103]

Rabbi Jung wrote in the preface of *Israel of Tomorrow*: "Poland was chosen as the most significant Jewish community of yesterday; America and Palestine as all important for Israel of tomorrow." Before World War II, Poland was the center of Jewish education, and also of scribes who wrote Torah scrolls. Before the war, there were 27 Jewish dailies in Poland, over 100 weeklies, and dozens of periodicals. There were Jewish museums and archives.[104] Rabbi Jung wrote:

> We, American Jews, the remnants sent to our shores... must rise above our present level of moral consciousness if we are to prove of real assistance to the scattered remnant of our people.[105]

Rabbi Jung felt that to live up to the task, American Israel—which included Orthodox, Reform, and Conservative organizations—had to cooperate and work together.[106]

---

102 Yeshiva University Archives, Jung Collection, Box 23, Folder 2—Jung, "Program for 5701," 43. Also in *B'nai Brith Messenger* and the *Jewish Community Press* (September 27, 1940): 25.
103 Harry Schneiderman, "Review of the Year 5701—United States," *American Jewish Year Book* 43 (1941–1942): 33.
104 Wolf Blattberg, "Polish Jewry: Yesterday, Today, Tomorrow," in *Israel of Tomorrow*, ed. Leo Jung, 369.
105 Yeshiva University Archives, Jung Collection, Box 21, Folder 11—excerpts from Rabbi Jung's sermons, second day of the Jewish New Year.
106 Ibid.

Rabbi Jung, through the JDC, continued to be attentive to the needs of the refugees. This help was often a prelude to the refugees immigrating to North America. One group with which Rabbi Jung was familiar included the 15,000 refugees in Shanghai, which included Rabbi Meir Ashkenazi (the Chief Rabbi of Shanghai) and the Mir Yeshiva (until the war, located in what was Poland but is now in Belarus). Rabbi Jung did his best to attend to their needs.[107]

Yeshiva University also continued its efforts. Dr. Samuel Sar, dean of Yeshiva College, was appointed to head JDC's "Continent Drive" to improve religious conditions. Dr. Sar was also charged with the organization of schools, synagogues, kosher slaughtering, and other religious functions basic to the continuance of Orthodox Judaism on the continent of Europe.[108]

Education

If America and Israel had to share the mission of preserving Jewish cultural and spiritual life, then certainly after World War II, there was a new role for Jewish educational institutions. Jewish education would be the greatest influence shaping the future. With knowledge of Judaism, the Jewish people would be bolder in their demands and more able to work for democratic rights. Rabbi Jung continued to feel that:

> ...For our self-defense, our children must receive a Jewish education, academic, social, and crowned by the pattern of Jewish communal enterprises that will give them self-knowledge and a sense of historic importance.[109]

A critique of Rabbi Jung's view of parochial schools by the Reform Rabbi Emil W. Leipziger, and Rabbi Jung's rebuttal in March 1945, gave a clear picture of the Modern Orthodox view of Jewish education

---

107 Yeshiva University Archives, Jung Collection, Box 1, Folder 5—correspondence with Bernard Turk, October 28, 1945, and November 21, 1945.
108 Yeshiva University Archives—"Mr. Sar Journeys Abroad for JDC." *The Commentator* 27, no. 1 (February 19, 1948): 1.
109 Leo Jung, "New Years Program," in *Crumbs and Character*, 155–56.

and the state of its Jewish institutions. Rabbi Jung promoted parochial schools, as he felt that parochial schools were the main hope for producing knowledgeable, enthusiastic Jews and Americans. He wrote: "…it has been my conviction for a long time that unless we obtain a well-informed laity, American Israel will be doomed."[110] Rabbi Jung's theme in the 1940s was that parochial school attendance was a symbol that the American Jew had come of age. Cultural pluralism was the American way of life; therefore, Jews who adhered to Judaism were practicing the American way. Rabbi Leipziger's views were opposite to those of Rabbi Jung; the former felt that parochial schools and the American way of life were a contradiction, that parochial school was divisive and contrary to an opposite trend of inclusiveness in American life. In his response to Rabbi Leipziger, Rabbi Jung lamented that the average Talmud Torah, which was attended by only a small fraction of the Jewish population, did not seem capable of supplying either sufficient knowledge or staunch allegiance to Torah-true Judaism. At the same time, Rabbi Jung's work as chairman of the Education Committee of the UOJCA showed his devotion, desire, and effort to improve the parochial school system. By the end of the 1940s, it was reported that there was an increase of 3,000 children attending the Jewish day schools as well as an increase of 60 day schools. This, however, still represented only a small percentage of the total population eligible to attend.[111]

Orthodox Jewish educational organizations established authoritative bodies to represent the traditional viewpoint in Jewish education and to strengthen the cause of Torah through study. The Long Island Board of Orthodox Jewish Education is an example. The board agreed to seek the counsel and cooperation of Yeshiva and Yeshiva College in formulating educational policies and projects.[112] Hence, Yeshiva was represented; Yeshiva called for the rallying of Orthodox forces, and it was involved in formulating educational policies and projects. Yeshiva,

---

110 Yeshiva University Archives, Jung Collection, Box 1, Folder 5—"Response to Critique," March 15, 1945.
111 Yeshiva University Archives, Jung Collection, Box 1, Folder 5 Response to Reform rabbi's critique of his stance on parochial schools.
112 Yeshiva University Archives—"NYC Academic Progress Hindered By Lack of Unity," *The Commentator* 29, no. 1 (February 24, 1949): 2.

the voice of Modern Orthodoxy, became more directly linked with Jewish education, and became more influential.

Here was a new interest in learning the Hebrew language, which could be traced to Israel's nationhood. Yeshiva University, representative of Modern Orthodoxy, promoted Hebrew studies. After World War II, there were several new Hebrew clubs at Yeshiva. Yeshiva was pleased when New York University created a new Professorship of Hebrew Culture and Education, the first of its kind in United States.[113] Rabbi Jung helped to establish this position.[114] The *New York Times*, on November 9, 1947, reported that an important step in the promotion of interfaith understanding had been taken by New York University with the creation of this new professorship.[115] By 1949, New York University offered 25 different Hebrew courses.[116]

By 1948, classes in modern Hebrew in New York public high schools were gaining pupils faster than any other foreign language. Hebrew was made an accredited course for graduation and for state scholarships.[117] "*Ivrit be-Ivrit*," which Jung had placed in his curriculum proposal for the Talmud Torahs, increased in popularity.[118] This employed the technique of teaching Hebrew using the Hebrew language.

Yeshiva

Yeshiva took firm leadership of Modern Orthodoxy after the war.[119] Yeshiva's role in matters pertinent to Jewish education grew, and it

---

113 Yeshiva University Archives—"Executive Board Formed," *Yeshiva College Quarterly* 4, no. 5 (December 1941): 1.
114 Yeshiva University Archives—Dr. S. Margoshes, "Department of Hebrew Culture at N.Y. University, the Hebrew Contribution to Civilization, on Interracial Understanding," *News and Views* 38 (November 20, 1947): 1.
115 Yeshiva University Archives, Jung Collection, Box 16, Folder 11—letter to James M. Hester (president of New York University) from Jung, May 12, 1971.
116 Yeshiva University Archives—"Courses in Hebrew Culture at NYU," *New York Times*, November 9, 1947.
117 Editorial, "Modern Hebrew in the Public Schools and its Inspirational Source," *Jewish Forum* 31, no. 8 (August 1948): 166.
118 Yeshiva University Archives—"Bible Courses Required For Future Rabbis," *The Commentator* 24, no. 3 (November 21, 1946): 1.
119 Yeshiva University Archives—"Y.U.—A National Asset (Secretary of Defence Johnson) Program of Americanism Praised By Barkley," *Yeshiva University News* 7,

became even more indispensable to Modern Orthodoxy. The concerns of Yeshiva included reorganization and expansion.

In 1940, the college admitted its largest class ever; 40% came from the public high schools.[120] This enlarged enrollment demonstrated that the college had appeal to those seeking a secular education; possibly, it showed an increased interest in a Jewish environment. In 1941, for the first time, courses were offered to adults at Yeshiva.[121] This was a sign that there was a feeling that the times necessitated deeper knowledge reinforced by a concern for a sense of values.[122]

Yeshiva became more successful and competitive on two fronts—the religious and secular—living out the ongoing theme of synthesis, which was key to Modern Orthodoxy.[123] In 1941, renowned scholars like Rabbi Jung, Dr. Belkin, Dr. Pinchas Churgin, Rabbi Joseph Lookstein, and Dr. Solomon Zeitlin were lauded in one of Yeshiva's newspapers for their outstanding publications and invaluable contribution in Jewish and Semitic studies.[124] Rabbi Weiss, national president of the UOJCA, announced that Rabbi Jung's *Essentials of Judaism* (one of the Jewish Library Series of the Orthodox Union) had gone into its seventh edition with the printing of another 10,000 copies.[125] On the secular side, Yeshiva's journal, *Scripta Mathematica*, had earned a national reputation.[126]

However, Yeshiva had been in trouble at the start of the 1940s; it was plagued with financial woes. As well, two of Yeshiva's great leaders died, leaving it in a precarious situation. However, this

---

no. 1 (September 1949): 1.
120 Yeshiva University Archives—"College Admits Largest Class," *News Bulletin: Yeshiva College* 2, no. 5 (December 1940): 1.
121 Yeshiva University Archives—"Extension Courses For Adults and Students Introduced At Yeshiva College," *Yeshiva College Quarterly* 4, no. 5 (December 1941): 2.
122 Yeshiva University Archives—Bernard Revel, "Our Hope and Thought," *News Bulletin: Yeshiva College* 2, no. 5 (December 1940): 5.
123 Yeshiva University Archives—"Discuss the Role of Synthesis at Third Session," *The Commentator* 27, no. 5 (December 1948): 1.
124 Yeshiva University Archives—"Yeshiva College Noted for Publications," *Yeshiva College Quarterly* 4, no. 5 (December 1941): 1.
125 Schneiderman, "Review of the Year 5701—United States," 34.
126 Yeshiva University Archives—"Yeshiva College Noted for Publications," 1.

situation ultimately resulted in strengthening Yeshiva, therefore in strengthening Modern Orthodoxy. President Bernard Revel died in 1940; two months later, Rabbi Moses Soloveitchik (the *rosh yeshiva*) died as well, leaving the Yeshiva weakened.[127] Until the death of Revel in 1940, the Agudath Harabbonim had somewhat contained its antagonism toward the board of RIETS, an antagonism harbored since Yeshiva College opened its secular classes in 1928, as they respected Revel. Also, Rabbi Soloveitchik had a long-established admirable reputation as a Talmudic scholar among all the rabbis. However, with the death of Revel, there was an attempted takeover. Rabbi Silver of Cincinnati, president of Agudath Israel, sent a telegram informing the board that he had appointed a committee of seven to assume leadership of the school. Yeshiva's directors, which included Rabbi Bernard Levinthal and the Honorable Samuel Levy, rejected the Agudath Harabbonim.[128] An executive board of seven members, which had full authority over the administration of Yeshiva and Yeshiva College, was formed. The chairman was the Honorable Samuel Levy; executive vice chairman was Rabbi Lookstein; a major member was Rabbi Jung; and Dr. Sar, Dr. Belkin, Dr. Moses Isaacs, and Dr. Churgin represented the academic department. The board had a long and active association with the institution; it knew Revel's wishes.[129] Each appointee represented a special interest group within the school; Jung's Jewish Center included some of the most important supporters of RIETS. The board was set up to prevent another attempted takeover by the Agudath Harabbonim.[130] The board was to guide the school and to recommend candidates for the *rosh yeshiva* and presidency positions.[131]

---

127 Rakeffet-Rothkoff, *The Silver Era in American Jewish Orthodoxy*, 264–267.
128 Gilbert Klaperman, *The Story of Yeshiva University: The First Jewish University in America* (New York: MacMillan Co., 1969), 172; Rakeffet-Rothkoff, *The Silver Era in American Jewish Orthodoxy*, 264–267.
129 Yeshiva University Archives—"Executive Board Formed," *Yeshiva College Quarterly* 4, no. 5 (December 1941): 1.
130 Yeshiva University Archives —"A New Era," *Yeshiva College Quarterly* 4, no. 5 (December 1941): 4.
131 Klaperman, *The Story of Yeshiva University*, 172.

Leadership of the school was a most pressing problem. There was a somewhat turbulent reorganization of the leadership of the institution, including the selection of new heads of Yeshiva and Yeshiva College.[132] To replace Rabbi Moses Soloveitchik, two names were offered early on—Rabbi Jung had suggested Rabbi Chaim Heller, an Orthodox biblical scholar whose name would bring stature and prestige to Yeshiva, and Rabbi Herbert Goldstein had suggested Rabbi Joseph B. Soloveitchik, who had been Rabbi Heller's student and had been the unofficial chief rabbi of Boston since his arrival in 1932.

Rabbi Jung had written about Rabbi Heller in the *Jewish Forum* years before, praising him as an *iluy*, a scholar of extraordinary gifts in both Torah and secular studies and an "intellectual David," who was a scholarly and dedicated defender of the integrity of the Bible against the school of gentile academics, who had written copious commentaries critiquing the Bible. Heller employed the scientific method for his responses, and his research was built upon *Torah im derekh eretz* in that he combined "the latest scholarly method with deep reverence of a present day savant for the great minds of the past."[133] Rabbi Jung wrote that Rabbi Heller also reintroduced a method of studying rabbinic literature that—but for few exceptions—had been dead since the demise of the great Gaon of Vilna.[134]

However, Rabbi Joseph Soloveitchik (the son of Rabbi Moses Soloveitchik), supported by the Agudath Harabbonim and many students, was appointed as the *rosh yeshiva* in 1941, succeeding his father; he was the *rosh yeshiva* until 1984. He was acceptable to most factions, although he did have serious detractors. He became the new Talmudist and became known as "The Rav" and ultimate spiritual guide for Modern Orthodoxy, the most influential Orthodox religious leader during the second half of the 20th century.[135] Rabbi Soloveitchik held a PhD degree from the University of Berlin; he stood for the

---

132 Yeshiva University Archives—"A New Era," 4.
133 Leo Jung, "Chaim Heller," *Jewish Forum* 8, no. 9 (October 1925): 506.
134 Ibid., 505.
135 Zev Eleff, "Freedom and Responsibility: The First Orthodox College Journalists and Early Yeshiva College Politics, 1935-1941" *American Jewish Archives Journal* 62, no. 2 (2010): 76.

integration of secular and religious studies. Under his leadership, Modern Orthodoxy's reputation was greatly enhanced.[136] Rabbi Soloveitchik, as the senior *rosh yeshiva*, became increasingly visible and prominent on the Modern Orthodox scene. Rabbi Jung never displayed a negative reaction to the election, as that would be disrespectful of democratic means and would be politically unsavvy, thus would be out of keeping with Rabbi Jung. There is also no evidence to show that Rabbis Jung and Soloveitchik had any relationship at all, not even a formal relationship.

Rabbi Jung was also on the committee to elect a new president. In fact, there were board members who were his congregants, and wanted him to be the new president. According to historian Rabbi Zev Eleff, it was well known that the two frontrunners for president of Yeshiva were Rabbi Soloveitchik and Rabbi Jung.[137] Jeffrey S. Gurock suggested that Rabbi Jung's candidacy had flaws, as Rabbi Jung did not have ordination from a leading *yeshiva* in Eastern Europe and was not known as a Talmudic scholar.[138] Four decades later, when Gurock interviewed Rabbi Jung, he insisted that he was not at all disappointed with the choice of president, but Gurock said that he sensed that he was.[139] In 1941, Dr. Belkin was made head of Yeshiva after the death of Revel. Belkin, who held a PhD from Brown University, had been secretary of the graduate school since it opened in 1937. With Belkin's appointment, the Modern Orthodox leaders were firmly in charge.[140] The gap widened between the Agudath Harabbonim and Modern Orthodoxy as the latter became even more distinct an entity. However, the Modern Orthodox continued to look over their shoulders at the more right-wing faction. *The Commentator*, a Yeshiva newspaper, reported that "it is no secret that there are forces in Orthodox Judaism which would be

---

136 William Helmreich, "Old Wine in New Bottles: Advanced Yeshivot in the United States," *American Jewish History* 69, no. 2 (December 1979): 249.
137 Eleff, "Freedom and Responsibility the First Orthodox College", 74.
138 Jeffrey S. Gurock, *The Men and Women of Yeshiva: Higher Education, Orthodoxy, and American Judaism* (New York: Columbia University Press, 1988), 138–139; Rakeffet-Rothkoff, *The Silver Era in American Jewish Orthodoxy*, 271.
139 Personal interview with Gurock, December 17, 1996.
140 Rakeffet-Rothkoff, *The Silver Era in American Jewish Orthodoxy*, 271.

quite content to let the influence of the entire movement initiated by Dr. Revel be eradicated by time."[141]

Added to the faculty were European rabbis who had been rescued. Examples were Rabbi Isaac Rubinstein, former chief rabbi of Vilna and a member of the Polish senate representing the Jewish community, and Rabbi Moshe Shatzkes, commonly known as the Lomza Rav.[142] These appointments added prestige to Yeshiva and added to its credibility as a major Orthodox center.

Samuel Belkin, President of Yeshiva University from 1943 to 1976. Courtesy of Yeshiva University Archives

It has been amply demonstrated that Rabbi Jung influenced the financial destiny of Yeshiva. In 1939 to 1940, Yeshiva was in dire straits and in need of $130,000, according to Rabbi Jung. Revel had come to Rabbi Jung in great need of his help. The latter was able to raise $50,000 from an anonymous donor, a nonobservant, secret Jew, who was impressed with how Rabbi Jung presented Judaism and how he had presented Yeshiva's needs. In 1946, Rabbi Jung revealed that the donor was Enrico Garda, Ambassador of Italy to San Marino.[143] Previously revealing his name would have been dangerous for Garda, as he and Mussolini had been friends. Rabbi Jung was also able to raise money from many of his loyal congregants.[144] He raised the remainder of the funds with the help of Mendel Gottesman, Abraham Mazer, and Joseph Golding.[145] All these men played an important part in saving the institution from financial ruin.

---

141 Yeshiva University Archives—"Eidenu Appears in Tribute to Memory of Dr. Revel," *The Commentator* 15, no. 4 (March 26, 1942): 2.
142 Yeshiva University Archives—"Faculty Promotions Honor Yeshiva College Scholars," *Yeshiva College Quarterly* 4, no. 5 (December 1941): 1.
143 Jung, *The Path of a Pioneer*, 110–111.
144 Gurock, *The Men and Women of Yeshiva*, 139.
145 Jung, *The Path of a Pioneer*, 111.

In 1946, at a meeting of the National Council of Organizations for Yeshiva University, Belkin read a message from his long-time friend (a supporter of Yeshiva), Albert Einstein: "I am convinced that Yeshiva is of great importance for the preservation of Jewish tradition and for the deeper spiritualization of youth in general..."[146] Einstein continued to be enlisted to attract new supporters to the cause of Yeshiva, and he continued to work with Rabbi Jung. It is to be noted that even Einstein seemed to emphasize religious values, though he meant different things than Orthodox Jews meant with the same terms. Though Einstein's definition of religion was not Modern Orthodox, he liked Modern Orthodox thinkers and the philosophy of Yeshiva, as it saw a positive relationship between religion and science; in this way, Einstein could represent Yeshiva. Einstein is quoted as saying: "I think that science without religion is lame, and conversely, that religion without science is blind. Both are important and should work hand in hand."[147] Einstein said: "Science can only ascertain what is, but not what should be, and outside of its domain value judgments of all kinds remain necessary. Religion, on the other hand, deals only with evaluation of human thought and action: It cannot justifiably speak of facts and relationships between facts."[148] In a letter to Einstein, Rabbi Jung demonstrated that he respected both the religious and the scientific approach.[149] Belkin said in his inaugural address: "We prefer to look upon science and religion as separate domains which need not be in serious conflict and therefore need no

---

146 Yeshiva University Archives—"Conference Held: Plans Y.U. Future," *The Commentator* 23, no. 6 (May 9, 1946): 1.
147 Peter A. Buckly and Allen G. Weakland, *The Private Albert Einstein* (Kansas City, MO: Andrews and McMeel, 1992), 85–87.
148 Albert Einstein, Religion and Science, Science and Religion II, *Science, Philosophy and Religion, A Symposium* (New York: The Conference on Science, Philosophy and Religion in Their Relationship to the Democratic Way of Life, Inc., 1941), http://www.sacred-texts.com/aor/einstein/einsci.htm.
149 Yeshiva University Archives, Jung Collection, Box 1, Folder 4—letter to Albert Einstein from Leo Jung, March 1943.

reconciliation." He felt that only within the personality of the individual could synthesis be achieved.[150]

By 1946, it was clear that a greater future lay ahead for Yeshiva University; it began to expand. Plans for the establishment of professional schools were revealed; a dental, medical, and law school were being planned.[151] It had an expansion plan for a 15-story building. Buildings were added, and a blueprint for a nonsectarian medical school was developed. Yeshiva received university status in 1945, and it had enlarged enrollment and expanded courses of study. Twenty-five new courses were added.[152] Yeshiva was competing ably with other American universities, and it was advancing the cause of Modern Orthodoxy; it was visible and attractive to the American public.

Zionism

Just as there was a new role for America, there was a new role for *Eretz Israel*; Jews were determined to be masters of their own fate and rebuild a homeland. The Jew had been seen as helpless and passive in the concentration camp experience. However, out of the concentration camps came a new type of Jew, one who was bold, proud, and less fearful of public opinion. The advent of the State of Israel itself infused more energy and passion into Zionism. Palestine represented a better tomorrow; Jews were looking for better days. The 1940s saw an increasing aggressive and nationalistic policy on the part of American Zionism.[153] The virulent anti-Semitism of the 1930s, along with the Holocaust and World War II catastrophes of the 1940s, helped to overcome the factionalism that plagued Zionism in the 1930s, though some factionalism remained.[154]

---

150 Yeshiva University Archives, Yeshiva and Yeshiva College News, Box 19, Folder 4— "President Belkin," *Yeshiva College News* 3, no. 2 (January 1946): 7.
151 Yeshiva University Archives—"Conference Held: Plans Y.U. Future," 1.
152 Yeshiva University Archives—"Ed. School Grows New Courses, Faculty," *Yeshiva University News* 7, no. 2 (November–December 1949): 1.
153 Melvin I. Urofsky, *American Zionism from Herzl to the Holocaust* (Garden City, NY: Anchor Press and Doubleday, 1975), 421; Yeshiva University Archives, "Zionist Youth Take a Stand," *The Commentator* 22, no. 3 (November 29, 1945): 2.
154 Urofsky, *American Zionism from Herzl to the Holocaust*, 424.

The Reform movement reversed its official non-Zionist stance. At the famous Biltmore Hotel Conference in 1942, chaired by Reform rabbi and Zionist leader Stephen Wise, there was a call for a Jewish state. Before Biltmore, Palestine was seen primarily as a place of refuge by American Jews After Biltmore, world Jewry saw Palestine as a future Jewish state, where Jewish nationhood and justice was to be restored.[155] Also after Biltmore, American Zionist organizations could claim that they spoke for the majority of American Jews.

In 1942, after the Biltmore Conference, in defiance of the pro-Zionist stance of the national leadership, a number of dissident Reform rabbis founded the American Council for Judaism (ACJ), an organization that rejected any effort to impose Jewish nationality upon all Jews, as it felt that it was against Jewish interests and American patriotism. These ideas had resonated better two decades before.[156] It was the first and only Jewish organization created at that point to fight against Zionism and the establishment of the State of Israel. However, it did not represent mainstream Jews. The advent of the state was a major defeat for the ACJ.

The national Orthodox Union conference, which was held in January 1944 and which was attended by over 1,200 delegates representing every important Orthodox community in America, denounced the ACJ and others who equated loyalty to the Holy Land with disloyalty to America. The conference demonstrated the rising strength of Orthodoxy and its unanimity of purpose in facing a vital issue confronting Jewry. As well, the conference denounced the dejudaized and self-appointed ACJ as high treason to all Jewry, and it accepted unanimously as its official view a statement read by Belkin that referred to the ACJ as a "disoriented fringe divorced from their people's past…"[157]

---

155 Thomas A. Kolsky, *Jews Against Zionism: The American Council For Judaism, 1942–1948* (Philadelphia: Temple University Press, 1990), 39–40.
156 Ibid., 80 and 197.
157 Yeshiva University Archives—"Dr. Samuel Belkin Reads Important Statement Before National Orthodox Conference," *Yeshiva and Yeshiva College News* 1, no. 6 (March 1944): 2; Urofsky, *American Zionism from Herzl to the Holocaust*, 429.

Rabbi Jung referred to the ACJ as an organization that is "…un-American, un-Jewish, and has no counsel of significance to offer."[158]

Modern Orthodoxy and Zionism

The RCA and the UOJCA recognized and welcomed the State of Israel without reservations and were committed to religious Zionism.[159] The majority identified with Mizrachi and Hapoel Hamizrachi, also known as Mizrachi laborers, as they supported *kibbutzim* and *moshavim*, which represented collective, agricultural community living. Only a small number identified with the anti-Zionist Agudath Israel. Yeshiva hailed the new state as opening a new chapter in Jewish history.[160] Modern Orthodoxy wholeheartedly supported the State of Israel; it lost its ambiguity with respect to Israel.[161] The Modern Orthodox leadership did feel that the birth of the State of Israel had to be interpreted in terms of the Modern Orthodox religious philosophy of history, and it warned of any attempt of secularization of Jewish life in Israel.[162] *Eretz Israel* was the epitome of Modern Orthodoxy, as it combined tradition and modernity.

Rabbi Soloveitchik ridiculed as false the theory that the establishment of Israel was not in keeping with Jewish law, and he felt that Torah would be fruitful in Palestine even if a majority of secular Jews ran the state. Rabbi Soloveitchik said: "Orthodoxy may not have a big share in the new state, yet Torah will be fruitful in Palestine. Religious Jews will be able to live better in a Palestine ruled by *Hashomer Hatzair* than in an American Jewish ghetto like Williamsburg."[163] Rabbi Soloveitchik was

---

158 Leo Jung, Preface, *Jewish Leaders: 1750–1940*, Jewish Library, First Series, vol. 6 (Jerusalem: Boys Town Jerusalem Publishers, 1953 and 1964), v.
159 L. Bernstein, *Challenge and Mission*, 211-212.
160 Yeshiva University Archives—"Yeshiva Hails Birth of Jewish State; Assemblies, Celebrations Mark Event," *The Commentator* 26, no. 4 (December 11, 1947): 1.
161 Yeshiva University Archives—"Dr. Soloveitchik Asks Palestine Aid; School of Education to Open in the Fall," *The Commentator* 24, no. 6 (January 15, 1948): 1; Yeshiva University Archives, "Synagogue Council Acclaims Truman," *The Commentator* 29, no. 7 (June 9, 1949): 1.
162 L. Bernstein, *Challenge and Mission*, 53.
163 Yeshiva University Archives—"Dr. Soloveitchik Asks Palestine Aid: $15,000 Goal for Campaign," *The Commentator* 26, no. 6 (January 15, 1948): 1. *Hashomer*

careful to see that issues regarding Palestine would comply with *halakhah*. When Mizrachi asked the RCA to distribute a service that Mizrachi had composed for *Yom Ha'atzmaut*, Rabbi Soloveitchik ruled against a service conducted in a non-*halakhic* fashion. He also felt that the RCA, a rabbinic group, should not disseminate material of another group, particularly a lay group.[164] RCA, unlike Mizrachi, was not supposed to be a political organization.

Rabbi Jung wrote that the *galut* (outside the Holy Land) had built up the Holy Land but that *Eretz Israel* would pour new strength into the *galut*.[165] He felt that *Eretz Israel* would release great religious energies.[166] Rabbi Jung felt that Palestine represented "full stature" for Jews—they had a country, like everybody else did, and now they were equals among equals.[167] He wrote that Israel was a sign that Jews fit into the modern world.[168] Rabbi Jung was talking about *Eretz Israel* and less about America as "the promised land," the second chance for culture, or a haven from tyranny. Rabbi Joseph Lookstein said that there would be a "two-way pipeline connecting the Jews of America with the *Yishuv* of Palestine." From American Jews they would get money, weapons, and manpower, and from Palestine they would get "pure Jewish tradition."[169] Belkin talked about the importance of Zionism for Jewish spiritual life. Zionism would provide Jewish awareness and Orthodox religious life, said Norman Lamm.[170] Rabbi Meyer Berlin, chair of World Mizrachi,

---

Hatzair is a nonreligious, socialistic, Zionist youth group that emphasizes Jewish identity and culture.

164 L. Bernstein, *Challenge and Mission*, 52.
165 Yeshiva University Archives, Jung Collection, Box 48, Folder 5 (published articles)—Jung, "Palestine Today," *Jewish Forum* 30, no. 9 (September 1947), second page.
166 Yeshiva University Archives, Jung Collection, Box 48, Folder 5—Jung, "The Problem of Sovereignty and Minorities, Judaism and the New World Order," *American Journal of Economics and Sociology* 4, no. 4 (July 1945): 521.
167 Yeshiva University Archives, Jung Collection, Box 46, Folder 4—paper headed Kislev 1947.
168 Marty Noam Pencower, *The Holocaust and Israel Reborn: From Catastrophe to Sovereignty* (Champaign-Urbana, IL: University of Illinois Press, 1994), 435.
169 Yeshiva University Archives—"Present Validity Seen in Ancient Galuth Judaism," *The Commentator* 27, no. 2 (March 11, 1948): 1.
170 Yeshiva University Archives—"Symposium Studies Jewry in America," *The Commentator* 29, no. 5 (May 12, 1949): 4.

said that only in Palestine could Judaism exist on a permanent basis and that Hebrew culture depended upon the influence and nourishment it derived from Palestine.[171]

Rabbi Jung saw Jews in Palestine as being "chosen" to set a good example. It would not be a nation like other nations; it would lead by the example of virtuous behavior. This was a classic Orthodox view that derived from biblical sources:

> In accordance with the religious teachings of the Holy Torah, continuing its exemplary pioneering in national righteousness and stimulated by the dynamic influence of the new awareness all over the world, the Jews will take up again the challenge of the social imperatives of the Torah, and by applying precedent to the new conditions make contributions towards a better world of tomorrow.[172]

Contrasting Orthodox Views

In the 1940s, Mizrachi and Agudath Israel's rivalry intensified. As late as 1942, Rabbi Jung was addressing audiences on the significance of Agudath Israel. However, he quit his membership after there was a State of Israel when Agudath Israel would not cooperate with the Israeli government, even on nonreligious affairs.[173] Although Rabbi Jung had understood the fear of Agudists about the modern godless world and a Palestine dominated by secular Zionism, he, too, lost his ambiguity regarding Zionism. Rabbi Jung moved closer to Rav (Rabbi) Avraham Yitzhak Kook's philosophy, which could accept man's intervention in the creation of the State of Israel.[174] Rabbi Jung still felt that Israel was indeed a Jewish state and not a secular one; he cited as proof

---

171 Yeshiva University Archives—"Mizrachi Head Speaks Before Gala Assembly," *The Commentator* 26, no. 6 (January 15, 1948): 1.
172 Jung, "Jewish Foundations of the New World Order," 18.
173 Yeshiva University Archives—"Dr. Jung Addresses Yeshiva Chapter on Agudah Significance," *The Commentator* 15, no. 4 (March 26, 1942): 1 and 4.
174 Milton R. Konvitz, "Leo Jung—Rabbi for All Jews," *Midstream* 39, no. 6 (August/September 1993): 40.

that there were kosher kitchens in workingmen's hospitals and health resorts, even those belonging to the leftist groups.[175]

Though Rabbi Silver (the president of Agudath Israel of America) favored a Jewish state, Agudath Israel as an organization did not.[176] A symposium in 1946, under the auspices of the Jewish Affairs Committee of RIETS, exposed these politically discordant and divergent views. Agudath Israel, unlike Mizrachi, could not accept any politics infused into the Zionist idea, though both groups agreed that Zionism began at Sinai and not in London, recognizing the religious component.[177] Mizrachi felt that Orthodox interests could best be served by remaining in the government.

Also, Agudath Israel was fearful that Mizrachi was interfering with its schools in *Eretz Israel*. They set up the *Vaad Hayeshivot* to prevent Mizrachi from interfering and to see that no secular and alien trends entered their schools.[178] After World War II, there was also friction between Mizrachi and Agudath Israel's *roshei yeshivot*, who were becoming a prime force in American Orthodoxy.[179]

Rabbi Jung's Efforts

Rabbi Jung accepted an invitation to be a member of the enlarged Jewish Agency. His congregation raised money for the Jewish National Fund, which he described as an organization that united all shades of political and religious opinion.[180] Rabbi Jung became affiliated with Poalei Agudah (Agudah laborers), which more readily supported the Jewish nationalist movement.[181] Poalei Agudah was a strongly social-minded and kibbutz-oriented movement that made a significant mark on the Israeli scene. It had ties with Zionism through the Jewish Agency

---

175 Yeshiva University Archives, Jung Collection, Box 48, Folder 5—Jung, "Palestine Today," third page.
176 Rakeffet-Rothkoff, *The Silver Era in American Jewish Orthodoxy*, 262.
177 Ibid., 171; Yeshiva University Archives—"Opposing Factions Review Zionist Stand," *The Commentator* 24, no. 4 (December 5, 1946): 1.
178 Yeshiva University Archives—"Opposing Factions Review Zionist Stand," 1.
179 Rakeffet-Rothkoff, *The Silver Era in American Jewish Orthodoxy*, 247.
180 Yeshiva University Archives, Jung Collection, Box 48, Folder 5—Jung, "Palestine Today," second page.
181 Konvitz, "Leo Jung—Rabbi for All Jews," 40.

and took an active role in building the land, which led to a breach with Agudath Israel. It became distinct from its parent organization, Agudath Israel.[182] Rabbi Jung commented that the Orthodox working men, Poalei Hamizrachi (Mizrachi laborers), and Poalei Agudah did not generally ask questions about political affiliation, but worked together to make Judaism safe in the Holy Land. In the interwar years, Poalei Hamizrachi emerged as a group that (like Poalei Agudah) placed importance on Torah, based on social ideals. Poalei Hamizrachi gained members and was strengthened by settlers from Nazi-ravaged lands. Its accomplishments were great in pioneering the creation of religious collective and cooperative farming settlements. The organization developed a stronger following in America than Poalei Agudah and they, unlike Poalei Agudah, did eventually reunite with their parent organization Mizrachi.

Rabbi Jung was sent to Palestine by the American Fund for Palestine Institutions (AFPI), which supported 86 institutions from opera to Beth Jacob, from *Habimah* (the national theater) to *yeshiva* institutions. It was established in 1942 to coordinate fundraising for Palestinian institutions. There were two special committees in charge of traditional institutions, one in New York and one in the Holy Land, both composed of prominent Mizrachists, Agudists, and other Orthodox leaders—Sephardim and Ashkenazim. Rabbi Jung was part of this committee. It examined applications and made recommendations to the AFPI; Rabbi Jung thus reported that the AFPI had become important in the life of religious institutions. Rabbi Jung remarked that the nonreligious institutions connected with the AFPI—as institutions—observed the Sabbath and Holy Days.[183]

Rabbi Jung also went as the chairman of the JDC Cultural Committee, as the JDC needed help in supporting *yeshivot*. However, the Jewish Agency was overburdened and could not support Jewish culture, thus the AFPI filled the gap, which was most welcomed. In addition, Rabbi Jung

---

182 Saul Bernstein, *The Renaissance of the Torah Jew* (New York: Ktav Publishing House, 1985), 62–63.
183 Yeshiva University Archives, Jung Collection, Box 48, Folder 5—Jung, "Palestine Today," third and fourth pages.

represented the American Beth Jacob Committee, which was building a seminary in Jerusalem to honor the 93 Beth Jacob girls who had committed suicide rather than submit to Nazi violation.

In 1947, on his second trip to *Eretz Israel*, Rabbi Jung visited the Ashkenazic Chief Rabbi of Israel, Rabbi Isaac Herzog, to consult with him on *halakhic* problems. He met with leaders of both Mizrachi and Agudath Israel. He met with Rabbi Berlin (president of World Mizrachi), Rabbi I. M. Lewin of Agudath Israel, and Dr. Jacob Engel of Mizrachi, and he spoke at the Beth Jacob Seminary for Girls. He also visited Rabbi Avraham Yeshayahu Karelitz (known as the *Hazon Ish*), one of the great sages of modern times—an authority on matters relating to Jewish law and a strong influence on religious life and institutions in B'nai Brak. Rabbi Jung said that the *Hazon Ish* encouraged him to come to live in *Eretz Israel* and to bring his congregation along with him. Rabbi Jung returned to America, where he encouraged Jews to visit and to send their children to *Eretz Israel*, at least for a visit.[184]

New Approach After World War II: The Age of the Pioneer

The *Hazon Ish* requested that Rabbi Jung encourage *aliyah*, which represented a new approach for what Rabbi Jung referred to as the "age of the pioneer." There were periods in history when philanthropists loomed very large; there were other times when the *shtadlan* (one who pleaded for his people) was important. But now, according to Rabbi Jung, the pioneer was important.[185] Rabbi Jung described two types of pioneers—the pioneers who worked the land and fought for the land, and the pioneers of the Torah who constituted the spiritual army.[186] The pioneers of the land fought to restore the land and the others fought to restore the soul. Both were important to Modern Orthodoxy.

Yeshiva established scholarships to send rabbis to Israel, feeling that they would get inspirational training at the source of Torah.[187]

---

184 Ibid., fourth page.
185 Ibid., second page.
186 JDC Archives, File 2409—minutes of executive meeting of the JDC, September 17, 1947, "Report by Rabbi Leo Jung," 2–3.
187 Yeshiva University Archives—"S.O.Y. To Award Free Israel Trips," *The Commentator* 29, no. 3 (March 24, 1949): 1.

3. MODERN ORTHODOXY IN THE 1940S

Leo Jung after receiving an honorary degree. 1949. Courtesy of Yeshiva University Archives

Yeshiva newspapers highlighted former Yeshiva University students who had gone to live in Palestine and work on *kibbutzim*.[188] The message from Yeshiva was that Yeshiva students must form the backbone of religious pioneering; that is what Modern Orthodoxy was espousing.[189] In 1949, Yeshiva University gave a platform to Rabbi Isaac Herzog, the Ashkenazic Chief Rabbi of Israel, who said that "American students of Jewish law should spend five years of study in Israel."[190] Yeshiva urged its students to at least visit Israel even if they did not plan to remain.[191]

Halakhic Issues

Increased Attention

Toward the end of World War II and in the postwar period, there began a demand for total ideological consistency and a demand for unequivocal observance of *halakhah* on the part of the Modern Orthodox movement. Pulpit rabbis were asked by their rabbinic organizations to carry the message to their congregants and to be knowledgeable regarding the particulars of *halakhah*.[192] Rabbi Soloveitchik said that in religious and *halakhic* matters, Orthodox leaders must be autonomous and militant.[193] This contrasted with the fear of demanding too much, which was prevalent in the 1920s and 1930s. There was increased interest in the area of *halakhah*, which was good for the Orthodox movement and the Orthodox way of life, as adherence to *halakhah* is what Orthodoxy stood for.

With the State of Israel, Jewish law received new impetus.[194] In the area of *halakhic* issues, the decisions required by the modern rabbi

---

188 Yeshiva University Archives—"Former Yeshiva University Students Now Chalutzim in Israel," *Yeshiva University News* 7, no. 2 (November and December 1949): 2.
189 Yeshiva University Archives—"Dr. Soloveitchik Asks Palestine Aid; $15,000 Goal for Campaign," 1.
190 Yeshiva University Archives—"Chief Rabbi Talks on Halachic Topic," *The Commentator* 29, no. 3 (May 12, 1949): 4.
191 Ibid.
192 Yeshiva University Archives—"The Yeshiva Rabbi in the Province," *News and Views* 1, no. 5 (April 1944): 1 and 4.
193 Yeshiva University Archives—"Rabbi Soloveitchik's Address," 4.
194 Basil F. Herring, *Jewish Ethics and Halakhah for Our Time: Sources and Commentary* (New York: Ktav Publishing House, 1984), 19.

3. MODERN ORTHODOXY IN THE 1940S

pertaining to the war, the State of Israel, and new technology necessitated the expansion of the rabbi's areas of expertise. At the end of the 1940s, the Jewish State and Jewish law became important and often-discussed topics of *halakhic* discourse.[195]

During World War II, the *responsa* committee of CANRA (of which Rabbi Jung was the Orthodox representative) faced questions on disinterment and reinterment, autopsies, *kohanim* (the priestly group of Jews, who are not allowed to come in contact with the dead) coming in contact with the dead on the battlefield, dietary laws, conditional *gittin* (Jewish divorces; plural of *get*), marriages, time of the Sabbath in the Arctic, and new technology. The RCA, in particular, was concerned with the *agunah* problem—Rabbi Mordecai Stern prepared a document to be signed by a soldier before he left for war, which constituted a "conditional *get*."[196] The *agunah*, a topic about which Rabbi Jung cared greatly, received increased attention; the RCA devoted an entire session to the problem of the postwar *agunah*.[197] Still, many Orthodox leaders agree that the problem remained unsolved because the Orthodox did not make a definite stand on the issue.

The State of Israel brought to the fore many *halakhic* complexities and the rediscovery of special injunctions. The discourse centered on the application of traditional Jewish law in the State of Israel. There was a need for a comprehensive analysis of Torah concepts and the establishment of legal precedents that would govern the Jewish state. There were active *halakhic* discussions concerning issues such as the status of Jerusalem as an international city. The challenge was to harmonize the ancient Jewish tradition with the requirements of a modern industrialized state.[198] This was like Modern Orthodoxy itself, which

---

195 Yeshiva University Archives—"Rabbi Drazin's Lecture on Jewish State, Law," *The Commentator* 27, no. 6 (January 13, 1949): page number not available. One of many examples.
196 Hoenig, "The Orthodox Rabbi as a Military Chaplain," 42.
197 L. Bernstein, *Challenge and Mission*, 241. See the chapter on the 1950s for more on Rabbi Jung's devotion to the *agunah* problem.
198 Yeshiva University Archives—"Torah's Use Urged by Agency Expert," *The Commentator* 27, no. 2 (March 11, 1948): 1.

had to adjust to the modern technological world while observing the life of Torah.

The 1940s saw an expansion in technology and in medical and scientific knowledge. This led to new questions, and these new situations needed careful *halakhic* examination.[199] Rabbis had to be prepared with answers; they had to learn the *halakhah* well and to consult with *halakhic* authorities. The American rabbi, in short, had to become more learned.

Mehitzah

Mixed seating was still an issue, but there was a call for a well-defined and definite policy regarding mixed pews. Mixed pews were denounced in 1947 by Dr. Samuel Belkin, who felt that a synagogue could not be considered a traditional synagogue if there were mixed pews. He was quoted as saying:

> The Yeshiva cannot and will not sanction this abrogation of the most essential and most characteristic element in the synagogue.[200]

On the other hand, in 1947, Louis Ginzberg (a Conservative rabbi) changed his mind and agreed that there could be mixed seating—that the resisting minority should yield to the majority who wanted this.[201] In the 1920s and 1930s, he had been against mixed seating. The difference between Orthodox and Conservative would no longer be one of degree of actual observance, but of ideology. An example of this is that Orthodoxy claimed that its decision regarding the *mehitzah* was based in *halakhah* and the Conservative factions also claimed that their decision was based in *halakhah*. The point is that the Modern Orthodox and Conservative movements were moving further apart; Rabbi Jung

---

199 L. Bernstein, *Challenge and Mission*, 34.
200 Yeshiva University Archives—"Dr. Belkin Opens Synagogue Panel," *The Commentator* 25, no. 3 (March 20, 1947): 1.
201 Wertheimer, ed., *The American Synagogue*, 380; Marshall Sklare, *Conservative Judaism: An American Religious Movement* (Glencoe, IL: Free Press, 1955), 88.

was no longer calling the Conservative movement "the other Orthodoxy," but advocating that Conservatives "conserve" Judaism.[202] Modern Orthodoxy was defining its stance on issues in a clearer, more definite way.

Microphone

The issue of the use of the microphone in an Orthodox synagogue on *Shabbat* and holidays was raised. Though Simcha Levy (the chairman of the *Halakhic* Committee of the Rabbinical Council) eventually gave his approval for using microphones, this issue remained controversial in the 1940s, because 1) the majority of the Agudath Harabbonim was against its use, 2) the Chief Rabbinate in Palestine prohibited its use, 3) Rabbi Soloveitchik had not given his approval, and 4) not all the RCA *Halakhic* Committee members had given approval.[203] Levy's approval was given, citing the scientific knowledge that was available.[204] As Louis Bernstein pointed out, the American rabbis were still too timid and unsure of themselves to make a definite decision on their own; this issue was an example of that.[205] Some rabbis stated that the *roshei yeshiva* should be consulted; others felt that they should rely on themselves. The growing power and influence of the *roshei yeshiva* would be felt even more in the following decades, and that conflict would remain in Modern Orthodox circles. Rabbi Jung was consulted on this issue, but his answer could not be found; however, there was never a microphone used in his own synagogue.[206] The discussion and background work on the microphone issue that was ongoing in the 1940s led to its resolution in the 1950s.

Kashrut

---

202 Jung, "Program for 5701," 25.
203 L. Bernstein, *Challenge and Mission*, 38.
204 Ibid., 37–41.
205 Ibid., 38.
206 Yeshiva University Archives, Jung Collection, Box 1, Folder 5—letter to Rabbi Jung, December 4, 1945. Please note that this question came two years before the official decision of the *Halakhic* Committee to okay microphone use.

Questions posed by the consumer in the area of *kashrut* lessened as there was more packaged food, although packaged food meant more complicated supervision.[207] Rabbi Jung continued to fight those who issued individual *hekhsherim* by strengthening the efforts of the RCA, and in the 1940s, there were fewer private *hekhsherim*.[208] All *mashgihim*, or *kashrut* supervisors, had to be paid through the office of the Orthodox Union.[209] This prevented corrupt practices (such as bribery) and ensured uniformity and consistency in *kashrut* supervision. Rabbi Jung wrote that *hillul Hashem* (desecration of God's name) had been caused by these corrupt methods; he was vehement in his condemnation:

> I had taken measures to assure the unanimous passing of a resolution that would prohibit any individual rabbi from endorsing for gain any article advertised as kosher. I need not grow eloquent to you on the catastrophic consequences of this evil custom.[210]

Rabbi Jung continued to criticize the members of the Agudath Harabbonim who, he said, had for the last 25 years received payment for individual *hekhsherim*. The OU symbol challenged the older rabbis' way of earning a living, and Rabbi Jung acknowledged that the members of the Agudath Harabbonim resented him personally for his efforts, which they saw as contrary to their interests.[211] Rabbi Jung was chairman of the *Vaad Hakavod*, the RCA's court of honor, which was involved with the problem of withdrawing *hekhsherim* from two

---

207 L. Bernstein. *Challenge and Mission*, 34.
208 Ibid., 92–93 and 100.
209 Yeshiva University Archives, Koenigsberg Papers, Box 9, Folder 2—minutes from the meeting of the *Kashrut* Committee of the RCA and the Orthodox Union, June 27, 1940, and minutes from the RCA, September 16, 1948.
210 Yeshiva University Archives, Jung Collection, Box 41, Folder 1—letter to Rabbi Simcha Levy, member of the *Kashrut* Committee of the RCA and the Orthodox Union, from Rabbi Jung, July 7, 1941.
211 Yeshiva University Archives, Koenigsberg Papers, Box 41, Folder 1—minutes of the *Kashrut* Committee of the RCA and the Orthodox Union, June 27, 1940; L. Bernstein, *Challenge and Mission*, 99.

Agudath Harabbonim rabbis.[212] The case was fought in the courts; it was the *Kashrut* Commission of the RCA versus the two rabbis, and the victory went to the RCA. The RCA's determination to maintain *kashrut* as a public trust on the American scene was strengthened.[213] This case led the RCA and the UOJCA to refine and make more definite policies regarding applications, endorsements, and supervision in the 1940s.[214]

Rabbi Jung continued to lobby government officials to prevent fraud in the *kashrut* industry.[215] He worked with state Senator Walter Mahoney of New York, who helped to see that kosher laws were clarified and proper inspectors and supervisors were in place. The Advisory Board, which in 1940 became a statutory official board of the Department of Agriculture and Markets for New York, assisted in appointing qualified inspectors. Rabbi Jung was chairman of this board for 30 years. From 1934 to 1964, close to 3,000 cases were prosecuted by this board; this had a positive effect on the *kashrut* industry.[216] Rabbi Jung claimed that New York was the first state to punish fraud and protect consumers with fair pricing to improve *kashrut* facilities.[217]

Non-kosher affairs by Jewish organizations continued.[218] Rabbi Jung had joined the American Jewish Committee to promote unity among American Jews, but with regard to its dinner, he wrote: "I feel that no Orthodox Jew should ever accept any invitation to a Jewish affair that is not prepared and served in accordance with Jewish

---

212 L. Bernstein, *Challenge and Mission*, 95.
213 Ibid., 98.
214 Ibid., 99; Yeshiva University Archives, Koenigsberg Papers, Box 9, Folder 2—minutes of the *Kashrut* Committee of the RCA and the Orthodox Union, June 27, 1940. Benjamin Koenigsberg was chairman of the *Kashrut* Committee of the Orthodox Union—many of the minutes of this committee are in this file. They attest to the statement of the establishment of definite policies with regard to applications, endorsements, and supervision made in the 1940s.
215 Yeshiva University Archives, Jung Collection, Box 41, Folder 1—letter to Senator Walter J. Mahoney from Rabbi Jung, May 1, 1941.
216 Jung, *The Path of a Pioneer*, 249.
217 Ibid., 248.
218 L. Bernstein, *Challenge and Mission*, 120.

Law."[219] Rabbi Jung would not accept even if kosher food were provided for him.

Rabbi Jung became chairman of the *Kashrut* Committee of Beth Israel Hospital, which he had initiated. Also on the committee were Rabbis Lookstein and Goldstein.[220] This facility's participation in *kashrut* was an important incentive for patients to keep kosher, even during hospitalization.

Decorum

In the 1920s and 1930s, Rabbi Jung had written a great deal about the need for "decorum," but not in the 1940s. He was occupied with other issues, yet decorum always remained an important issue for him, even if not for Modern Orthodoxy. Chaplain Norman Siegel, supervisor of Jewish chaplains of the Pacific Ocean Area, speaking at a gathering of friends of servicemen sponsored by the Yeshiva College Alumni Association, felt that the boys who had become more religious during the war needed to come back to a "clean orderly synagogue."[221] Decorum still was a Modern Orthodox issue, but it is as if the discussion needed reopening—and a defense. This need to defend decorum was a harbinger of things to come.

Sabbath

Rabbi Jung always maintained a membership in the Sabbath Alliance, but was never a major player. The effort continued, without ultimate success, to see to it that those who followed the *halakhah* of Sabbath observance were able to do so without too many difficulties. On January 14, 1945, under the auspices of the Council of Religious Observance of Washington Heights, the first rally was held to urge Jewish shops to close and to encourage Sabbath observance.[222] In 1947, the UOJCA called together several representatives of Jewish organizations

---

219 Jung, *The Path of a Pioneer*, 259.
220 Yeshiva University Archives, Jung Collection, Box 41, Folder 1—letter from Nathan Ratcoff, the medical director of Beth Israel Hospital, November 30, 1942.
221 Yeshiva University Archives—"Chaplain Siegel Speaks at Edison," 1.
222 Yeshiva University Archives—"Shomer Shabbos Rally Held; Urge Jewish Shops To Close," *The Commentator* 20, no. 6 (January 18, 1945): 1.

to enact legislation to enable Sabbath observers to remain open on Sundays, as they were unable to keep open on Saturdays. All organizations were urged to contact their legislators.[223] This represented another effort in a long history of efforts to amend the law and to obtain suitable legislation to permit Sabbath-observing merchants to operate on Sunday.

Conclusion

The decade of the 1940s was marked with despair, with discontent with the status quo, and with hope with the end of World War II and the advent of the State of Israel. The Holocaust had given the American Modern Orthodox movement, as well as all Jewish movements, a new role. The Holocaust was the ultimate example that modernity had failed, and for many it meant that they were open to a new, more positive look at religion. There was a new, improved image of the rabbi, of religion itself, and of the Jewish people. The American Modern Orthodox Jew showed the ability to adapt, to lead, to inspire, and to compete. The movement's many varied outreach programs showed some signs of success.

The 1940s saw new and very capable leadership for Modern Orthodoxy. Rabbi Joseph B. Soloveitchik emerged as leader, which was a sign that there would be some unity and direction in the movement. In the Land of Israel, the Chief Rabbinate served to centralize, unify, and provide leadership for Orthodoxy in Israel as well as in America. There was also new leadership at Yeshiva University. Because of the new leadership, issues and what Modern Orthodoxy stood for became better defined and would continue to be better defined in the 1950s.

There was expansion and further development in the areas of education, *kashrut* facilities, and participation in social, political, and cultural endeavors. Orthodox newcomers to America, after the war,

---

[223] Yeshiva University Archives, Koenigsberg Papers, Box 11, Folder 6—letter from Koenigsberg, chairman of the UOJCA Committee on Jewish Observance, to Mr. Pfeiffer, November 22, 1948.

made Orthodoxy more visible; they provided examples of dedicated religious living.

All these happenings bode well for Modern Orthodoxy; the groundwork for achievements was being laid as the Modern Orthodox faced the decade of the 1950s.

4. MODERN ORTHODOXY IN THE 1950S

•••

"If I have seen further… it is by standing upon the shoulders of Giants."
(Sir Isaac Newton[1])

Introduction

There were many things that had gone on before and during the 1950s that prepared the way for the movement to the right, to more observance, to more identification with the tenets of Orthodox Judaism, and to the tightening of religious standards. This chapter will deal with these foundational issues; the most intense movement to the right in Modern Orthodoxy would come in later decades. Rabbi Leo Jung helped put in place criteria for leading a more religious life; other rabbis continued his work.

The increase in Orthodoxy's participation in the Jewish and non-Jewish community, which occurred in the 1940s, had important consequences, as it prepared its leaders for dealing with the government, for effective outreach, and for better experience in attracting adherents. There were certain trends that were good for Modern Orthodoxy. The modern age was under critical scrutiny; the disappointment in the hope

---

1 John Bartlett, *Bartlett's Familiar Quotations*, 14th edition, ed. Emily Morison Beck (Boston and Toronto: Little, Brown and Company, 1968), 379B. Letter from Sir Isaac Newton to Robert Hooke, February 5, 1675.

that science would produce a just society led to a new appreciation of religion, which opened the way to a religious revival. The advent of the State of Israel strengthened the position of Modern Orthodoxy. In America, Modern Orthodoxy had to face the intensified *halakhic* standards of newly arrived Holocaust survivors without abandoning its commitment to university education and general culture.

The Holocaust, however, had killed huge numbers of the carriers of tradition. There were fewer examples of knowledgeable and observant people in Eastern Europe, who had served as an important reservoir for Jewish learning. Adult examples and peer behavior could no longer be counted on to transmit the ways of religious life; according to Haym Soloveitchik, this led to an increased reliance on texts, beginning in the 1950s. This new reliance on learning from the inflexible words of the texts led to more stringency in observance of Jewish laws.[2]

This chapter will explore the activity in the Orthodox movement that translated into reinvigoration, such as more attention to Jewish education, more affiliation of Jews with synagogues, Jewish organizations, Jewish causes, and more infusion of Jewish tradition into the home. There were new trends in religious practice, observance, and administration. Rabbi Jung and other leaders of the 1920s, 1930s, and 1940s had made Orthodoxy in America a viable and attractive option. In describing the progress of Orthodoxy in America, Rabbi Jung wrote:

> We have seen the rise of a revitalized Orthodoxy, with its institutions improved in manner and method, with its teaching better presented and gaining wider acceptance… American Israel has moved from uneasy adolescence towards a solid measure of maturity… From the founders of our institutions to their grandchildren there has been preserved the purity of vision, the quality of service and the stubborn determination to make America safe for Judaism untrimmed, unbarbered and infinite in its potentialities.[3]

---

2 Haym Soloveitchik, "Rupture and Reconstruction: The Transformation of Contemporary Orthodoxy," *Tradition* 28, no. 4 (Summer 1994): 65–66.
3 Yeshiva University Archives, Public Relations Files, 1942–1980—Leo Jung, "Greetings, 1957."

New leaders emerged in the 1950s with different approaches and different priorities. Rabbi Jung and others had laid the groundwork from which the new leaders could build.

The Modern wing of Orthodoxy had ambitious plans and made headway. There was organizational progress.[4] Learning and scholarship became more respected, which changed the character of Modern Orthodoxy. More learning led to better knowledge and adherence to *halakhah*, or Jewish law.

Rabbi Jung was active in religious, educational, political, cultural, and social undertakings that truly exemplified *Torah im derekh eretz*, the philosophy of Modern Orthodoxy. His activities demonstrate that he was an able exponent of Orthodox Judaism and of the American spirit.

What Facilitated the Movement to the Right?

Religious Revival

Rabbi Emanuel Rackman wrote in 1952 that "a spiritual quest is now going on. Orthodox Judaism is only beginning to recover from the initially devastating effects of the Enlightenment."[5] There was relatively more respect for religion and less respect for secularism in this period; Orthodoxy thus had a chance to be seen in a more positive light. Modern Orthodoxy embraced the values of modernity, as well as the values of Torah Judaism; however, Enlightenment values had made it difficult for Modern Orthodoxy to put forth its philosophy. This milieu made it easier.

Orthodoxy, like all other groups, was helped by a postwar revival in religion. There was enough interest in religion that one of Rabbi Jung's sermons, delivered at his synagogue on the Sabbath of January 3, 1953, was reviewed in the *New York Times*. In this review, it was reported that many of his remarks were addressed to college students home on vacation, and that he had said that the character of its average citizen, which should be shaped by civil leaders, clergy, and teachers,

---

4 Will Herberg, "The Postwar Revival of the Synagogue: Does It Represent a Religious Awakening?" *Commentary* 9, no. 4 (April 1950): 319.

5 Emanuel Rackman, "Orthodox Judaism Moves with the Times: The Creativity of Tradition," *Commentary* 13, no. 6 (June 1952): 550.

would determine the character and destiny of a nation.[6] Though no evidence was found to suggest that Rabbi Jung knew in advance that this sermon would be reviewed, it can be said nonetheless that newspaper coverage of such things is rarely accidental. The point is that it was felt that the sermon had appeal to a larger audience and that there was interest in a religious point of view.

Will Herberg, in his important article, "Religious Trends in American Jewry" (written in 1950), described a general Jewish revival. This revival trend bode very well for Orthodoxy.[7] Herberg said that the revival had benefited the Conservative group the most, but noted that the Modern wing of Orthodoxy had made "impressive headway."[8] He wrote that the Orthodox who were attending synagogue were no longer primarily older and of immigrant stock, but were American born, in their 20s and 30s.

The veterans of World War II, in many instances, were active in initiating and building synagogues, a result—Herberg felt—of the activity of the chaplains in the army.[9] The return to the synagogue meant more synagogue construction, more synagogue attendance, and an increase in synagogue membership.[10] Jewish practices in homes, such as lighting Sabbath candles and reciting the Sabbath *kiddush*, increased.[11] Nathan Glazer—a professor at Harvard University, prominent sociologist, and an editor of the journal *Commentary*—also noted in 1955 that there was more attendance in Jewish schools and that synagogue membership was up. He noted that "even Orthodoxy shows a new vigour that is particularly evident in its all-day schools."[12] This certainly

---

6 Yeshiva University Archives, Jung Collection, Box 40, Folder 7—review of Rabbi Jung's sermon, *The New York Times*, January 4, 1953; Yeshiva University Archives, Jung Collection, Box 49, Folder 2—letter to Rabbi Jung from Bernard Baruch, January 5, 1953.
7 Will Herberg, "Religious Trends in American Jewry," *Judaism* 3, no. 3 (Summer 1954): 229. A movement away from secularism and assimilation; a movement of "return" leads to return to synagogue and observance.
8 Herberg, "The Postwar Revival of the Synagogue," 315.
9 Ibid.
10 Herberg, "Religious Trends in American Jewry," 232.
11 Herberg, "The Postwar Revival of the Synagogue," 315.
12 Nathan Glazer, "The Jewish Revival in America, I: A Sociologist's Report," *Commentary* 20, no. 6 (December 1955): 495.

is tangible evidence that there was greater interest in the Jewish religion and Jewish education. Modern Orthodox values had a chance to be taught and presented to an increased audience.

Prosperous Times
Glazer stated that the temper of the times brought people back to religion; Jews were more prosperous and living with—and among—non-Jews.[13] Many Orthodox people by the 1950s had begun to establish themselves in upper-class and upper middle-class areas, leaving the areas of second settlement, such as the Bronx.[14] A socialist working-class community had become middle class. Herberg wrote that the militant secular, radical, and antireligious attitude of the Eastern European Jewish socialist was almost gone, and that the growing acceptance of religion as an integral part of Americanism made socialism irrelevant.[15] Modern Orthodoxy would get its share of those returning to religion.

Influx of Orthodox Immigrants
The Orthodox who came to settle in America after the war, as discussed in the previous chapters, played a large role in the movement to the right, and Rabbi Jung played an important role in getting these immigrants to America. Norman Lamm commented on Rabbi Jung's role in facilitating the immigration of these immigrants:

> "To his [i.e., Rabbi Jung's] great credit, he brought over many refugees during and after the war; it was a major contribution. He performed historically and did whatever he could to get Jewry to come to America."[16]

Working through the Joint Distribution Committee (JDC), Rabbi Jung's mandate was to bring the immigrant to America at this time.

---

13 Ibid.
14 Marshall Sklare, *Conservative Judaism: An American Religious Movement* (Glencoe, IL: Free Press, 1955), 267.
15 Herberg, "Religious Trends in American Jewry," 233.
16 Personal interview with Norman Lamm, the president of Yeshiva University, January 16, 2003.

These efforts did not mean that the JDC, or Rabbi Jung, discouraged *aliyah* to Israel, as the JDC and Rabbi Jung were involved in other projects that brought Jews to Israel. However, there was tension in the postwar years between Israel and the diaspora as destinations for Holocaust survivors.

For traditional Orthodox groups, teaching by example still continued, and they began to influence other Jewish groups.[17] The rank and file continued to follow the example of their leaders and to take their advice, which provided them with an exciting intellectual and emotional experience. They were visible, strongly committed, proud, and self-confident. Not only did they practice the rules, they derived joy from practicing them. They taught in Modern Orthodox institutions, which provided exposure to their ideas and ways. Modern Orthodoxy was stimulated by the emotional and intellectual fervor of the traditional and Hasidic Orthodox groups.[18] However, it took time for this influence to be noticed.

Organizational Progress

In general, there was an expansion of Modern Orthodox organizations and institutions.[19] The activities of the organizations were an example of the religious reinvigoration.

UOJCA

Rabbi Jung continued to be active in the UOJCA.[20] By the end of the 1950s, there were more Orthodox synagogues under its auspices.[21] The UOJCA convention in 1951 in New York dealt with the

---

17 Nathan Glazer, "The Jewish Revival in America, II: Its Religious Side," *Commentary* 21, no. 1 (January 1956): 23.
18 Ibid., 23–24.
19 Marc H. Tanenbaum, "Communal Affairs," Organizational Expansion, *American Jewish Year Book* 60 (1959), 53.
20 Yeshiva University Archives—"UOJCA Will Seek to Establish Discipline of Orthodox Jewish Life and Education," *The Commentator* 24, no. 4 (December 10, 1951): 4.
21 Author unknown, *American Jewish Year Book* 56 (1955), 231; Yeshiva University Archives, Koenigsberg Papers, Box 11, Number 3—minutes of UOJCA meeting, April 29, 1958, 1. The president of the OUJCA, Moses I. Feuerstein, reported *incorrectly* at the meeting that there were 3,000 Orthodox synagogues under the UOJCA—we can assume that he was reporting the number because it had expanded.

reinvigoration of Jewish personal and communal life. The members at the convention set the direction Modern Orthodoxy would take in the future. The UOJCA became less tolerant and more demanding, also a sign of a movement to the right. Modern Orthodoxy became more defined as goals were analyzed and clearer demands were made. Modern Orthodox issues, pertinent in the 1950s, were discussed. Synagogue standards, such as the *mehitzah*, adult education, youth activities, and the lack of Jewish education for women, were areas of concern for the UOJCA.

This convention brought together a most representative and authoritative assembly of Modern Orthodox Jewry. Among the outstanding Orthodox leaders who participated were: Rabbi Joseph B. Soloveitchik, a professor of Talmud at Yeshiva University; Dr. Samuel Belkin, the president of Yeshiva University; Rabbi Oscar Fasman, the president of the Hebrew Theological College in Chicago; Rabbi Joseph Lookstein, a professor of sociology at Yeshiva University; Rabbi Herbert Goldstein; Max Etra, the newly elected president of the UOJCA; Rabbi Jung; and Herman Wouk, a noted author.[22]

The UOJCA wanted assurances that Jewish institutions that were supported by the Jewish community observed Jewish law; the United Jewish Appeal and the Long Island Jewish Hospital were criticized in this respect. Rabbi Jung had always been active in insisting that *kashrut* be observed in all Jewish organizations.

More stringent measures were called for, yet modern issues were also recognized. The topic of education for women was discussed, leading to more attention and support for education for women. This issue also made Modern Orthodoxy a unique group within Orthodox Judaism, as the other Orthodox groups were for the status quo. Though the Beth Jacob schools (for girls) in America grew in the 1950s, the education provided did not represent Modern Orthodoxy. The schools' primary purpose was to prepare students to be good Jews, mothers, and wives, and contributors to family and community. Secular studies were often secondary, though still considered important. Girls in Beth Jacob schools did not learn law from the text of the Talmud itself, but could

---

22 Yeshiva University Archives—"UOJCA Will Seek to Establish Discipline of Orthodox Jewish Life and Education," 4.

study its nonlegal portions of aggadah. This contrasted with the approach of the Modern Orthodox.

Rabbinical Council of America (RCA)

The RCA made advancements in the area of *kashrut,* and the OU became the symbol of authority in this area. It was noted by Rabbi Louis Bernstein that it was in the 1950s that the RCA finally cut the "umbilical cord" to the Agudath Harabbonim.[23] According to Bernstein, the RCA became the most important Orthodox organization in the world by the end of that decade.[24] The RCA became a powerful and authoritative force in expressing the views of American Orthodox Jewry.[25] Rabbi Joseph Soloveitchik became chairman of the *Halakhic* Committee of the RCA in 1954, replacing Rabbi Simcha Levy. In this role, he brought prestige and stature to the RCA, even among other Orthodox groups.[26] The *Halakhic* Committee claimed final authority on religious matters for Modern Orthodoxy. Many *halakhic* issues were resolved under Rabbi Soloveitchik's leadership. The *Halakhic* Committee of the RCA underwent its greatest period of growth in the 1950s under Rabbi Soloveitchik. By the 1950s, RCA members—part of the UOJCA—occupied an increasing number of pulpits, while the European rabbis who had been active in Agudath Harabbonim occupied fewer pulpits. The influence of these European rabbis thus decreased. The 1950s was a time of assertive stands. Modern Orthodoxy did not wish to be confused with the Conservative movement. Many of the RCA's accomplishments were factors enabling a movement to the right as it made it easier for its members to comply with a stricter standard of Jewish observance. In 1954, the RCA officially prohibited individual rabbis from issuing *hekhsherim*. The procedure of granting OU endorsement was formalized by the *Kashrut* Committee in 1953. The RCA and UOJCA established a joint *kashrut* department

---

23 Louis Bernstein, *Challenge and Mission: The Emergence of the English-Speaking Rabbinate* (New York: Shengold Publishers, 1982), 157.
24 Ibid., 180.
25 Ibid., 206.
26 Ibid., 51 and 71.

administered by laymen to take fiscal responsibility and controlled by rabbis to deal with *halakhic* and religious aspects.[27] By 1953, *kashrut* had become big business, as there were many endorsements and an increasing number of products available for the kosher market. This was extremely important, as the availability of kosher food was the greatest inducement to keeping kosher. The greatest inducement was thus neither aesthetic nor scientific, but practical.[28]

There was a lot of activity to promote *kashrut*, including fact finding regarding how many people bought given products and how to better reach the consumer. Surveys were conducted to obtain such information.[29] The committee had a busy outreach program that distributed information on *kashrut* to nonkosher homes.[30] The committee worked through the synagogues, Jewish organizations, and Jewish newspapers.[31] Thus, in the *Jewish Center Bulletin*, there began a column under "educational notes" called "Jewish Domestic Science," which tried to acquaint its readers with the kosher kitchen and provided recipes.[32] Rabbi Jung's wife, Mrs. Erma Jung, ran a class teaching women how to keep a kosher kitchen.[33]

The first issue of the *OU News Reporter* was published in May 1956 with two purposes: as a newsletter designed for use as a poster for congregational bulletin boards and as a mailing flyer to individuals. The publication let the public know about OU products and where they could be purchased. There were even proposals for material to be used in children's education and adult programs; a conference was held with Dr. Joseph Kaminetsky of Torah Umesorah to develop a program for this purpose. They worked to interest editors and publishers of

---

27 Ibid., 103.
28 Jenna Weissman Joselit, *The Wonders of America: Reinventing Jewish Culture, 1880–1950* (New York: Hill and Wang, 1994), 187.
29 Yeshiva University Archives, Koenigsberg Papers, Box 9, Folder 3—UOJCA report to the Joint Kashrut Commission on the Public Relations Program, May 22, 1956.
30 L. Bernstein, *Challenge and Mission*, 104.
31 Yeshiva University Archives, Koenigsberg Papers, Box 9, Folder 3—UOJCA report to the Joint Kashrut Commission on the Public Relations Program, May 22, 1956.
32 Jewish Center Synagogue Archives—"Jewish Domestic Science," *Jewish Center Bulletin* (February 2, 1951).
33 Personal interview with Martin Schwarzschild, November 11, 1996.

Anglo-Jewish weeklies, including Conservative and Reform journals, editors of food magazines, executives of food chains, and the general media.

As the RCA's presence at large fundraising affairs of the 1950s and 1960s increased, and as Orthodoxy's participation in the wider Jewish community increased as well, national organizations became increasingly careful in the observance of *kashrut*.[34] It is evident that the objectives that Rabbi Jung had worked so hard to achieve were coming to pass, such as banning individual endorsements for *kashrut* and seeing to it that Jewish organizations, out of respect for all Jews, kept the dietary laws at public functions.

The RCA acted independently and had successful projects of its own. The RCA became active in the political and social scene nationally and internationally.[35] It had a leading role in aid for Russian Jewry and lobbied the government on their behalf.[36] It fought for social issues, such as labor rights. Headway was made in securing rights for Sabbath observers taking university exams.[37]

Joint Distribution Committee (JDC)

A major contribution of the JDC was providing for the sustenance and the spiritual revival of Jewish communities in every part of the world along religious and cultural lines. This was done through its Cultural and Religious Committee, and the JDC executive agreed that Rabbi Jung was one of the "mainstays of the religious and cultural committees."[38] Rabbi Jung's involvement was instrumental in seeing to it that Orthodox needs were met. As chairman of the religious board of the JDC, he saw to it that religious needs were met for Jews in other lands, such as North Africa, Iran, South America, and Israel. Rabbi Jung—who spoke German, Yiddish, Hebrew, and Spanish—was sent by the JDC to various areas of the world, including Buenos Aires, where his

---

34 L. Bernstein, *Challenge and Mission*, 120.
35 Ibid., 184.
36 Ibid., 167.
37 Ibid., 185–186.
38 Joint Distribution Committee (JDC) Archives, File 2409—titled, "Rabbi Leo Jung," May 17, 1957.

daughter lived. In this way, Jung helped to spread Orthodox influence and affirm America's new leading role.³⁹

As the 1950s began, financial aid to *yeshivot* and *yeshiva* students was critical, and *yeshiva* programs were in need of revision, as they lacked updated educational programs and capable teachers. The JDC's role was investigation, planning, remedying, and encouragement. For example, the JDC supported a Jewish teacher's seminary in Iran. This was important, as these graduates in Teheran became the first group of locally trained teachers available for Jewish schools in Iran, alleviating an acute shortage of teachers. The JDC supplied Israel and various areas of the world with necessary items, such as Talmuds, *tefillin* (phylacteries), Torah scrolls, and books.⁴⁰

Hassidic *yeshivot*, such as Lubavitch and Vishnitz, began to accept support from the JDC after having been persuaded to do so by the JDC. This made the JDC more representative of all Jews, as it now included most Orthodox groups.⁴¹ These groups had found it difficult to accept the leadership of the JDC, which included non-Orthodox Jews, and preferred Orthodox organizations such as *Vaad Hahatzala*.

Fighting for the American Dream—the Social and Political Situation in the 1950s that Affected Modern Orthodoxy

Rabbi Jung worked to ensure that the American dream would exist so that religion and—in particular for him, Orthodoxy—could thrive. He, as the vice-president of the National Committee to Repeal the McCarran Act, worked to repeal the McCarran Acts of 1950 and 1952. The McCarran Act was legislation proposed by Senator Patrick Anthony McCarran and enacted by Congress in 1950, which aimed to seek out alleged members of designated Communist-action organizations. Under the McCarran Act, the customs bureau banned the import of certain books and periodicals that were neither obscene nor revolutionary. The

---

39 JDC Archives, File 2409—letter #1459, June 16, 1950, to JDC Buenos Aires, Julius Lomnitz, Re: Rabbi Jung.
40 JDC Archives, File 3390—minutes, November 21, 1950.
41 Yeshiva University Archives, Jung Collection, Box 19, Folder 1—letter to Solomon Tarshansky, director of the American Friends of the Jewish Joint Distribution Committee, November 26, 1952.

United States Information Agency libraries abroad confiscated hundreds of books and discarded them because authors were associated with subversive groups or those considered subversive. People were deportable for what they said or for the ideas expressed by the people in groups that they had joined, and American citizens were denied passports. People were kept in detention camps without just cause or proof of crime. Jews who had been associated with communism became targets, hence, Jewish organizations became involved.[42] The McCarran Act was implemented in the midst of the Cold War, when there was a tremendous fear of communism and of the power of the USSR, and when the United States was fighting communist aggression in Korea. In 1950, the Senate and the House of Representatives overrode President Truman's veto and enacted the McCarran Act despite widespread opposition of religious, educational, professional, labor, Black, Jewish, fraternal, and veteran organizations. Rabbi Jung was active with—among others—Zecharia Chafee Jr., who wrote a book denouncing the Act, called *The Blessing of Liberty*, and with Professor Paul Tillich, a well-known Protestant theologian.[43] Rabbi Jung, as a member of the Planning Committee of The National Committee to Repeal the McCarran Act, wrote to the editor of the *New York Times* denouncing the Act on at least two occasions.[44] It was a long and hard

---

42 Jung, *The Path of a Pioneer: The Autobiography of Leo Jung*, Jewish Library, Second Series, vol. 8 (London and New York: Soncino Press, 1980), 265; Yeshiva University Archives, Jung Collection, Box 41, Folder 2—letter to the editor of the *New York Times* from Rabbi Jung and Carey McWilliams, December 14, 1951; Milton Konvitz, "The Swing of the Pendulum," Book Review (review of the book *The Blessing of Liberty* by Zecharia Chafee Jr.), *Midstream* 3, no. 1 (Winter 1957): 96-98.

43 Jung, *The Path of a Pioneer*, 265; Yeshiva University Archives, Jung Collection, Box 41, Folder 2—letter to Rabbi Jung from Secretary of Committee, May 7, 1951; Yeshiva University Archives, Jung Collection, Box 41, Folder 2—letter to the editor of the *New York Times* urging repeal of the McCarran Act, June 5, 1951; Yeshiva University Archives, Jung Collection, Box 41, Folder 1—letter from John B. Thompson, dean of the Rockefeller Memorial Chapel at the University of Chicago, December 11, 1950, requesting that Rabbi Jung become a leader in the opposition to this bill.

44 Yeshiva University Archives, Jung Collection, Box 41, Folder 2 (photocopied letters)—letter to the editor of the *New York Times* for Rabbi Jung, Carey Williams, and Olive O. Van Horne, December 14, 1951, and copy of letter in the *New York Times*, "Repeal of Subversives Bill Urged," June 6, 1951.

fight to have the Act repealed. Rabbi Jung recalled in his autobiography that the outright repeal of the Act was urged by 1,200 prominent Americans, among whom were several rabbis.[45] On the stationery of the National Committee to Repeal the McCarran Act, the only rabbi who appeared was Rabbi Jung.[46] There is no evidence to show that the Jewish community disapproved of Rabbi Jung's activity, although the majority of Jewish leaders kept their voices still, as they were anxious to appear to be loyal Americans and anti-Communists.

The McCarran Act led to the Permanent Subcommittee on Investigations, chaired by Senator Joseph McCarthy and the era known as "McCarthyism." The RCA, in 1954, joined the chorus of religious voices critical of Senator McCarthy and his proposal to investigate the churches. The RCA conference in 1954 passed anti-McCarthy resolutions; the theme of the conference was "Challenges to Religious Freedoms."[47] The resolutions asserted the RCA's disapproval of McCarthy's activities and its willingness to be involved. The RCA protested as a group; not many individual members took up the fight on their own.[48] Rabbi Jung's involvement and that of the RCA showed courage and are examples of Modern Orthodoxy's interest in the broader community, in the social issues of the day, and in vigilance in maintaining a fertile environment for religion.

The 1950s was a time of patriotism, and Rabbi Jung was caught up in the tide of enthusiasm. Rabbi Jung's speeches in the 1950s were inspirational and patriotic.[49] He stated: "My pulpit has taught Washington on its highest level as an echo of Mount Sinai and as a

---

45 Jung, *The Path of a Pioneer*, 265.
46 Yeshiva University Archives, Jung Collection, Box 41, Folder 2—letter to Rabbi Jung from Olive O. Van Horne, Secretary of National Committee to Repeal the McCarran Act, May 7, 1951.
47 L. Bernstein, *Challenge and Mission*, 188–189.
48 Ibid., 186.
49 Yeshiva University Archives, Jung Collection, Box 41, Folder 2—letter to Mr. Arthur LeVine, February 12, 1951; Yeshiva University Archives, Jung Collection, Box 49, Folder 2—copy of *New York Times*, January 4, 1953, "Destiny of Nation Put To Individual."

Rabbi Jung and President Truman. Courtesy of Anne Etra, granddaughter of Rabbi Jung

partial fulfillment of the divine promise."[50] For Rabbi Jung, America encouraged the development of group culture. In the 1950s, Rabbi Jung hoped that the Jew recognized that one's major contribution to America and the highest expression of one's patriotism must come from searching for and living up to the Jewish tradition. Thus, he promoted observance of religion as being a good American.

Zionism

In the 1950s, there was a very positive identification with Zionism by American Jews. In the 1930s and 1940s, anti-Semitism had been an important cause of the spread of Zionism. However, the Jewish people saw the advent of the State of Israel in 1948 as a return to their self-affirmation as Jews. The State of Israel gave Jews collective pride, and helped reverse the trend to assimilation.[51] According to Herberg, the antireligious, socialist Zionist, or Yiddish cultural Jews, lost heart as their cause no longer seemed relevant. There still remained some devoted to this cause, however.[52]

In particular, the State of Israel had very positive ramifications for Modern Orthodoxy. Orthodox Jews saw Israel as a means of preserving Torah Judaism. There was a realization that it was easier in Israel than elsewhere to incorporate Jewish laws and philosophy into one's life. Dr. Eliezer Berkovits wrote: "...The State of Israel itself points to the adequate place for Jewish living, the natural home of Judaism."[53] The Chief Rabbinate in Israel enjoyed exclusive jurisdiction in religious matters; that fanned the hope in Orthodox circles of overcoming the division in American synagogues by uniting it in obedience to the Chief Rabbinate in Jerusalem. Orthodox Jews saw the Israeli Chief Rabbi as a unifier. The analogy was made that the Chief Rabbi would be like the Pope for the Catholics. Rabbi Israel Tabak (the head of the RCA), Samuel Belkin (the president of Yeshiva University), and others

---

50 Yeshiva University Archives, Jung Collection, Box 41, Folder 2—letter to Mr. Arthur LeVine, February 12, 1951.
51 Herberg, "The Postwar Revival of the Synagogue," 316.
52 Will Herberg, "The Triple Melting Pot," *Commentary* 20, no. 2 (August 1955): 498.
53 Eliezer Berkovits, "Jewish Living in America," *Judaism* 2, no. 1 (Winter 1953): 73.

endorsed this idea, but it naturally did not appeal to Conservative and Reform leaders, nor to nonmodern Orthodox elements.[54] Though many Orthodox Jews saw the Chief Rabbi as a unifying force for Orthodox Jewry in America, this unity certainly did not eventuate, as different Orthodox factions remained with their different ideologies intact.[55]

American Modern Orthodoxy became heavily involved in a new aspect of work regarding Israel—lobbying congressmen and senators to plead for Israel's rights.[56] Israel was important and needed defending in any way possible. During the 1956 war known as the Suez War, or the Sinai Campaign, Egypt sealed off the Israeli port of Eilat, effectively stopping Israel's sea trade with much of Africa and the Far East. In response to this violation of international agreements, Israel launched a military operation in 1956. As well, Egypt's nationalization of the Suez Canal threatened British and French interests in oil supplies and trade, thus they launched their own campaign. United States government officials, caught by surprise, were upset that Britain, France, and Israel had secretly planned the campaign and had not informed them. The United States campaigned to force Israel to withdraw from the areas it had conquered; the campaign included a threat to discontinue all United States assistance, to impose United Nations (UN) sanctions, and to expel Israel from the UN. One reason Israel complied was that it received assurance from the United States that it would maintain the freedom of navigation in the waterway; in addition, Washington sponsored a UN resolution creating the United Nations Emergency Force to supervise the territories vacated by Israeli forces.[57] Rabbi Jung, as one of the leaders of Orthodox Jewry, wrote to John Foster Dulles, United States Secretary of State, to appeal for American assistance for Israel in the 1956 war. Rabbi Jung wrote: "I know that the overwhelming majority of my co-religionists are profoundly disturbed as I am about the failure of our government to assist Israel in her hour of great

---

54 Herberg, "The Postwar Revival of the Synagogue," 320.
55 L. Bernstein, *Challenge and Mission*, 130.
56 Ibid., 225.
57 Maurice D. Atkin, "United States of America—Relations with Israel," *Encylopaedia Judaica* (Jerusalem: Keter Publishing House Jerusalem Ltd., 1972), vol. 15, 1666.

4. MODERN ORTHODOXY IN THE 1950S

danger."[58] The relationship of Israel's leaders with American leaders eventually became a closer one as they realized that both of their democratic countries needed each other; it was important to note that Modern Orthodox leaders played a key role in this process.

Rabbi Jung was intimately involved with the Israeli leaders and with what was going on in Israel. Prime Minister Ben-Gurion of the Mapai party, later called the Labor Party, was interested in Rabbi Jung's article in *Israel of Tomorrow*, which pointed out that Jewish law had always been labor minded. Rabbi Jung showed in this article how religious and labor ideals went together; Ben-Gurion was particularly interested that Jewish law stressed labor practices. Chief Rabbi Isaac Herzog enlisted Rabbi Jung's help to secure Sabbath observance in Israel. Rabbi Jung was able to help Rabbi Herzog restore Sabbath observance at the Hadera Paper Mills as the owner, Mr. Mazer, was a Jewish Center congregant. Rabbi Herzog had hoped that this example would prevent more Sabbath desecration.[59]

At the request of the president of the Jewish Agency for Israel, Nahum Goldmann, Rabbi Jung was on the Advisory Committee on Cultural Applications, which arose from the conference on Jewish Material Claims Against Germany. It worked for the cultural rehabilitation of Jewish victims of Nazi persecution and for the restoration of cultural treasures destroyed by the Nazis. The committee was made up of representatives of various cultural trends. Rabbi Jung served on the committee with Professor Salo W. Baron (who was the chairman), Dr. Belkin, Dr. Louis Finkelstein, Dr. Oscar Handlin, Dr. Abraham Sachar, Rabbi Leo Baeck, Rabbi Israel Brodie (Chief Rabbi of Great Britain and the Commonwealth), and Rabbi Jacob Kaplan (Chief Rabbi of France).[60] Rabbi Jung's presence, as well as Belkin's, once again

---

58 Yeshiva University Archives, Jung Collection, Box 41, Folder 1—letter to the Honorable John Foster Dulles, from Rabbi Jung, February 9, 1956.
59 Yeshiva University Archives, Jung Collection, Box 10, Folder 1: Letter from Rabbi Isaac Herzog (Chief Rabbi of Israel) to Rabbi Jung, September 22, 1957; letter to Rabbi Jung, October 24, 1957, from Sarah Herzog; letter to Rabbi Herzog, October 3, 1957.
60 Yeshiva University Archives, Jung Collection, Box 40, Folder 3: Letters to Rabbi Jung from Dr. Nahum Goldmann, President of Israel, December 11, 1953; letter to

ensured that Modern Orthodox perspectives would be included, and demonstrated that American Modern Orthodoxy was playing an important role.

Examples of the Movement to the Right

Return to Halakhah

The movement to the right was exemplified by a return to *halakhic* creativity and interest, which began in the 1940s. Orthodoxy was concerned in the 1950s with the difficulty of resolving questions of Jewish law along traditional and authentic lines, while at the same time adapting *halakhah* to new situations and conditions.[61] While change within *halakhah* is unthinkable, creativity is essential. Rabbi Rackman illustrated how the responsa by Rabbis Soloveitchik and Menahem M. Kasher "reveal the vitality of the *halakhah* for the resolutions of uniquely modern problems."[62] However, it should be noted that Conservative Judaism was also calling for a return to *halakhah* and that the Conservatives did generally remain within *halakhah* as they defined it. Solomon Simon wrote in his article, "A Renewed *Halakhah*," that "there were times when it was necessary to stand up against an inflexible *halakhah*, but at the present moment it is necessary to return to *halakhah*."[63] Simon's article was published in the journal *Judaism*, edited by the prominent Conservative rabbi and scholar, Robert Gordis. Marshall Sklare, in his book *Conservative Judaism: An American Religious Movement*, talked about working out a more consistent pattern of observance and a desire to raise standards.[64] In past decades, the key challenges for Modern Orthodoxy had been to discuss and impress upon the Jewish population issues of Sabbath observance, adherence to family law, and some basic knowledge of Judaism. This challenge

---

Goldmann from Rabbi Jung, December 14, 1953.
61 Jacob Sloan, "Communal Affairs," Religion, *American Jewish Year Book* 58 (1957): 154; Solomon J. Sharfman, Forward, *Tradition* 1, no. 1 (Fall 1958): 5–6.
62 Rackman, "Orthodox Judaism Moves With the Times," 549–550.
63 Solomon Simon, "A Renewed Halakhah," *Judaism* 3, no. 1 (Winter 1954): 52.
64 Sklare, *Conservative Judaism*, 154, 215, and 224.

Rav Soloveitchik with students. 1960-s. Courtesy of Yeshiva University Archives

remained, but added was discussion of the role of the Torah, *halakhah*, and observance of the other *mitzvot*.

Rabbi Soloveitchik, chairman of the *Halakhic* Committee of the RCA, was by the 1950s very influential as a spokesman for American-style Orthodoxy; his worldview was based on *halakhah*.[65] The *Halakhic* Committee in the first 25 years of the RCA had two distinct periods, the Levy and Soloveitchik eras. The Soloveitchik period brought to the RCA and to Orthodoxy greater prestige, and the greatest growth occurred in the 1950s.[66] The increased interest in *halakhic* discourse on the part of rabbinic students is demonstrated by the packed attendance at Rabbi Soloveitchik's *halakhic* addresses. His words set precedents, and this exchange provided inspiration for rabbis, who went out to disseminate his message throughout the

---

65 Seth Farber, "Reproach, Recognition and Respect: Rabbi Joseph B. Soloveitchik and Orthodoxy's Mid-Century Attitude Toward Non-Orthodox Denominations," *American Jewish History* 89, no. 2 (June 2001): 193.
66 L. Bernstein, *Challenge and Mission*, 71.

United States. His message was that *halakhah* offered an approach towards the social, economic, and political problems that confronted society; *halakhah* was the principal of intellectual activity and was a guide in forming a well-regulated life. Rabbi Soloveitchik volunteered to speak on *halakhah* before the Jewish New Year at Yeshiva University. This became a very important annual event in New York's Torah life.[67]

The microphone was an issue that was finally resolved in the 1950s. Rabbi Simcha Levy had ruled that it could be used, which tested the authority of the RCA's *Halakhic* Committee, as many Agudath Harabbonim members and *roshei yeshiva* had banned the use of the microphone.[68] The RCA was being challenged. Then, as Louis Bernstein wrote, came the anti-climax. Rabbi Soloveitchik, at a Detroit convention in 1954, ruled against the use of a microphone on the Sabbath on *halakhic* grounds.[69] It can be deduced that the Agudath Harabbonim and *roshei yeshiva* had some influence in this case. Jonathan D. Sarna claims that the extreme position of the Agudath Harabbonim led to the middle ground of an American Orthodoxy and that the separation of Conservative and Orthodoxy owed a considerable amount to the uncompromising stance of Agudath Harrabonim rabbis.[70] The banning of the microphone was another issue that distinguished Modern Orthodoxy from the Conservative movement.

Orthodoxy made efforts to defend traditional Judaism and made issues of such matters as the *mehitzah*.[71] The *mehitzah* became a definer of Orthodox communal norms by the second half of the 1950s.[72] On the question of the *mehitzah*, Rabbi Mordecai Lewittes, an attendee at a UOJCA meeting, said that it was an unquestionable necessity, but it did not "have to reach the ceiling."[73] Two issues were present in that

---

67 Ibid., 28.
68 Ibid., 40.
69 Ibid., 41.
70 Jonathan D. Sarna, *American Judaism* (New Haven, CT and London: Yale University Press, 2004), 191–193.
71 Glazer, "The Jewish Revival in America, II," 19.
72 L. Bernstein, *Challenge and Mission*, 138.
73 Yeshiva University Archives—"UOJCA Will Seek to Establish Discipline of Orthodox Jewish Life and Education," 4.

declaration. Though Orthodoxy had always maintained that a *mehitzah* was a requirement, it was not until the 1950s that the discussion became a central focus of the divisions between the Modern Orthodox and Conservative movements. Only when the Reform movement removed the *mehitzah* were there *responsa* written requiring a *mehitzah*.[74] Added to the discussion was the necessary height of the *mehitzah*. In Norma Joseph's article, "Mechitza: Halakchic Decisions and Political Consequences," she noted that Rabbi Moses Feinstein felt that a minimum standard regarding the height of the *mehitzah* was not adequate and that it was best to have a high *mehitzah*.[75] The height of the *mehitzah* would also distinguish Modern Orthodoxy from traditional or Hasidic Orthodoxy. One important resolution adopted at this convention was that Orthodox Jews were not to be allowed to worship in Conservative and Reform synagogues. The lack of a *mehitzah* was a major reason for this decision.[76] Again, this is seen as a more definite and more stringent approach.

The *mehitzah* was not only a contentious issue between the Modern Orthodox and traditional Orthodox, as the latter had never compromised on this issue. It was a divisive issue between the Conservative and Orthodox movements, and in the 1950s, it became another defining moment for Modern Orthodox Judaism.[77]

The *mehitzah* was not a new issue; the 1940s had pointed to the direction that Modern Orthodoxy would take. However, it was not until the 1950s that the debate became a big issue, as there was confrontation between the Orthodox and Conservative movements over control of important Orthodox synagogues, some of which were defecting to Conservative Judaism. Sklare reported that an overwhelming majority of Conservative synagogues had mixed pews.[78] RCA members had offici-

---

74 Norma Baumel Joseph, "Mechitzah: Halakhic Decisions and Political Consequences," in *Daughters of the King: Woman and the Synagogue*, eds. Susan Grossman and Rivka Haut (Philadelphia, New York, and Jerusalem: The Jewish Publication Society, 1992), 118. Norma B. Joseph is a professor of religion at Concordia University.
75 Ibid., 125.
76 Yeshiva University Archives—"UOJCA Will Seek To Establish Discipline of Orthodox Life and Education," 4; Joseph, "Mechitzah," 126.
77 Ibid., 128.
78 Sklare, *Conservative Judaism*, 88.

ated in synagogues with mixed pews, permitted only if they worked to have that situation changed; this situation came to an end.[79]

Jeffrey S. Gurock pointed out that the separation of the Conservative and Orthodox movements was a slow process that began in the 1920s, and that there was not one single moment along the way when the separation took place.[80] However, the *mehitzah* became a symbol in the struggle between the Orthodox and Conservative ideologies, as well as a focus of controversy and agitation. According to Norma Joseph, the conflict was political, though couched in legal terms. The issue was not only to keep men separate from women in the synagogue, but also to keep Orthodox Jews separate from Conservative and Reform Jews.[81]

As discussed, the UOJCA had adopted a resolution that a *mehitzah* was a necessity. The RCA had played a leading role in cooperation with the UOJCA in the fight against mixed pews.[82]

Rabbi Feinstein wrote 14 *responsa* in his book of *responsa* (*Igrot Moshe*) about the *mehitzah*, arguing that the *mehitzah* was a biblical law rather than a rabbinic enactment.[83] As biblical law or Torah law was most authoritative, this accentuated how important the *mehitzah* was considered to be. The Modern Orthodox rabbis, headed by Rabbi Solomon J. Sharfman, president of the RCA, ruled against mixed pews.[84] Rabbi Norman Lamm declared that the *mehitzah* was not a custom, but a *halakhah*. He wrote that rabbis of the last generation, such as Rabbi Israel Meir Hakohen (also known as the Hafetz Hayyim) and Chief Rabbi Avraham Yitzhak Kook, had upheld this *halakhah*, and that contemporary rabbis, such as Rabbi Herzog of Israel, Dr. Belkin, and Rabbi Soloveitchik, also affirmed the law. Rabbi Lamm felt that the debate reflected on the validity of the Jewish tradition and its survival intact in the modern world.[85]

---

79 L. Bernstein, *Challenge and Mission*, 140.
80 Personal interview with Jeffrey S. Gurock, December 17, 1996.
81 Joseph, "Mechitzah," 131.
82 L. Bernstein, *Challenge and Mission*, 138.
83 Joseph, "Mechitzah," 120.
84 Arthur Hertzberg, "Communal Affairs," Religion, *American Jewish Year Book* 59 (1958): 119.
85 Norman Lamm, "Separate Pews in the Synagogue: A Social and Psychological Approach," *Tradition* 1, no. 2 (Spring 1959): 141.

The Conservative movement had maintained that the *mehitzah* was not an essential requirement. From the Orthodox point of view, this stance was considered illegitimate, and Rabbi Feinstein wrote that one must not pray in a non-Orthodox synagogue or in a synagogue without a *mehitzah*.[86] As already discussed, Rabbi Soloveitchik was in agreement. The attention given to this *halakhic* detail and imposed strictness was one example of a movement to the right. The *mehitzah* was one barometer that the Modern Orthodox synagogue was moving to the right.

In the 1950s, the Orthodox had to address the women's issue; its opponents made an accusation that separation gave women inferior status and that husbands and wives worshipping next to each other make for better families.[87] In 1959, Rabbi Lamm said that the opposite occurred; confusion in roles had led to divorce and juvenile delinquency. Therefore, separation of roles reinforced the family and was good from a social and psychological point of view. Rabbi Lamm wrote that women who wanted equality in seating should also have to take on all the men's duties prescribed by Jewish law—all the synagogue duties as well as the spiritual duties. This was a weak argument, because some women were indeed ready to do this. Rabbi Lamm made another argument when he wrote that equality in value did not mean equality in function and that mixed seating represented a "pagan-Christianization of the synagogue."[88] What was significant was that Modern Orthodoxy's new leadership was forced to defend their *halakhic* Jewish attitude towards women and to think about the role of women in Judaism.

Definite decisions were made; the movement had come a long way since the 1930s when Rabbi Jung had asked Rabbi Jacob Agus to research the question of the *mehitzah*. However, the Jewish Center Synagogue always had a *mehitzah* even if it was not high enough for some traditional Orthodox. Rabbi Lamm told of one rabbi who used to come to the synagogue on Friday nights to pray, but never on Saturday morning. Rabbi Lamm later found out that it was because the *mehitzah*

---

86 Joseph, "Mechitzah," 126.
87 Lamm, "Separate Pews in the Synagogue," 146–151.
88 Ibid.

was not high enough for him and that, at that time, there were no women on Friday nights, thus he felt able to come then.[89]

Conservative Bet Din and Ketubbah: Another Example of the Widening Gap Between Conservative and Orthodox Judaism

As Orthodoxy became more concerned with *halakhic* integrity and as the Conservative movement did not shy away from issues that alienated the Orthodox movement, the gap between Conservative and Orthodox Judaism widened. The rejection by the Orthodox of the Conservative *ketubbah* (marriage agreement) is another example. The *ketubbah* is related to the *agunah* issue. It was set up to restrict the husband's absolute power to divorce or not divorce his wife. The Conservative movement established its own *bet din* (court) and introduced its own *ketubbah*. In 1954, Professor Saul Lieberman of the Conservative Jewish Theological Seminary (JTS) introduced a new clause to the Conservative *ketubbah*, amending the traditional *ketubbah* text. As part of the Conservative *ketubbah*, couples agreed to turn to the Rabbinical Assembly *bet din* and accept its ruling in cases of divorce.[90] Professor Lieberman maintained that the civil courts could uphold the *bet din* decision if the husband did not accept the *bet din* ruling. Lieberman's proposal was rejected by the Orthodox rabbinate for many reasons. The Orthodox discredited the competence of the religious Conservative court, as they felt that Conservative rabbis were not qualified to make *halakhic* decisions. A non-Orthodox *bet din* was not acceptable, and civil courts could not enforce the *ketubbah*, which was viewed as a religious document. Added to the critique was that the amendment had no bearing on the *agunah* whose husband had disappeared or was missing in military action, it did not discourage frivolous divorces, and it could force unwilling spouses to consent to divorce.[91]

---

89 Personal interview with Lamm, January 16, 2003.
90 L. Bernstein, *Challenge and Mission*, 192.
91 Lamm, "Religious Additions to the Ketuba: A Halakhic Critique," *Tradition*, 2, no. 1 (Fall 1959); Aaron Rakeffet-Rothkoff, *The Silver Era in American Jewish Orthodoxy: Rabbi Eliezer Silver and His Generation* (New York: Yeshiva University Press; Jerusalem: Feldheim Publishers, 1981), 295.

These issues united the Orthodox factions and served to accentuate and clarify the line of demarcation between Orthodox and Conservative.⁹² Orthodox leaders agreed that the problem had to be solved by genuine *halakhic* means. Rabbi Lamm commented that nothing concrete emerged on the part of Orthodoxy to solve this problem, which he felt was a failing of Orthodoxy in general.⁹³

Rabbi Jung did attempt to become more involved in the area of *halakhah*. Asking questions concerning Jewish law and answering those questions, called *responsa*, became more important in the 1950s. Rabbi Jung sponsored an annual *halakhic* volume, *Noam* ("Grace"); he assumed financial responsibility, with help from Samuel C. Feuerstein and Max Stern. Jehiel Jacob Weinberg—the last rector of the Hildesheimer Rabbinical School, a victim of Hitler, and a resident of Montreux, Switzerland—was his consultant on several issues. Rabbi Jung chose Rabbi Kasher and his son Rabbi Moshe Shlomo Kasher to do the major work, but Rabbi Jung was involved in both method and approach.⁹⁴ *Noam* dealt with modern questions such as artificial insemination, autopsy, transplants, and the problem of the *agunah*, some of which were controversial issues. Rabbi Jung commented on this major difficulty, as follows:

> There was a double difficulty to overcome: One, a certain unwillingness on the part of some Torah authorities to deal with these, to them, unusual and too delicate questions; and there was the additional primary need to get absolutely authoritative opinions and decisions.⁹⁵

The series included 19 annual volumes. The first volume appeared in 1957; the tenth volume contained an index of hundreds of *responsa* that had brought the laws of Torah up to date. *Noam* included the writings of Rabbis Joseph Elijah Henkin, Feinstein, Weinberg, Kasher, and the Chief Rabbis of Israel. Rabbi Lamm commented:

---

92 L. Bernstein, *Challenge and Mission*, 134 and 138.
93 Personal interview with Lamm, January 16, 2003.
94 Jung, *The Path of a Pioneer*, 126–130.
95 Ibid., 127.

Noam was very important and it dealt with very important issues, but for some reason it did not have the resonance of the *halakhic* community that it deserved. Most people, if you refer to *Noam*, won't know what you are talking about. The idea was Jung's and he raised the money for it. It was a major contribution by Jung.[96]

Rabbi Jung got Rabbi Kasher—a great scholar of rabbinical thought and literature, the editor of *Torah Shleima*, and a writer of *responsa*—and his son to collect and edit these *responsa*. Rabbi Jung had written about what a "master mind" Rabbi Kasher was and praised his commentary on the Torah in the *Jewish Forum* in January 1927.[97] Rabbi Jung appointed three committees—one composed of three physicists, one composed of three lawyers, and one composed of three physicians—that were to study the questions addressed to the sages before submitting them, to make sure that the scientific material was free from inaccuracies or other flaws.

Rabbi Jung wanted his mentor, Rabbi Weinberg, to write a volume on the *agunah*, an issue that had always caused him pain. He felt that he needed an authority who was courageous enough to undertake this. Rabbi Jung wrote:

> I begged Dr. Weinberg to write such a thesis, telling him that it would immortalize his name not only as a profound scholar, but as a benefactor of the most sorely afflicted human being in the camp of Israel, the *agunah*.[98]

Rabbi Weinberg, because of his poor health, recommended his best student, Dr. Eliezer Berkovits, of the Hebrew Theological College in Chicago, to do this.[99] According to Rabbi Jung, he himself encouraged and financed Berkovits to write a volume on the history and elucidation

---

[96] Personal interview with Lamm, January 16, 2003.
[97] Rabbi Jung, "M. M. Kasher's Torah Sh'lemah: A Brief Appreciation," *Jewish Forum* 10, no. 1 (January 1927): 79.
[98] Jung, *The Path of a Pioneer*, 129.
[99] Yeshiva University Archives, Jung Collection, Box 13, Folder 8—letter to Lamm from Berkovits, undated but in the box with mail from the 1970s.

4. MODERN ORTHODOXY IN THE 1950S

of the *halakhic* problems involved with the *agunah*.[100] In his writing, Berkovits argued in favor of a certain form of conditional marriage that would eliminate the possibility of a woman becoming an *agunah* because of her husband's refusal to grant a divorce. Rabbi Weinberg seemed to approve of Berkovits's suggestion, but in the end, Rabbi Weinberg refused to support Berkovits. Rabbi Jung remarked:

> It was at a time when Dr. Berkovits had finished his book which the Gaon had cordially endorsed that some unknown rabbi upset [Rabbi] Weinberg's peace of mind and made him retract his enthusiastic endorsement of Dr. Berkovits' opus. It was originally supposed to have appeared in one of the volumes of *Noam*.[101]

Marc B. Shapiro, in his biography of Rabbi Weinberg, suggested that the latter never changed his mind but was fearful of approving the suggestion and did not want to get involved, as this issue of "conditional marriage" was a major point of dispute between the Conservative and Orthodox movements. Also, Shapiro raised the possibility that Weinberg sent one letter of approval to Rabbi Jung, as he felt that Rabbi Jung supported this type of *halakhic* approach, and another to Rabbi Kasher, who he felt might not approve. Berkovits said that, according to Rabbi Jung, Rabbi Kasher had written to him saying that he was very pleased with Berkovits's manuscript, but then, later on, he had second thoughts, saying that it was Rabbi Weinberg who had objections. Berkovits, however, did not believe this to be true.[102] Rabbi Kasher did not want the article included in *Noam* partially because of fear of the religious right.[103]

---

100 Jung, *The Path of a Pioneer*, 129.
101 Ibid., 129-130.
102 Yeshiva University Archives, Jung Collection, Box 13, Folder 8—letter to Lamm from Berkovits (undated).
103 Marc B. Shapiro, *Between The Yeshiva World and Modern Orthodoxy: The Life and Works of Jehiel Jacob Weinberg, 1884–1966* (Oxford, UK, and Portland, OR: The Littman Library of Jewish Civilization, 1999), 190-191. Berkovits's work, "Concerning Conditional Marriage," ultimately appeared in Hebrew (*Tenai be Nissuin v' Get*) in 1966 as a publication of the Mossad ha-Rav Kook, Jerusalem.

This is an example that some Modern Orthodox leaders feared, and they gave into the more right-wing rabbinic authorities. At the same time, they were worried about the perception that they were allied with the Conservative movement in any way. The Modern Orthodox movement wanted to define itself with respect to Conservative Judaism. The leaders wanted no overlaps with the Conservative movement; yet, at the same time, they created blurred lines with the more right-wing traditional Orthodox movements, and also created factions in Modern Orthodoxy.

Rabbi Jung stood firm in his judgment and opinion. He showed courage and willingness to tackle difficult issues and to try to implement what he felt "Torah Judaism" stood for. Rabbi Oscar Fasman, the president of the Hebrew Theological College and a pulpit rabbi for almost 35 years in Skokie, Illinois, supported Rabbi Jung. Rabbi Jung felt that the problem of the *agunah* could not be evaded, and hoped that "the suggestions of the brilliant scholar, Dr. Berkovits, would lead to an alleviation of the *agunah* all over the world."[104] However, most Modern Orthodox leaders still showed timidity or caution when it came to *halakhic* change or interpretation, and were not ready to face what they considered uncomfortable problems. Norman Lamm agreed that the handling of the *agunah* issue "is a failing of Orthodoxy in general."[105]

The project was in the hands of great people; according to Lamm, Rabbi Weinberg was very much a Torah personality and giant. However, one cannot help noticing the absence of Rabbi Soloveitchik. The fact that Rabbi Soloveitchik, chairman of the *Halakhic* Committee of the RCA, did not contribute to *Noam* is somewhat curious. Rabbi Soloveitchik already had a reputation as a major *halakhic* scholar and major philosopher for *halakhic* problems; yet Rabbi Jung still referred to Rabbi Weinberg in Europe for his questions and aid in his *halakhic* journal. Perhaps this is why, as Lamm said, the series did not have as much success, popularity, or recognition as it deserved. No records have been found to shed light on the reason for Rabbi Soloveitchik's lack of participation, thus one can only surmise why *Noam* did not include the new American *halakhic* leadership,

---

104 Jung, *The Path of a Pioneer*, 129.
105 Personal interview with Lamm, January 16, 2003.

the new generation of rabbis. Rabbi Jung knew Rabbi Weinberg from Switzerland, as Rabbi Jung's in-laws were from there and he visited regularly, thus it was understandable that he referred to Rabbi Weinberg. It could be said that Rabbi Jung was not supportive of the new leadership of Modern Orthodoxy; he had voted for Rabbi Chaim Heller, not Rabbi Soloveitchik, as the chairman of the *Halakhic* Committee, or perhaps the new leadership was not supportive of Rabbi Jung. Rosalie Rosenfeld, Rabbi Jung's daughter, wrote: "So far as I know, my father had no relationship with the Soloveitchiks."[106] The fact that Rabbi Soloveitchik did not publish in *Noam* speaks to that lack of relationship. It is an example of the fact that Rabbi Jung was not considered a prime *halakhic* scholar.

Rabbi Jung's Philosophy

Rabbi Jung's philosophy and theme in the 1950s became less secular and more based in Jewish law than before, and he articulated his belief that the core of Jewish living was *kedushah*, which means "holiness." For Rabbi Jung, *kedushah* came from following the *halakhah*. This reflected a new emphasis on *halakhah*. In previous decades, Rabbi Jung had stressed ethics, morality, and human decency; in the 1950s, he stressed that these came from following the *halakhah*. In the 1950s, reverence, righteousness, and *rahmanut* (which he referred to as the three "R's" of *kedushah*) applied to many things, including married love.[107] Reverence for God and man was essential to ensure righteousness or justice, personal worth, and human dignity. Rabbi Jung wrote:

> The key to Judaism is "*kedushah*" (holiness), the endeavor to plant heaven on earth through divine values. Religion as such is co-extensive with life, holding us close to God. It may be neither divorced from life, nor divorced from God. The Hebrew term *kedushah* appears in connection with every

---

[106] Rosalie Rosenfeld (Rabbi Jung's daughter), letter dated October 7, 1997, answering questions sent to her by Maxine Jacobson. In the possession of Jacobson.

[107] Yeshiva University Archives, Jung Collection, Box 48, Folder 3 (published articles)—"The Three R's of Married Love," *Jewish News* 61, no. 36, Denver, Colorado, September 9, 1954.

aspect of Jewishness, from marriage to business, from dietary laws to the laws of mourning... I would fain say of holiness within the Jewish scheme of life that it is composed of three "R's": Reverence, Righteousness and, for the moment unexplained, *Rahmanut*... The crowning quality is *Rahmanut* for which there is as yet no word in the English language. *Rahmanut* is usually translated as "mercy" or "compassion" but etymologically it means "mother's love"—the unselfish dedicated love of a mother for her little one, her passionate desire to spend herself... for the purpose of raising her baby from helpless infancy towards self-sufficient maturity.[108]

His concept of *kedushah* is that it "amounted to a total program for a noble, wise, and generous life."[109] The sixth and seventh volumes of the First Series of the Jewish Library, *Jewish Leaders* and *Guardians of our Heritage*, respectively, are about the teachings and judgments of selected Jewish scholars. Rabbi Jung felt that these teachings and judgments stemmed from *kedushah*.[110]

Education

There were signs of revival in Jewish education in America, for which assumptions had been made that Torah learning and observances were relics of the past. There was a greater demand for intensive religious education in the 1950s as there was more interest in religion and efforts to reach the youth were expanded.[111] There was greater emphasis on all-day education programs as opposed to afternoon schools.[112] Identification with the Jewish religion led to Jewish education, which was seen as a good thing

---

108 Yeshiva University Archives, Jung Collection, Box 48, Folder 3 (published articles)—Jung, "Kiddushah," Thought of the Week, *Torah Vodaath*, April 19, 1957.
109 Rabbi Jung, ed., *Jewish Leaders: 1750–1940*, Jewish Library, First Series, vol. 6 (Jerusalem: Boys Town Jerusalem Publishers, 1953 and 1964), 5.
110 Ibid.
111 Morris N. Kertzer, "Communal Affairs," Religion, *American Jewish Year Book* 56 (1955): 233.
112 Ibid., 236.

for Jewish survival.[113] The reverse was also true; the revival of Judaism was in part due to increased concern for Jewish education, which laid the groundwork for the movement to the right. Glazer wrote that Orthodoxy showed new vigor, particularly in its all-day schools; the number of Jewish children getting some kind of Jewish education increased. Only one who appreciates Judaism can be led to practice it; thus, Jewish education played a big role in the movement to the right. More children were being sent to parochial schools, and almost all of the parochial schools were conducted under Orthodox auspices, imposing Orthodox religious observances.[114] Sklare noted that it was the Orthodox movement, not the Conservative movement, that had promoted the all-day school.[115]

The Torah Umesorah movement, a national agency for the founding of day schools, spearheaded building new schools and developed educational programs for children and parents.[116] Although initiated in the 1940s, the movement made headway in the 1950s. In several cities, the day school began with groups of Yeshiva students canvassing from door to door to sign up new students. Joseph Kaminetsky, who received a doctorate from Columbia Teacher's College, was educational director of the Jewish Center Synagogue from 1934 to 1946, and he wrote "Model Program for the Talmud Torah" with Rabbi Jung. He helped develop the Torah Umesorah day school movement that was originally begun by Rabbi Shraga Feivel Mendlowitz.[117] Kaminetsky headed the movement from 1945 until 1980. He went from community to community to sell the idea of the Jewish day school, as still more parents needed to be encouraged to send their children to parochial schools. Kaminetsky tried to see that there would be a day school in every Jewish community.[118]

---

113 Herberg, "The Postwar Revival of the Synagogue," 317.
114 Glazer, "The Jewish Revival in America, I," 495.
115 Sklare, *Conservative Judaism*, 156.
116 Jewish Synagogue Center Archives—*Jewish Center Bulletin*, December 8, 1950.
117 Alexander Gross and Joseph Kaminetsky, "Shraga Feivel Mendlowitz," in *Men of the Spirit*, ed. Leo Jung (New York: Kymson Publication Company, 1964), 571 and 717.
118 Jonathan Rosenblum, Rosenblum's Columns, "Dr. Joe, we owe you," *Jerusalem Post*, March 26, 1999, Jewish Media Resources, http://www.jewishmediaresources.com/198/dr-joe-we-owe-you.

New day schools opened under Torah Umesorah auspices, resulting in a shortage of teachers. Well-trained teachers were a prerequisite for good schools; Torah Umesorah thus established a board of license to standardize requirements for teaching certificates. Kaminetsky, in the article "Spiritual Values for Our Children" (which appeared in the *Jewish Center Synagogue Bulletin*), said that "the day school movement has made tremendous strides in the last decade."[119]

Parents sent their children to the day schools for various reasons. Public schools were overcrowded, *yeshiva* education was now more modern and progressive, and the school buildings were more physically attractive than they had previously been. Parents were not particularly religious or observant in many cases, yet the children learned Judaism and had to wear *tzitzit* (fringes) and *kippot* (skullcaps) to school. The children became more proud of their Jewish roots, and more comfortable with Jewish life, than their parents.[120] Children in parochial schools affected the parents. They often had to join the synagogue as a prerequisite. Parents incapable of answering children's questions about being Jewish soon got drawn in.[121] Looking back, Haym Soloveitchik wrote that "the hour of education arrived." Mimesis of the home was replaced by instructional and religious apprenticeship.[122]

Herberg claimed that there was a religious revival on university campuses; books on religion were read more than before, and religious speakers were invited and and their lectures attended more. The student who was looking for meaning and spiritual values could not find these examples in the previous generation.[123]

---

119 Jewish Synagogue Center Archives—*Jewish Center Synagogue Bulletin*, December 8, 1950.
120 Harold U. Ribalow, "My Child Goes to Parochial School," *Commentary* 17, no. 1 (January 1954): 64–65.
121 Glazer, "The Jewish Revival in America, I," 497.
122 Soloveitchik, "Rupture and Reconstruction," 91.
123 Will Herberg, "The Religious Stirring on the Campus," *Commentary* 13, no. 3 (March 1952): 244.

Yeshiva University

Yeshiva University extended its scope and activities. Rabbi Jung still worked closely with the president of Yeshiva University, Dr. Belkin, making recommendations and raising funds.[124] Belkin continued to struggle with the Conservative movement; however, he was able to launch a program of academic and physical expansion in the 1950s. There was increased enrollment and an increased number of faculty at Yeshiva University, as well as expanded courses of study.[125] In 1951, it was reported that the college enrollment set an all-time record, with a 17.5% increase over the previous year's student body, the largest registration since the inception of Yeshiva.[126] From 1945 to 1955, Yeshiva attracted a more homogeneous group of Orthodox students who had a Jewish educational background.

A charter was granted for the creation of a medical and dental school. This was the first medical school to be established in New York in 52 years and the first medical school in the world under Jewish auspices. The medical school opened in 1953, five years and one month after Yeshiva was elevated to university status.[127]

A definite example of the movement to the right was when RIETS instituted its own *kollel* in 1950, a place where advanced students could devote their life to Jewish learning. Gurock pointed out that this was in response to the Eastern European *yeshivot* and rabbis who had come to America after the war. The Talmudic scholar had become more attractive to the Jewish layperson, and respect for Jewish learning increased.[128]

Yeshiva University maintained its philosophy of *Torah Umadda*; religious and secular studies would be conducted under one roof. When

---

124 Yeshiva University Archives, Jung Collection, Box 1, Folder 8—letter to Dr. Samuel Belkin, president of Yeshiva University, from Rabbi Jung, May 1, 1955.
125 Yeshiva University Archives—"New School Year Sees Enrollment Up, Faculty Additions," *Yeshiva University News* 8, no. 1 (November 1950): 6.
126 Yeshiva University Archives—"College Enrollment Sees All Time High," *The Commentator* 24, no. 2 (November 1950): 1.
127 Yeshiva University Archives—"Charter Granted for Medical and Dental School—$25 Million to be Sought—Wide Acclaim Greets Plan," *Yeshiva University News* 8, no. 1 (February 1951): 1.
128 Jeffrey S. Gurock, "Resisters and Accommodators: Varieties of Orthodox Rabbis in America, 1886–1983," in *American Jewish Orthodoxy in Historical Perspective*, ed. Jeffrey S. Gurock (New York: Ktav Publishing House Inc., 1996), 66.

a debate occurred as to whether Jewish courses at the university should be mandatory, as this prevented the student from taking other secular courses, the policy was defended. Dr. Gershon Churgin stated:

> ...The purpose of this institution, as an Orthodox Jewish college, is to produce laymen well versed in the treasure of Jewish knowledge. In order to insure this aim... Jewish studies are required in the college... If we remove these courses or lessen their importance... by removing the credits... we would... be removing the necessity and purpose of Yeshiva College.[129]

Yeshiva would not accommodate any watering down of what it stood for.

The rabbinical seminary reorganized its *semikhah* program to recruit and train rabbinical students along lines that were uniquely Modern Orthodox. Talmud and codes were to be studied, and more attention was to be given to Biblical studies, homiletics, and pastoral counselling. RIETS students were required to take 90 credits in the Bernard Revel Graduate School that led to a master's of the arts in Hebrew Literature. They were to take courses in Jewish philosophy along with the history of *halakhah* and *aggadah*. Rabbinical students were also to serve as apprentices with rabbis.[130] The rabbis would be educated and knowledgeable in religious as well as secular studies, and would be equipped to be capable pulpit rabbis.

Yeshiva University was unique among Talmudic seminaries because Stern College, a college for women, was founded as part of Yeshiva University in 1954.[131] Women were to be secularly and religiously educated. This was a sign of Yeshiva's uniqueness and status, and it helped further define what Modern Orthodoxy stood for.

---

129 Yeshiva University Archives—"Required Jewish Curriculum in College Discussed by Margolith, Churgin, Arfa," *The Commentator* 24, no. 3 (November 26, 1951): 2.
130 Marc H. Tannenbaum, "Communal Affairs," Religion, *American Jewish Year Book* 60 (1959): 54.
131 William B. Helmreich, *The World of the Yeshiva: An Intimate Portrait of Orthodox Jewry* (New York: Macmillan/Free Press, 1982), 196.

Jewish Scholarship More Respected—More Reliance on the Text

Haym Soloveitchik wrote an article on the movement to the right in Orthodoxy in the 1990s, in which he looked back and gave reasons why the text became more relied on, why there was a new respect for knowledge, and why this led to stricter observance. This process began in the 1950s, gathering force in the 1960s and 1970s. Soloveitchik called this the shift from practice to text.[132] He talked of "augmented tradition" because of the loss of mimetic tradition, in which one learned by copying a living example. This loss led to reliance on texts in which "religious observance is both amplified and raised to new, rigorous heights."[133]

Soloveitchik wrote that traditional conduct yielded to the demands of theoretical knowledge. This outlook, according to Soloveitchik, began in the 1950s.[134] In a traditional society, tradition was relayed from person to person as a way of life. In America, alternatives existed, and knowledge of the Jewish way of life was far from a given. Knowledge and authority had to come from the text, not from observing religious behavior.[135] Soloveitchik called this the shift of authority to texts, which led to a desire for accuracy and stringency.[136]

The Image and Role of the Rabbi

As texts took on new importance, the desire to have them interpreted correctly also became important. The rabbi had to be a Jewish scholar, knowledgeable in Talmud.[137] It is the emphasis that the Modern Orthodox rabbi must be a scholar that is new, though there were always examples of "scholar rabbis."

The RCA rabbi represented a new type of Orthodox rabbi—dignified, English-speaking, and conversant with Torah, Talmud, the secular culture of the day, and believing in the divine origin of the law. The demand for rabbis in America in previous decades had been for good

---

132 Soloveitchik, "Rupture and Reconstruction," 4.
133 Ibid., 68.
134 Ibid., 69.
135 Ibid., 70–71.
136 Ibid., 72, 74.
137 L. Bernstein, *Challenge and Mission*, 138.

speakers, who demanded little, partook in community work, and were personally appealing. Rabbi Jung fit the criteria of that sort of rabbi, although he was always involved in scholarly endeavors. However, in the 1950s, a new image for the rabbi (along with new expectations) emerged. Dr. Nahum Glatzer wrote in 1950 that "scholar rabbis" should be men of knowledge, in addition to being able to inspire and be warm, in order to dispel the long held notion that Jewish scholarship was cold-natured.[138]

Norman Lamm said that, when he was a student in the 1940s, there were three major Modern Orthodox rabbis: Rabbis Jung, Lookstein, and Goldstein. "Joseph Lookstein was very powerful, [Leo] Jung was very dignified, and Herbert Goldstein was very involved in Zionist causes."[139] Gurock said:

> ...You had Herbert Goldstein, Joseph Lookstein and Leo Jung, not many out there that had that combination of academic training and articulate English; they were the speakers that Orthodoxy could have as poster boys. They were the spokesmen for American-style Orthodoxy. Their lay leadership was proud of them in terms of putting them out to represent Orthodoxy.[140]

However, the heroes of the generations of the 1950s and 1960s changed; the students looked to Rabbi Soloveitchik and the *roshei yeshiva*, who were expected to be expert in the religious texts and to be able to interpret them.[141] The modern Jew was turning to classical sources of Jewish life; this revived interest in classical sources demanded interpretation and explanations by scholarly rabbis.[142] The fact that

---

138 Yeshiva University Archives—"Yeshiva Men Should Inspire Community, Says Dr. Glatzer," *The Commentator* 21, no. 1 (February 27, 1950): 4.
139 Personal interview with Lamm, January 16, 2003.
140 Personal interview with Gurock, December 17, 1996.
141 Soloveitchik, "Rupture and Reconstruction," 95–96; Rakeffet-Rothkoff, *The Rav: The World of Rabbi Joseph B. Soloveitchik*, Vol. 2, ed. Joseph Epstein (Hoboken, NJ: Ktav Publishing House, 1999), 239; Bernard Rosensweig, "The Rabbinical Council of America: Retrospect and Prospect," *Tradition* 22, no. 2 (Summer 1986): 10.
142 Soloveitchik, "Rupture and Reconstruction," 94.

Rabbi Soloveitchik had such a dedicated following was seen as a strength in Modern Orthodoxy. This phenomenon was wider than just the Modern Orthodox constituency. Those who followed the *roshei yeshiva* were in the more traditional Orthodox camp. The students of Agudath Harabbonim rabbis, who had followed them faithfully, also began to turn to the *roshei yeshiva* by the 1950s, which weakened the state of the Agudath Harabbonim.[143] This can be seen as an indictment of the rabbinical leadership, of which Rabbi Jung was prominent. Then again, that generation also paved the way for the next generation of rabbis to lead. They had opened channels of communication with the contemporary generation. Rabbi Jung had always tried to elevate the importance of the rabbi and widen the rabbi's role, to make what the rabbi said important and authoritative.[144]

Literature

The movement to the right was seen in literature: there was an increase in the sale of guidebooks on Judaism, the Bible, Bible-related books, and books for children, indicating a desire to learn more about the Jewish religion and an example of a text-based culture.[145] Not all the books in the market represented an Orthodox understanding of religion, but they did represent a religious point of view. There was an effort by the Orthodox leadership to see that there were guidebooks on Orthodox Judaism. Two of them were published in the 1950s: *The Jewish Way of Life* by Isidore Epstein, editor of the Soncino Talmud, and *This Is My God* by Herman Wouk.

Rabbi Jung's edited book, *Guardians of Our Heritage*, depicted leaders who led traditional and observant lives. These leaders served as examples of "ethical conduct" and Torah-true leadership. He felt that, at this time, Jews were ready and open to "a missionary movement of Judaism by Jews

---

143 Rakeffet-Rothkoff, *The Silver Era in American Jewish Orthodoxy*, 292.
144 Yeshiva University Archives, Jung Collection, Box 49, Folder 2—review of Rabbi Jung's sermon, *New York Times*, January 4, 1953.
145 Isidore Epstein, "Step by Step in the Jewish Religion," book review, *Tradition* 1, no. 2 (Spring 1959): 249; Sloan, "Community Affairs," The American Jewish Community, *American Jewish Year Book* 58 (1957), 152.

among Jews."¹⁴⁶ The book *Guardians of Our Heritage* is an argument for Orthodox Judaism and a critique of those who assimilated and veered from Orthodox precepts. Rabbi Jung felt that Reform and Conservative Judaism had been harmful to the quality of Jewish life. He wrote:

> What is now indicated is, indeed, not name calling but a clear appreciation of the solid facts and a determination of Torah-true Jewry to invest all its efforts in the upbuilding of Judaism, both in America and in Israel. No argument against rootless, bootless reform, no evidence as to their destruction of Jewish religious life, no matter how eloquent, will basically help the situation.¹⁴⁷

Rabbi Jung felt that the field of Jewish study had not received sufficient attention from researchers and historians due to the fact that there had not been a lot of interest in Orthodoxy by Jewish readers. *Guardians of Our Heritage* was one of three biographical books edited by Rabbi Jung; the others were *Jewish Leaders* and *Men of the Spirit*.¹⁴⁸ All these books were similar in intent. Rabbi Jung's desire was to encourage a move toward a renaissance of Jewish learning and observance. His desire was to investigate and appreciate Torah-true Jewry, those who had invested all their "efforts in the up-building of [Orthodox] Judaism."¹⁴⁹ Rabbi Jung wrote:

> ...It has been my aim to include every vital variety of rabbinic leader from patient saint to impatient pioneer, from the *Tzaddik* in Eastern lands to the *Gaon* in central Europe, from the protagonist of *Torah im derekh eretz* to the builder-up of

---

146 Jung, Preface, *Jewish Leaders*, x.
147 Ibid., ix.
148 Author unknown, "Book Review of Guardians of Our Heritage," *Tradition* 1, no. 2 (Spring 1959): 248. Rabbi Jung also wrote *Harvest, Sermons, Addresses, Studies* (New York: Philip Feldheim Inc., 1956). Also: Yeshiva University Archives, Jung Collection, Box 49, Folder 2 (newspaper clipping)—"Review of Jewish Leaders," *The Jewish News*, December 18, 1951.
149 Jung, Preface, *Jewish Leaders*, ix.

spiritual waste places, the marks of thoughtless assimilation or ruthless persecution, or both.[150]

For Rabbi Jung, there was no typical rabbi; their approaches and achievements varied, but all the leaders chosen were loyal to Orthodox Judaism and had made noble contributions.

Rabbi Sharfman, president of the RCA, suggested that teaching Torah to modern minds had been neglected as "we have been too occupied with other concerns to provide for that."[151] He probably was referring to the fact that the main attention had been given to modernizing Orthodoxy and making it viable in America. This would also be a reason why the study of Torah scholars had been neglected.

Correspondence with Herman Wouk

As already mentioned, it was important to Modern Orthodoxy that guidebooks represented that philosophy; Rabbi Jung thus encouraged Herman Wouk, a well-known American novelist, to use his talents to write about Judaism, as he would have a large, receptive audience. Wouk had heard Rabbi Jung speak, and he was inspired. Wouk studied with Rabbi Jung, who exposed him to the classics of Judaism.[152] According to Wouk, Rabbi Jung helped him through "his intellectual doubt and moral position."[153] Rabbi Jung's religious ideas inspired Wouk and rekindled the religious experience of his youth with his Hassidic grandfather, though Wouk's renewal was to Modern Orthodoxy. Wouk thanked Rabbi Jung for encouraging him to write *This is My God*, published in 1959, which Wouk claimed he had begun 13 years earlier when Jung had lent him *The Nineteen Letters of Ben Uziel*, Samson Raphael Hirsch's book of Modern Orthodox philosophy.[154]

---

150 Jung, Preface, *Men of the Spirit*, v.
151 Sharfman, Foreword, *Tradition* 1, no. 1 (Fall 1958): 5–6.
152 Yeshiva University Archives, Jung Collection, Box 20, Folder 4—letter to Rabbi Jung from Wouk, January 12, 1953.
153 Yeshiva University Archives, Jung Collection, Box 20, Folder 4—letter from Rabbi Jung to Wouk, January 12, 1953.
154 Yeshiva University Archives, Jung Collection, Box 20, Folder 4—letters to Wouk from Rabbi Jung, November 4, 1943 and December 22, 1943.

Rabbi Jung helped Wouk with editing and correcting the manuscript for *This Is My God*.[155] Rabbi Jung went through his manuscript very carefully and sent detailed suggestions, correcting information regarding Jewish holidays, *halakhic* details, mistranslations, interpretations, and discrepancies of fact and law. As well, Rabbi Jung advised some changes in thought and style, referring Wouk to his own books. It can thus be seen that Herman Wouk found Rabbi Jung's books to be essential references for Judaism and Jewish issues.[156] *This Is My God* was written for laymen, not for rabbis, yet it dealt with difficult themes: the quest for holiness, the problem of praying in English, separate seating in synagogue, family purity and the *mikveh*, and the principles of Orthodox Judaism. The fact that Wouk dealt with family purity, a difficult and seldom discussed topic, is testimony to Rabbi Jung's influence.

The book made the bestseller list, and became a standard text on the Jewish faith, of interest to both Jewish and Christian readers.[157] That this type of book was written by a Pulitzer Prize novelist whose works had been a top attraction on Broadway and in Hollywood was good for Modern Orthodoxy. Here was an author who lived as an Orthodox Jew in the modern world.[158] It showed that Modern Orthodoxy was part of the American scene. Wouk acknowledged that *This Is My God* was similar in intent to Jung's book, *Guardians of Our Heritage*.[159] The intent of the book was to teach about Judaism and Jewish values, and to excite the readers to want to inculcate in their life

---

155 Yeshiva University Archives, Jung Collection, Box 20, Folder 4—letter to Rabbi Jung from Wouk, June 5, 1959 from St. Thomas, U.S. Virgin Islands, and letter to Wouk from Rabbi Jung, in response, June 9, 1959.

156 Yeshiva University Archives, Jung Collection, Box 20, Folder 4—letter to Wouk from Rabbi Jung, March 31, 1959, and letter to Rabbi Jung from Wouk, March 26, 1959 (request that Rabbi Jung read the manuscript).

157 Yeshiva University Archives, Jung Collection, Box 20, Folder 4—letter to Wouk from Rabbi Jung, April 27, 1959, and letter to Wouk from Rabbi Jung, April 13, 1959.

158 Yeshiva University Archives, Jung Collection, Box 20, Folder 4—letter to Rabbi Jung from Wouk, May 4, 1959.

159 Yeshiva University Archives, Jung Collection, Box 20, Folder 4—letter to Wouk from Rabbi Jung, October 30, 1959 (recognizing that "This is My God" is on the best seller list)

what was taught. The reviewer in the journal *Tradition* felt that it took courage for Wouk to have written this type of book, as presenting himself as an advocate for Orthodox Judaism could have jeopardized his popularity as a novelist.[160] Wouk set an example and provided the tools for observant living. There was a change going on; the audience was receptive and eager to learn, a necessary requirement for a movement to the right to occur.

New Orthodox Journal

The RCA wanted a journal to represent Modern Orthodoxy.[161] Rabbi Solomon Sharfman, the president of the RCA, asked Norman Lamm, as the head of the Publications Committee of the RCA, to begin a new journal. Lamm went to Rabbi Jung to see if he would undertake the task, but Rabbi Jung was too busy. Lamm turned to Rabbi Sydney Hoenig and others, but they, too, did not have the time. Thus, Lamm took on the task himself and became the editor of a new journal, called *Tradition*. Lamm commented that he was younger than any other editor that he knew at that time. Hence, the journal was in the hands of a new generation of rabbis. The demise of "the popular" *Jewish Forum* and the rise of "the scholarly" *Tradition* seemed to be indicative of a generational gap in the perceived needs of Orthodoxy during this period, highlighting a tension that existed between different generations of American Orthodox rabbis.

The beginning of this journal had no correlation with the ending of the *Jewish Forum*, one of the first journals to represent Modern Orthodoxy in the English language, which stopped publication at the start of the 1960s. Lamm said that, at the time, he really did not know much about the *Jewish Forum*, since he was a student and had just gotten his *semikhah* in 1951. The goal of *Tradition* was clearly explained by Lamm in its first edition in the fall of 1958: it was to discuss, interpret, and illustrate Orthodox issues in such a way as to address the doubts of the modern mind and strengthen the faith of modern man. Rabbi Jung, a frequent contributor to the *Jewish Forum*, never wrote an article for

---

160 E.F., "This is My God," Book Review section, *Tradition* 2, no. 2 (Spring 1960): 333.
161 L. Bernstein, *Challenge and Mission*, 27.

Tradition. The *Tradition* articles were on a high scholarly level; the journal showed a confidence that the tradition fit into and represented contemporary times. Lamm referred to Rabbi Jung's writings as "popular" and was looking for scholarly works for *Tradition*. Though Lamm said that Rabbi Jung was too busy to write for the journal, one could be left with the impression that Rabbi Jung was not asked.[162] In this context, the *Jewish Forum* became the "old guard." The *Jewish Forum* had set out to be a journal containing "reliable studies prepared for popular digestion," but the readers were no longer interested in "popular" presentation.[163] Charles Raddock, who became the editor of the journal right before its demise, was calling for more scholarly articles and talked about "selling the public short" in that the *Jewish Forum*'s articles were not "solid enough."[164] But it was too late for the *Jewish Forum*. Raddock talked about the second generation of Jews, who were learning Torah and *daf yomi*, *humash* and Rashi; they needed books with substance written by Orthodox scholars.[165]

Though Robert Gordis, a leading Conservative rabbi and philosopher, had been on the board of the *Jewish Forum* since the 1940s, in the early 1960s, the journal was criticized for having a Conservative rabbi on the editorial board. Gordis resigned in 1962 since he was unhappy with Raddock's response to this criticism.[166] This represented the new relationship between Orthodox and Conservative Judaism.

The *Jewish Forum* was a key factor in the development of American Modern Orthodoxy from the 1920s to the 1960s. It can be considered a pioneer in the formation of English-language literary activity in the field of Torah study for those unable to study the original Hebrew sources. Jung's lack of participation seems to highlight a tension that existed between the different generations of rabbis. The "popular"

---

162 Personal interview with Lamm, January 16, 2003.
163 Editorial, *Jewish Forum* 17, no. 1 (January 1934).
164 Charles Raddock, "Must Jewish Books Fail?" *Jewish Forum* 43, no. 2 (February 1960): 19–20.
165 Charles Raddock, "Judaism and the Lost Intellectuals," *Jewish Forum* 35, no. 8 (September 1952), 98.
166 Robert Gordis, "Dr. Gordis Bows Out," *Jewish Forum* 45, no. 4 (April 1962), 8.

versus the "scholarly" seems to be indicative of this generational gap in the perceived needs of Orthodoxy at this time.

Modern Orthodoxy Became Better Defined—
The Gap Between Traditional Orthodoxy and
Modern Orthodoxy Grew

Modern Orthodox rabbis had maintained principles of inclusion and cooperation with other groups of Jews. These rabbis respected and supported non-Orthodox colleagues and worked with them in communal work. Mixing with Conservative and Reform colleagues remained unchanged, but by the 1950s, this relationship was in more need of defense, as traditional Orthodox groups exerted an influence.

Roshei yeshiva came to America after the war and espoused a policy of separation, opposing the participation by Orthodox Jews on mixed boards. They felt that this gave status and legitimacy to the non-Orthodox and that withdrawal from mixed bodies would result in closer cooperation within Orthodox circles.[167] The dilemma as to what extent Orthodoxy might collaborate with other rabbinic groups was solved in the 1950s, though the issue was certainly reopened later.[168] Rabbi Soloveitchik had written in 1954 that, for things pertaining to Jewish interests and to all Jews, all groups should be united and should fight together against the common enemy. However, for spiritual-ideological issues and for the unity of a Torah community, Orthodox rabbis must not join with the non-Orthodox, as any deviation or compromise in the area of *halakhah* was impossible and intolerable.[169] Rabbi Soloveitchik thus prohibited RCA members from participating in the Jewish Publication Society's Torah translation project, fearing that Orthodox rabbis would not have a veto in the final version.[170]

---

167 Agudath Harrabonim and Lubavitch Rebbe, editorial, *Der Yid* (a Satmar newspaper), March 16, 1956. They attacked Modern Orthodoxy as an introduction to Conservative and Reform Judaism.
168 Sloan, "Community Affairs," Religion, 153.
169 L. Bernstein, *Challenge and Mission*, 59. Translation of *Di Tog Morgen Zhurnal*, November 19, 1954.
170 Ibid., 53–56; Rosensweig, "The Rav as Community Leader," *Tradition* 30, no. 4 (Summer 1996): 210–218.

In 1950, the RCA became more active in the Synagogue Council of America (SCA), which had been organized in 1926 to bring together Orthodox, Reform, and Conservative rabbis in matters of common interest other than religious issues. At first, the relationship of the RCA with the SCA was ambivalent. Then the RCA realized that the SCA was the only vehicle for the RCA to voice its opinions on matters of church and state.[171] The RCA took a broader view of its role on the American scene; it saw the SCA as an avenue for the Orthodox to act in community situations. The UOJCA had been the Orthodox representative for the SCA from the latter's inception in 1926. It had been agreed that religious matters would not be discussed and that only matters affecting the welfare of the whole community would be on the agenda. Other Orthodox groups had no common language or interests with the SCA members. The RCA was asked to join shortly after it began in 1935. It did send delegates, but the SCA remained a minor concern of the RCA.

Participation in the SCA came to a head in the administration of David Hollander when the conflict was finally resolved. Hollander, president of the RCA, favored withdrawal from the SCA.[172] He had opted for a more insular Orthodoxy and appealed to Orthodox *yeshiva* directors who had signed a petition against interdenominational cooperation. In 1956, eleven leading *roshei yeshiva*, part of the Council of Torah Sages, which included Rabbis Feinstein, Jacob Ruderman, and Aaron Kotler, issued a public ruling that prohibited activities in mixed groups. The Council of Torah Sages, which began in America in 1941, consists of *roshei yeshiva* and Hasidic *rebbes* who championed the causes of the Agudath Harabbonim. Rabbis Feinstein and Kotler decided that, according to the Torah, mixed boards were prohibited. Hollander felt that the RCA should follow the Council of Torah Sages. Rabbi Soloveitchik refused to sign the petition,[173] and commented that Rabbis Feinstein and Kotler were not members of the SCA, thus the issue was not applicable to them. Therefore, the *Halakhic* Commission did not

---

171 L. Bernstein, *Challenge and Mission*, 142.
172 Ibid., 154.
173 Rakeffet-Rothkoff, *The Silver Era in American Jewish Orthodoxy*, 291–292.

deal with the issue, as it did not want to conflict with the *roshei yeshiva*.[174] This issue was never decided *halakhically*.[175] Though Soloveitchik would not go against the *yeshiva* leaders, he held that there could be cooperation in matters that were non-*halakhic*.[176]

When Hollander offered Rabbi Jung an appointment to the Division of Religious Affairs Commission (DRA) in 1955 on the condition that he would agree to fight mixed rabbinic boards, Rabbi Jung refused the appointment.[177] Rabbi Jung would not accept a conditional appointment, especially as he totally disagreed with the conditions. Hollander's view was voted down, making the RCA policy clear; they would continue to participate on mixed rabbinic boards.[178] Hollander and his right-wing ideas did not prevail in the RCA at this time.

Rabbi Rackman was the president of the RCA in 1956 as well as the president of the New York Board of Rabbis, which included Orthodox, Conservative, and Reform members. His view was that cooperation did not mean agreement, but rather respect, and that Modern Orthodoxy could make better gains from inside. Rabbi Rackman cited gains in *kashrut* facilities and observances at banquets.[179]

In 1954, the Men's Club of the Jewish Center held a symposium, "Tomorrow's Judaism—A Realistic Approach," with Rabbis David Max Eichhorn (Reform), Emanuel Rackman (Orthodox), and Edward T. Sanrow (Conservative). Rabbi Jung was the moderator.[180] This demonstrated Rabbi Jung's cooperative position; he had always felt that working with all Jews ensured that the voice of Modern Orthodoxy would be heard and that its position would therefore be strengthened.

Rabbi Jung joined other non-Orthodox and Orthodox rabbis to see what steps, if any, should be taken to expand the knowledge and

---

174 L. Bernstein, *Challenge and Mission*, 146–147.
175 Ibid. No *halakhic* issue is ever solved.
176 Seth Farber, "Reproach, Recognition and Respect," 193.
177 L. Bernstein, *Challenge and Mission*, 253.
178 Gurock, "Resisters and Accommodators," 65.
179 L. Bernstein, *Challenge and Mission*, 145.
180 Yeshiva University Archives, Jung Collection, Box 1, Folder 8—notice of symposium, March 11, 1954.

influence of the Jewish religion in various areas of the world.[181] It was felt that the historical situation was favorable; World War II and the founding of the State of Israel had gained the Jewish people more sympathy and respect. Rabbi Eichhorn (a Reform rabbi and a prolific writer, who had written a book on conversion), Robert Gordis (the founder of the first Conservative day school, the president of the Rabbinical Assembly and the SCA, and a professor at JTS), and Rabbi Jung called a meeting at JTS of a carefully selected group of Orthodox, Conservative, and Reform rabbis to discuss this. The attendees represented only themselves. Rabbis Leonard Rosenfeld, Emanuel Rackman, and Herschel Schacter (all from the Orthodox movement) were among the members of the committee. Rabbi Jung's goal was "to spread the truth about Judaism among non-Jews." Gordis was against missionizing but wanted "Information Centers," though some non-Jews would be led to Judaism through these centers. Rabbi Rosenfeld was in favor of "an all-out program designed to gain converts." Rabbi Bernard Bamberger, a Reform movement leader in the Central Conference of American Rabbis and a biblical scholar, also wanted the goal to be more than spreading information; he hoped that this process would result in acquiring converts.[182]

Conversion was on their minds, since there were non-Jews married to Jews in Israel, there were Jewish converts who had come to Israel whose conversions were not recognized, and there were former Jews who had converted to Christianity during World War II and wished to return to Judaism. The issue of conversion for the sake of marriage was not raised. Rabbi Jung insisted that these people must be converted under Orthodox rules.[183] Orthodox participation meant adherence to *halakhic* principles in the important area of conversion. Without Orthodox involvement, this point of view would not be enforced.

Modern Orthodox representatives continued to work in the SCA, the Division of Religious Activities of the National Jewish Welfare

---

181 Yeshiva University Archives, Jung Collection, Box 21, Folder 9—letter to Rabbi Emanuel Rackman, June 3, 1958, from conveners Rabbi Jung, Robert Gordis, and Rabbi Eichhorn.
182 Yeshiva University Archives, Jung Collection, Box 21, Folder 9—minutes of meeting, June 13, 1958.
183 Ibid.

Board, the New York Board of Rabbis, and the Jewish Military Chaplains Association. Though the *roshei yeshiva* grew in numbers, strength, and influence, they could not dictate to the Modern Orthodox group; but their opposing positions even helped define Modern Orthodoxy. The *roshei yeshiva* promoted the causes of the Agudath Harabbonim as they had condemned working with Conservative and Reform Rabbis in the SCA and on local boards, and they also championed the cause of using the Yiddish language. The Agudath Harabbonim found that its goals were being furthered by the wave of new immigrant rabbis to America, part of the Council of Torah Sages that would eventually replace it. The new *yeshiva* world was replacing the Agudath Harabbonim. This gave Modern Orthodoxy a new, very influential group to contend with.[184]

Denying Legitimacy to Non-Orthodox Denominations

At the same time, the *roshei yeshiva* influenced the Modern Orthodox movement, and this caused a tension and a pulling in two directions. In the 1950s, Modern Orthodoxy became more intolerant, though it maintained that it was not isolationist. Rabbi Soloveitchik, who approved the existence of mixed boards, discouraged pupils and disciples from granting legitimacy to non-Orthodox denominations.[185] Also in 1950, Israel Tabak (the president of the RCA), refused an invitation to the Rabbinical Assembly (Conservative) dinner saying that no unity was possible until all Jews returned to the principles of Torah Judaism. It became a precedent for RCA presidents to decline such invitations.[186] One of the reasons given for the change of attitude was that Conservative Judaism had gained momentum after the war and became more lenient in *halakhic* matters, which led to the mid-century Orthodox attacks. Gurock said that when the Conservative movement grew more attractive, it led to the Orthodox becoming more demanding.[187] However, the banning of mixed boards never became official Modern

---

184 Gurock, "Resisters and Accommodators," 64.
185 Farber, "Reproach, Recognition and Respect," 123.
186 L. Bernstein. *Challenge and Mission*, 136.
187 Jeffrey S. Gurock, "The Winnowing of American Orthodoxy," in *American Jewish Orthodoxy in Historical Perspective* (New York: Ktav Publishing House Inc., 1996), 299–313.

Orthodox policy, probably because the rabbis appreciated the value of the encounters.

Conclusion

There were changes occurring in the 1950s; after World War II, there was recovery and a sense of renewal and revival. American life was being reshaped as more traditional values were called for. The Holocaust had intensified distrust of the modern world and secularism; even though Modern Orthodoxy stood for interaction with this world, its emphasis on the importance of religion found a greater audience. As the attitude toward Western secular culture changed and religion gained more prominence, the desire to be more knowledgeable of Jewish texts, and to adhere to *halakhah*, became more important. It was in this environment that the qualitative character of Modern Orthodoxy began to change and to become more intense. Rejection of the status quo in Modern Orthodoxy began in this decade as the age and class structure of Modern Orthodox adherents changed. The Torah scholars and *halakhic* authorities became the new respected leadership. These forces led to more observance of religion and to an eventual movement to the right in Modern Orthodoxy, although in the 1950s, the right-wing movement was not that noticeable, being in its infancy.

Rabbi Jung had put a lot of energy into Americanizing Orthodoxy, which was necessary at the time; however, the focus changed in the 1950s. Modern Orthodoxy became less accommodating to American culture. Those born in America took it for granted and many of the new immigrants who came were more committed to practicing their religion and less focused on Americanization than the immigrants of previous generations. Norman Lamm commented that, by the 1950s, Modern Orthodox Jews had become like other groups in that there was unconscious acculturation and instincts calling for differentiation.[188]

There was a change of focus from ethics and social justice to observance of the law, as well as going to the sources oneself. There was resistance to ambiguity and ambivalence. This, in part, led to changes

---

188 Personal interview with Lamm, January 16, 2003.

in the leadership in Modern Orthodoxy. The new leaders introduced more accurate learning of the Jewish classical texts, becoming more demanding in terms of *halakhic* standards and higher levels of commitment. The desire and ability to observe the laws often comes with knowledge of the law and respect for the interpreters of the law; hence, the groundwork for this observance was laid in the 1950s.

Rabbi Lamm represented the new approach to Modern Orthodoxy. When he came to the Jewish Center Synagogue in 1958, he left a different stamp on the congregation as he created a more sophisticated, intellectual climate. He introduced an ideological motif and a sense of educational excellence, and his vision was more academically ideological.[189] However, in the 1950s, Rabbi Jung continued to stress morality and justice, repeating his popular theme of "reverence, righteousness, and *rahmanut.*" For the most part, except with *Noam*, he did not discuss or analyze *halakhah*; Rabbi Lamm filled this role.[190]

Modern Orthodoxy was no longer floundering; it had made definite decisions that separated it from the Conservative movement. In the 1970s, Sklare said that "having achieved a new sense of élan, Orthodoxy has proceeded to implement a policy of strict noncooperation with Conservatism."[191] The previous generation was more concerned with the Conservative movement on its left than the Modern Orthodox generation of the 1950s. However, the right-wing Orthodox who came after the war, both in America and in Israel, began to be influential. The Modern Orthodox movement now began looking over its right shoulder. There was some desire not to offend more traditional Jews, in some cases a desire to emulate them—coupled with the desire to maintain its Modern Orthodox influence. They went from desiring acceptance from their gentile neighbors to desiring approval from the traditional Orthodox.

---

189 Personal interview with Rabbi Jacob J. Schacter, November 11, 1996.
190 Personal interview with Lamm, January 16, 2003; Personal interview with Martin Schwartzchild, November 11, 1996.
191 Sklare, *Conservative Judaism*, 264.

CONCLUSION

Norms of Modern Orthodoxy in the Decades Under Discussion and Rabbi Jung's Contribution to the Development of Modern Orthodoxy in America

This is the story of the renaissance of American Modern Orthodoxy, from the disorganization of the older Orthodoxy to the new spirit of confidence that emerged after World War II. America went from being a "Jewish wasteland" to being a reservoir of Jewish life. Many modern Americans had viewed the religious person as an anachronism; this person was rehabilitated partly due to the efforts of the clergy and partly due to the changing times and the realization that modernity itself had failings. Much credit, then, goes to a generation of English-speaking rabbis who invigorated lethargic American Orthodox Jews in the mid-twentieth century. They rejuvenated a dying community.

The goal of the Modern Orthodox leaders was to disseminate Jewish knowledge and inculcate the principles of traditional learning, as well as to raise the dignity of Orthodox Judaism. The leaders sought to provide strength to those who wanted to follow an Orthodox life in America, to bring the Jewish intellectual back to the Jewish fold, and to win the allegiance of those Jews attracted to Reform or Conservative Judaism. At its demise in 1962, the *Jewish Forum*—a journal published from 1918 to 1962 in the English language to promote the religious and cultural values of Modern Orthodoxy—looked back to its beginnings, "when Orthodoxy was not as chic as it is today, nor even acceptable."[1]

The leaders worked hard to avoid a chasm arising between *halakhah* and life that encouraged the necessity for change. The leaders adopted the forms of the modern world, but remained within the boundaries of *halakhah*. The presentation of Modern Orthodoxy was changed, but never the tenets. These leaders created facilities enabling Orthodox Jews to practice their religion—they created educational facilities and tools that enabled them to appreciate Orthodox Judaism and take pride in what it stood for. Rabbi Jung mentored a new group of students who were both *yeshiva*-educated and professional, committed to Modern Orthodoxy, America, and Israel. The Modern Orthodox cause was advanced due to its landmark institutions such as Yeshiva University, the Union of Orthodox Jewish Congregations of America (UOJCA), and the Rabbinical Council of America (RCA), organizations that Rabbi Jung helped to set in place.

Rabbi Jung was a religiopolitical activist. He used the media, sermons, schools, newspapers, journals, and his Jewish Library series to teach about Judaism and to achieve goals of religious and social significance. Rabbi Jung embraced issues such as store openings on Saturdays or Sundays, the role of women, and ethnic rights. He exemplified the universalistic spirit that is inherent in Jewish particularism; his message was both particular to Orthodox Judaism and of value to humanity.

The beginning of his career overlapped with those of Rabbis Philip Klein, Bernard Drachman, and Moses Hyamson. They represented unusual deviations from the Eastern European rabbinical norm since they were secularly educated, were in tune with American values, and were models for many rabbis. One congregant wrote to Rabbi Jung reminiscing: "I remember the awesome impression that you made on me when I first met you—an Orthodox rabbi, who not only spoke English, a PhD from Cambridge—never before had I known an

---

1 David Stein, "Jew of the Month," *Jewish Forum* 45, no. 5 (Shavuot 1962): 13.

Orthodox rabbi of such background, such appearance."[2] Rabbi Jung was a pulpit rabbi *par excellence*. Norman Lamm commented: "I don't know how many *shomer shabbos* [Sabbath observant] Jews there were; there were more Jung worshippers than God worshippers—to his credit he kept his congregants."[3] All the congregants interviewed spoke of his interesting sermons, and they all commented on his kindness, his interest, and his participation in their lives.

There were Jews in the scientific age who completely chose the secular way and discarded Judaism; there were others who compromised and altered *halakhah* or the doctrine of divine revelation; and there were those, who at the opposite end, turned their backs on secular thought and immersed themselves only in the religious milieu. For Rabbi Jung, these extremes did not represent Torah-true Judaism.

Modern Orthodoxy made social, not religious, changes. Jeffrey S. Gurock described Modern Orthodoxy as an Orthodoxy that strived to be socially appropriate and yet *halakhically* correct.[4] Decorum meant that elements of religious observance were compatible with modernity and Americanism. Rabbi Jung tailored his message to be responsive to current needs.

Rabbi Jung helped make the environment conducive to the development of Modern Orthodoxy. He tried to clean up the Orthodox image by seeing that there were attractive facilities and appealing Orthodox institutions, and he saw to it that there were clean and proper *kashrut* facilities. Rabbi Jung fought a corrupt *kashrut* system and succeeded in replacing it with the reliable OU. He battled and campaigned to promote family purity and to replace the unsavory *mikvaot* with attractive buildings. As well, he fought for the rights of Sabbath observers, for the closing of Yiddish theaters on the Jewish New Year, and for reversing other public violations of Jewish law, which were then in vogue. Rabbi Jung also worked to see that schools provided good Jewish education, good educational materials, and

---

2   Yeshiva University Archives, Jung Collection, Box 3, Folder 3—letter to Rabbi Jung from David Miller, November 28, 1977.
3   Personal interview with Norman Lamm, January 16, 2003.
4   Personal interview with Jeffrey S. Gurock, December 17, 1996.

literature that taught about Judaism, as all these things were basic to developing a Torah-true life. Finally, he battled on behalf of the suffering Jews of Europe and all over the world, helping them remain loyal to Torah values.

Lamm feels that one of Rabbi Jung's major achievements was that the latter "brought to Orthodoxy a sense of dignity. He took it out of the kitchen into the dining room and gave it an aura."[5] Rabbi Jacob J. Schacter, who succeeded Rabbi Norman Lamm at the Jewish Center Synagogue, said that Rabbi Jung "left a dignified Orthodoxy, dignified, well-focused."[6]

Modern Orthodox leaders showed that *halakhah* addressed everyday problems. Rabbi Jung presented *halakhah* and religion as this-worldly and rational, in keeping with modernity and American values, and he provided attainable goals. Ethics for Rabbi Jung was Judaism in the concrete.[7] Ethics is part of *halakhah*, and this was the area that he emphasized.

Rabbi Jung saw the problems of his time. He believed in freedom of interpretation of Torah, for every generation had new problems and questions, and the answers lay in Torah.[8] The laws were not rigid and were to be applied to new situations.

Modern Orthodoxy was not insular; Modern Orthodox Jews had to identify and cooperate with other Jews. Rabbi Jung faced challenges of competitors, taking what was positive and good in their programs and adapting it within the *halakhic* scheme. He wrote: "We expect and respect our differences."[9] His motto was "cooperation without compromise." That was his interpretation of Jewish law, which coincides with what Modern Orthodoxy stood for.

---

5   Personal interview with Lamm, January 16, 2003.
6   Personal interview with Rabbi Jacob Schacter, November 11, 1996.
7   Personal interview with Martin Schwarszchild (a former president of the synagogue and a lifelong member), November 11, 1996.
8   Leo Jung, "The Rambam in True Perspective," *Jewish Forum* 18, no. 4 (April 1935); Leo Jung, *The Path of a Pioneer: The Autobiography of Leo Jung*, Jewish Library, Second Series, vol. 8 (London and New York: Soncino Press, 1980), xvi–xvii.
9   Yeshiva University Archives, Jung Collection, Box 45, Folder 4—"Intermein," 5.

Modern Orthodoxy was "man-centered," not "theo-centered," as the Modern Orthodox person had freedom to improve, correct, and be creative, and had a major role to play in one's own destiny. It stressed human responsibility and activity rather than passive submission or fatalistic resignation to one's condition, and it does not desire isolationism and blind obedience to rabbinic leaders. This became another defining point of Modern Orthodoxy.

The Movement to the Right

This study examined the religious status of Modern Orthodoxy with reference to increased observance of *halakhah* or Jewish law. The movement to the right only began in the 1950s, and intensified later. The Modern Orthodox person became, by the 1960s, more educated in religious and secular matters, more observant, and more self-confident and assertive. This person was not the old, uneducated, unacculturated, and poor Eastern European Orthodox Jew.

Even Rabbi Jung's adoring congregants acknowledged that the sermons of his successor (Rabbi Lamm) dealt with more profound religious issues, and they appreciated the educational excellence that Rabbi Lamm represented.[10] Lamm said that Rabbi Jung's sermons repeatedly dealt with "reverence, righteousness and *rahmanut*" and with "modernity of method," which were some of Rabbi Jung's favorite topics. The impression given by Rabbi Lamm was that the audience had tired of these topics and this approach.[11] Rabbi Jung's congregants began to want sermons that dealt with more than ethics.

They also began to select books with a more scholarly approach. Readers were ready for the authentic Jewish classics and content, and were no longer interested in just "popular" presentation. Books, such as Herman Wouk's *This Is My God* (which Rabbi Jung had encouraged Wouk to write), were critiqued for lack of depth. Rabbi Jung's Jewish

---

10 One can deduce this from interviews with Lamm, Rabbi Schacter, and Gurock.
11 This is substantiated by various congregants; personal interviews with various congregants (see the bibliography); personal interview with Lamm, January 16, 2003.

Library series would also likely fall under the rubric of "not solid enough."[12]

One of Rabbi Jung's key issues, Americanization, was no longer of great interest to the younger generation. There was less of a quest for Americanization and less accommodation to Americanism and modernity. Many Modern Orthodox Jews were, for the most part, born in America and already "Americanized." Lamm said that he was born in America and that he took the issue of Americanization for granted. He said that Rabbi Jung had made Americanism into a quasi-religion when he equated the American constitution with the Torah, wearing *tzitit* (fringes) with draping the American flag over oneself, and when he compared Washington to Sinai.[13] This was offensive to the younger generation, as they felt that the Torah, wearing *tzitit*, and Sinai were too holy to compare with American symbols.

Decorum (another key issue for Rabbi Jung) remained important in the synagogue, but the reason for it changed. No longer was decorum something observed to appear more American or modern; it was presented as a *halakhic* demand. *Davening* (praying) with *kavvanah* (true commitment and devotion) was a *halakhic* requirement. In this way, decorum was made legitimate since it was based in *halakhah*. With this change, Jenna Weissman Joselit referred to the Modern Orthodox group as the "post-decorous" generation.[14] Rabbis and officers in the Jewish Center continued to wear top hats, an anachronism in the twentieth century. Whenever a proposal was raised to discontinue wearing the top hats, there was a clamor to keep the custom; however, the custom became harder to maintain as younger people became involved in the synagogue. Rabbi Schacter himself came to appreciate what top hats symbolized, though at first the style made him uncomfortable.[15]

---

12 Charles Raddock, "Must Jewish Books Fail?" *Jewish Forum* 43, no. 2 (February 1960): 19–20. Raddock, who became the new editor of the *Jewish Forum* in 1961, was more right wing than the previous editor or the editorial board.
13 Personal interview with Lamm, January 16, 2003.
14 Jenna Weissman Joselit, *New York's Jewish Jews: The Orthodox Community in the Interwar Years* (Bloomington, IN: Indiana University Press, 1990), 43.
15 Personal interview with Rabbi Schacter, November 11, 1996.

Rabbi Jung's legacy of dignified Orthodoxy continued, but formal worship was not enough.

The traditional Orthodox Jews who came to America after World War II were an example of warmth and emotionalism that conflicted with the rationalistic approach of Rabbi Jung and his generation. The approach of the traditional Orthodox newcomers to America and their influence was in place in the 1950s. Rabbi Jung was out of sync with the new emotionalism. His rational, practical approach was out of date.

Modern Orthodoxy is itself a modern phenomenon; it is the reassertion of tradition in an innovative form. However, the movement to the right represents the sense that modernity has flaws; for Modern Orthodoxy, it presents a tension for living in this world. Keeping a balance between being part of the culture of the modern world and being different, participating in the world of science and the world of Torah, and being tolerant yet demanding, is an ongoing challenge for Modern Orthodoxy.

Some Anecdotes That Give a Glimpse of the Movement to the Right

Toward the end of his career, Rabbi Jung came to resist what he saw as the excesses to the right. The resistance tells the story of the development of Modern Orthodoxy. Rabbis Lamm and Schacter, who had been connected with the Jewish Center Synagogue, are repeatedly cited, as they represent the new outlook of the following generations and tell the story of what Modern Orthodoxy came to represent.

By the end of the 1950s, Sabbath attendance was beginning to increase. This attendance continued to increase in the following decades to the point that those who came late found it hard to get an available seat on the Sabbath.[16] The empty pews were part of the historical past. Over the years, the daily *minyanim* (prayer groups of at least ten men) tripled. Second, then third and more, *minyanim* were eventually opened, which created subgroups in a large synagogue. As a result of these smaller

---

16 Personal interview with Lamm, January 16, 2003.

groups, there was more intimacy, warmth, and emotionalism. Also, these smaller prayer groups replicated the old Eastern European style.

Rabbi Jung's synagogue lost the image of the "shul with the pool and the school." Two floors were rented out to a health club, the sixth floor was rented out to the Drisha Institute for women, and the ninth floor was rented out to an advanced Torah institute.[17] The synagogue was no longer the "rich man's club." According to Rabbi Lamm, before he came, the synagogue was a "closed club" and new members were not welcomed, but this changed over time.[18] With Rabbi Lamm already part of the Jewish Center Synagogue in the 1950s, Talmud study and the study of *daf yomi* (referring to the daily study of a page of Talmud) intensified.[19]

Rabbi Schacter told the story that when he *davened* the *Shemoneh Esreh* (the Eighteen Benedictions, a key prayer) with his *tallit* (prayer shawl) over his head, an example of being alone—though in a crowd—and undisturbed in one's devotion to God, Rabbi Jung requested that he not do this. Rabbi Schacter replied that he felt more comfortable doing this, if Rabbi Jung did not mind. This disturbed Rabbi Jung's sense of dignity; the demeanor was Eastern European in flavor, and he could not appreciate Rabbi Schacter's new passionate approach and emotional commitment.

Some younger rabbis continued to advocate a more important role for women in the synagogue. Rabbi Schacter gave Talmud classes for women, and other rabbis, such as Rabbis Avi Weiss and Moses Rifkin, advocated women's *tefilla* (prayer) groups.[20] Women started to partake more actively in holiday rituals; on *Simhat Torah* they began to dance holding the Torah, a custom previously carried out only by men. Regarding this issue of dancing with the Torah on *Simhat Torah*, Lamm said: "Jung's reaction was not strong, but he did leave early—Jung was a law and order man—*Simhat Torah* and *Purim* were too disorderly with all the

---

17 Personal interview with Rabbi Schacter, November 11, 1996.
18 Personal interview with Lamm, January 16, 2003.
19 Personal interview with Gurock, December 17, 1996.
20 Personal interview with Rabbi Schacter, November 11, 1996.

singing and dancing. *Purim* and *Simhat Torah* were dark days for Jung."[21] It appeared that Rabbi Jung was uncomfortable with women's new involvement and probably more uncomfortable with what he perceived as the lack of a dignified, rational approach.

There is no institutional policy in Modern Orthodoxy regarding women covering their heads; however, Modern Orthodox women cover their hair much more than the last generation, and there are more men wearing beards and *kippot* (skullcaps).[22] This is a sign that particularism is more emphasized, and that there is an increase in observant men and women. Rabbi Jung's wife wore a *sheitel* (wig), but only as it was a custom from her home town in Europe that she maintained in America. Jeffrey Gurock said that Mrs. Jung had told him that if she had to start over, she would not do it again.[23]

Being clean shaven was a sign of Americanization. Rabbi Lamm said that when he came to the Jewish Center, he did not have a beard but adopted one at a later time, and that when he first met Rabbi Soloveitchik, the latter did not have a beard.[24] Rabbi Jung always wore a well-trimmed beard. Perhaps this is an example of his independent thinking, his strong pride, and conviction in his Judaism—and most of all, his synthesis of modernism, Americanism, and Judaism. It is no longer true that members of the OUJCA and RCA are mostly clean shaven. This is an example of a lack of interest in visible Americanization, of a desire to be more particularistic, and of paying closer attention to *halakhic* details and interpreting *halakhah* in a more stringent way.[25]

***

Rabbi Jung's work was not ideological, and he made no contribution to the ideological definition of Orthodoxy. Lamm supported this contention and said that "he [Rabbi Jung] represented sophisticated dignity and his activities in government and secular circles enhanced the

---

21 Personal interview with Lamm, January 16, 2003.
22 Ibid.
23 Personal interview with Gurock, December 17, 1996.
24 Personal interview with Lamm, January 16, 2003.
25 Oscar Fasman, "After Fifty Years, an Optimist," *American Jewish History* 69, no. 2 (December 1979): 161.

reputation of Orthodoxy, but he never took off his ideological gloves."[26] Rabbi Jung showed no ideological consistency; if his ideology was clear in his own mind, he kept it hidden. He admired Samson Raphael Hirsch, yet he supported working with non-Orthodox Jews on issues common to both, and he became an ardent Zionist. He supported *yeshivot* in Israel that were non-Zionist, and his early affiliation with Agudath Israel was problematic in Modern Orthodox circles. Lamm pointed out that Rabbi Jung was very close with Rabbi Aaron Kotler, who headed the *Vaad Hahatzala*, a group that had been in conflict with the Joint Distribution Committee (JDC) and represented traditional Orthodoxy, and that Rabbi Jung became interested in Lubavitch through one of his congregants, Sam Kramer (a distinguished lawyer).[27] Rabbi Schacter pointed out that Rabbi Jung had come upon the works of Habad, which represent the Lubavitch movement, as the chair of the Cultural Committee of the JDC and that Rabbi Jung had a soft spot for Rabbi Joseph Isaac Schneerson. Rabbi Jung was a very generous and outreaching man, even if not ideologically consistent—maybe this, too, represents Modern Orthodoxy. He lacked hard, clear lines in his approach, a phenomenon characteristic of Modern Orthodoxy itself in his day. This story is of Modern Orthodoxy looking for a precise definition, which continues to elude the movement.

Rabbi Jung presented Modern Orthodoxy as an alternative to a purely secular or fundamentalist stance. In those who heard his message, he instilled respect for the modern world but also respect for religion. He was the epitome of Modern Orthodoxy, combining tradition and modernity. In other words, he was tolerant yet intensely observant and unyielding in his beliefs; he was part of the culture while maintaining his differences.

Rabbi Jung made a lasting contribution to Modern Orthodoxy in America. He revived and revised Orthodoxy, and the revision is ongoing. The religious status of generations ago should be appreciated as but a step along the way toward full-bodied Torah Judaism. His leadership was a key factor in the growth of Orthodoxy between the World Wars.

---

26 Personal interview with Lamm, January 16, 2003.
27 Ibid.

Rabbi Jung had fought for a more important role for religion, which was good for Modern Orthodoxy. However, when this goal was reached, followers looked to those who epitomized Torah scholarship and devotion to *halakhic* study. Rabbi Jung had been immersed in helping his fellow Jew and was no longer the hero of this generation, though without the foundation that he laid, they could not have gotten to this point. There was a change in the way one acquired knowledge—the new generation critiqued him for not being profound in his approach to Talmud learning, sometimes not appreciating the dilemmas of his time.[28]

Rabbi Jung's literary work, based in the secular world was written for an audience uneducated in Judaism; this waning appreciation of his writing was a sign of the movement to the right. However, his production of literature in English presented the values and ideals of Torah-true Judaism, and it was a forerunner of the ever-growing literary activity in the field of Torah study for those unable to study Hebrew originals. His practical organizational work laid a foundation upon which a more esoteric and spiritual life could be built.

It must be noted that not all Modern Orthodox rabbis are scholars; as well, not all Modern Orthodox laymen are involved in Talmud study, or committed to the observance of *halakhah,* but there is an increase in these types of people. Trained laymen and scholarly rabbis have brought vitality to Modern Orthodoxy.

The key terms in describing Modern Orthodoxy in America from 1920 to 1960 are change, acculturation, renewal, and considerable advance. The story of Modern Orthodoxy in America has been one of grave danger and hard, though successful, effort.

---

28 One can deduce this from personal interviews with Lamm, Rabbi Schacter, and Gurock.

BIBLIOGRAPHY

Almog, Shmuel, Jehuda Reinharz, and Anita Shapira, eds. *Zionism and Religion*. Hanover, New Hampshire: University Press of New England, 1998.

Baumel, Judith Tydor. *Unfulfilled Promise Rescue and Resettlement of Jewish Refugee Children in the United States 1934-1945*. Juneau, Alaska: Denali Press, 1990.

Bauer, Yehuda. *My Brother's Keeper: A History of the Jewish Joint Distribution Committee, 1929-39*. Philadelphia: Jewish Publication Society of America, 1974.

Berkson, Isaac Baer. *Theories of Americanization: A Critical Study*. New York: Arno Press, 1969.

Bernstein, Louis. *Challenge and Mission: The Emergence of the English Speaking Orthodox Rabbinate*. NewYork: Shengold Publishers, 1982.

Bernstein, Louis. "Generational Conflict in American Orthodoxy." *American Jewish History* 69, no. 2 (December 1979): 226-33.

Bernstein, Saul. *The Orthodox Story: A Centenary Portrayal*. Northvale, New Jersey, and Jerusalem: Jason Aronson Inc., 1997.

Bernstein, Saul. *The Renaissance of the Torah Jew*. New York: Ktav Publishing House, 1985.

Breuer, Isaac. *Concepts of Judaism*. Jerusalem and New York: Israel Universities Press, 1974.

Breuer, Jacob, ed., *Fundamentals of Judaism: Selections from the Works of Rabbi Samson Raphael Hirsch and Outstanding Torah-True Thinkers*. New York: P. Feldheim Publishers, 1949.

Breuer, Jacob, ed., *Timeless Torah: An Anthology of the Writings of Samson Raphael Hirsch*. New York: P. Feldheim Publishers, 1957.

Bulka, Reuven. *Dimensions of Orthodox Judaism*. New York: Ktav Publishing House Inc., 1983.

Bulka, Reuven. *The Coming Cataclysm: The Orthodox Reform Rift and the Future of the Jewish People*. Oakville, Ontario, and New York: Mosaic Press, 1984.

Bunim, Amos. *A Fire in His Soul: Irving M. Bumin, 1901–1980, The Man and His Impact on American Orthodox Jewry*. Jerusalem and New York: Feldheim Publishers, 1989.

Cohen, Alfred S., ed., *Halacha and Contemporary Society*. New York: Ktav Publishing House Inc. and Rabbi Jacob Joseph School Press, 1983.

Cohen, Michael R. *The Birth of Conservative Judaism*. New York: Columbia University Press, 2012.

Cohen, Naomi W., *American Jews and the Zionist Idea*. New York: Ktav Publishing House Inc., 1975.

Danziger, M. Herbert. *Returning to Tradition: The Contemporary Revival of Orthodox Judaism*. New Haven, Connecticut and London: Yale University Press, 1989.

Davis, Moshe. "Jewish Religious Life and Institutions in America." In *The Jews: Their History, Culture, and Religion*, 3rd edition, vol. 1, edited by Louis Finkelstein. Philadelphia: Jewish Publication Society of America, 1960.

Davis, Moshe. *The Emergence of Conservative Judaism: The Historical School in 19th-Century America*. Philadelphia: Jewish Publication Society of America, 1963.

Drachman, Bernard. *The Unfailing Light: Memoirs of an American Rabbi*. New York: Rabbinical Council of America, 1948.

Eisen, Arnold M. *The Chosen People in America: A Study in Religious Ideology*. Bloomington, Indiana: Indiana University Press, 1983.

Elazar, Daniel. *Community and Polity: The Organizational Dynamics of American Jewry*. Philadelphia: Jewish Publication Society of America, 1976.

Eleff, Zev. "Freedom and Responsibility: The First Orthodox College Journalists and Early Yeshiva College Politics, 1935-1941." *American Jewish Archives Journal* 62, no. 2 (September 2010): 54-88.

Ellenson, David H. *Rabbi Esriel Hildesheimer and the Creation of a Modern Jewish Orthodoxy*. Tuscaloosa, Alabama: University of Alabama Press, 1990.

Ellenson, David H. *Between Culture and Tradition: The Dialectics of Modern Jewish Religion and Identity*. Atlanta, Georgia: Scholars Press, 1994.

Entin, Nathaniel. "The Jewish Educational Committee of New York, 1939-65." Thesis, Dropsie University.

Farbridge, Maurice. *Judaism and the Modern Mind*. New York: The Macmillan Company, 1927.

Ferziger, Adam S. *Exclusion and Hierarchy*. Philadelphia: University of Pennsylvania Press, 2005.

Finkelstein, Louis, ed., *The Jews and Their Culture*, 4th ed. New York: Shocken Books.

Gastwirth, Harold P. *Fraud Corruption, and Holiness: The Controversy Over the Supervision of Jewish Dietary Practice in New York City*. Port Washington, New York: Kennikat Press, 1974.

Goldberg, Harvey E., ed., *Judaism Viewed From Within and Without*. Albany, New York: State University of New York Press, 1987.

Goldman, Karla. *Beyond The Synagogue Gallery*. Cambridge, Massachusetts and London, UK: Harvard University Press, 2000.

Gurock, Jeffrey S. *American Jewish Orthodoxy in Historical Perspective*, New York: Ktav Publishing House Inc., 1996.

_____. *The American Rabbinate*. Hoboken, New Jersey: Ktav Publishing House, 1985.

_____. *Men and Women of Yeshiva: Higher Education, Orthodoxy and American Judaism*. New York: Colombia University Press, 1988.

_____. *Orthodox Jews in America*. Bloomington and Indianapolis, Indiana: Indiana University Press, 2009.

_____ ed. *Ramaz: School, Community, Scholarship and Orthodoxy*. Hoboken, New Jersey: Ktav Publishing House, 1989.

_____, and Jacob J. Schacter. *A Modern Heretic and a Traditional Community*. New York: Columbia University Press, 1997.

Hadstrom, Matthew S. *The Rise of Liberal Religion*. Oxford, UK and New York: Oxford University Press, 2013.

Hain, Shmuel, ed. *The Next Generation of Modern Orthodoxy*. New York: Michael Scharf Publication Trust of the Yeshiva University Press, 2012.

Handlin, Oscar. *Adventures in Freedom: Three Hundred Years of Jewish Life in America*, New York, McGraw Hill, 1954.

Heilman, Samuel. *Defenders of the Faith*. New York: Schocken Books, 1992.

_____. *Portrait of American Jews, The Last Half of the Twentieth Century*. Seattle and London: University of Washington Press, 1995.

_____. *People of the Book*. Chicago and London: University of Chicago Press, 1976.

_____, and Steven Cohen. *Cosmopolitans and Parochials*, Chicago and London: University of Chicago Press, 1976.

Helmreich, William. *The World of the Yeshivah*, New York and London: New York Free Press, Collier Macmillan Press, 1982.

Herring, Basil, ed. *The Rabbinate as Calling and Vocation*. Northvale, New Jersey and London: Jason Aronson Inc., 1991.

Herzberg, Arthur. *Being Jewish in America*. New York: Schocken Books, 1979.

_____ ed. *The Zionist Idea*. New York: Antheneum, 1986.

Hirsch, Samuel Raphael. *Nineteen Letters*. Jerusalem: Feldheim Publishers, 1969.

Hyamson, Rabbi Dr. Moses. *Sabbath and Festival Addresses*. New York: Bloch Publishing Co. 1936.

Ish-Shalom, Binyamin. *Rav Avraham Itzhak HaCohen Kook: Between Rationalism and Mysticism*. Albany: State University of New York Press, 1993.

Jackson, Bernard, ed. *Modern Research in Jewish Law*. Leiden, The Netherlands: E. J. Brill, 1980.

Joselit, Jenna. *New York's Jewish Jews: The Orthodox Community in the Interwar Years*. Bloomingdale, Indiana: Indiana University Press, 1990.

_____. *The Wonders of America*, Bloomington, Indiana: Indiana University Press, 1983.

_____. "Orthodox Judaism." In *Varieties of American Religion*, edited by Charles Samuel Braden, 231-246. Chicago and New York: Willet, Clark and Co., 1936.

Kasher, M., Norman Lamm, and Leonard Rosenfeld, eds. *The Leo Jung Jubilee Volumn Essays on the Occasion of his Seventieth Birthday*. Copyright The Jewish Center, New York, 1962.

Katz, Jacob. *A House Divided: Orthodoxy and Schism in Nineteenth Century European Jewry*. Hanover, New Hampshire and London: Brandeis University Press, 1998.

Katz, Steven T. *American Rabbi: The Life and Thought of Jacob B. Agus*, New York and London: New York University Press, 1997.

Kaufman, David. *Shul With A Pool: The "Synagogue-Center" in American Jewish History*. Hanover, New Hampshire: University Press of New England, 1999.

Klaperman, Gilbert. *The Story of Yeshiva University*. London: Macmillan Company, Collier- Macmillan Ltd., 1969.

Klien, Isaac. *The Ten Commandments in a Changing World*. New York: Bloch Publishing House, 1944.

Kochan, Lionel. *The Jewish Renaissance and Some of Its Discontents*. Manchester, UK: Manchester University Press; New York: St. Martin's Press, 1992.

Kolsky, Thomas A. *Jews Against Zionism, The American Council For Judaism 1942–1948*. Philadelphia: Temple University Press, 1990.

Kurzweel, Zvi. *Modern Impulse of Traditional Judaism*. Hoboken, New Jersey: Ktav Publishing House, 1985.

Lamm, Norman. *Faith and Doubt, Studies in Traditional Judaism* New York: Ktav Publishing House, 1971.

Lamm, Norman, and Walter S. Wurtzburger, eds. *A Treasury of Tradition*, New York: Hebrew Publishing Co., 1967.

Landman, Leo, ed. *Rabbi Joseph H. Lookstein Memorial Volume*. New York: Ktav Publishing House, 1980

Leibman, Charles. "Changing Social Characteristics of Orthodox, Conservative and Reform Jews," *Sociological Analysis* Winter 1966: 210–22.

_____. "Orthodoxy in American Jewish Life." *American Jewish Year Book*, 1965 Edition. Philadelphia: Jewish Publication Society, 1965.

_____, and Eliezer Don-Yehija. *Aspects of Religious Behavior of American Jews*. New York: Ktav Publishing House, 1974.

Lookstein, Joseph. *Faith and Destiny of Man: Traditional Judaism in a New Light.* New York: Bloch Publishing Co., 1967.

_____. "Seventy five Yesteryears: A Historical Sketch of Kehilath Jeshuran," *Congregation Kehilath Jeshurun, Diamond Jubilee Year Book,* 17-236. New York: Congregation Kehilath Jeshurun, 1946.

Lowenstein, Steven M. *Frankfurt on the Hudson: The German Jewish Community of Washington Heights.* Detroit, Michigan: Wayne State University Press, 1989.

Marcus, Jacob Rader, and Abraham J. Peck, *The American Rabbinate: A Century of Continuity and Change, 1883–1983.* Hoboken, New Jersey: Ktav Publishing House Inc., 1985.

Meddling, P., ed. *Studies in Contemporary Jewry.* Bloomington, Indiana: Indiana University Press, 1986.

Meiselman, Shulamit. *The Soloveitchik Heritage: A Daughter's Memoir.* Hoboken, New Jersey: Ktav Publishing House Inc., 1995.

Mintz, Adam. *The Relationship of Orthodox Jews with Believing Jews of Other Religious Ideologies and Non-Believing Jews.* New York: The Michael Scharf Publication Trust of the Yeshiva University Press, 2000.

Mittleman, Alan L. *The Politics of Torah: The Jewish Political Tradition and the Founding of Agudat Israel.* Albany, New York: State University of New York Press, 1996.

Moore, Deborah Dash. *At Home in America: Second Generation New York Jews.* New York: Colombia University Press, 1981.

Neusner, Jacob. *The Alteration Of Orthodoxy,* vol. 8, New York: Garland Publishers, 1993.

_____, ed. *Sectors of American Judaism.* New York: Ktav Publishing House, 1975.

Newman, Louis I. *Biting on Granite: Selected Sermons and Addresses.* New York: Bloch Publishing Co.,1946.

Parzen, Herbert. *Architect of Conservative Judaism.* New York: Jonathan David Publishers, 1964.

Pelcovitz, Ralph. *Danger and Opportunity.* New York: Shengold Publishers, 1976.

Penkower, Monty Noam. "Jewish Cataclysm and Jewish Restoration: The Response of Leo Jung," in *The Holocaust and Israel Reborn: From*

Catastrophe to Sovereignty, by Monty Noam Penkower. Urbana, Illinois: University of Illinois Press, 1994.

Polland, Annie, and Daniel Soyer. *Emerging Metropolis*. New York and London: New York University Press, 2012.

Posner, Zalman. *Thinking Jewish: A Contemporary View of Judaism, A Jewish View of Today's World*. Nashville, Tennessee: Kesher Press, 1978.

Rakeffet-Rothkoff, Aaron. *Bernard Revel*. Philadelphia: The Jewish Publication Society of America, 1972.

_____. *The Silver Era*. New York: Yeshiva University Press; Jerusalem: Feldheim Publishers, 1981.

Raphael, Marc, ed. *Approaches to the Study of Modern Judaism*, vols. 1 and 2. Chico, California: Chico Scholars Press, 1983.

_____. *Profiles in American Judaism*. San Francisco, California: Harper and Row, 1984.

Reznikoff, Charles, ed. *Louis Marshall, Champion of Liberty: Selected Papers and Addresses*, vols. 1 and 2. Philadelphia: The Jewish Publication Society of America, 1957.

Rock, Howard B. *Haven of Liberty*. New York and London: New York University Press, 2012.

Rosenbloom, Noah H. *Tradition in an Age of Reform: The Religious Philosophy of Samson Raphael Hirsch*. Philadelphia: The Jewish Publication Society of America, 1976.

Rosenthal, Gilbert. *The American Rabbi*. New York: Ktav Publishing House Inc., 1977.

_____. *Contemporary Judaism, Patterns of Survival*. New York: Human Sciences Press, 1986.

Rotenberg, Mordechai. *Dialogue With Deviance*. Philadelphia: Institute for the Study of Human Issues, 1983.

Sacks, Jonathan. *Arguments for the Sake of Heaven*. Northvale, New Jersey and London: Jason Aronson Inc., 1991.

_____. *One People: Tradition, Modernity and Jewish Unity*. London and Washington, DC: Littman Library of Jewish Civilization, Bnai Brith Book Service, 1993.

_____. *Orthodoxy Confronts Modernity*, Hoboken, New Jersey and London: Ktav Publishing House Inc., 1991.

_____. *Tradition in an Untraditional Age*. London: Valentine, Mitchell, 1990.

Sarna, Jonathan. *JPS: The Americanization of Jewish Culture 1888-1988*. Philadelphia, New York, and Jerusalem: The Jewish Publication Society, 1989.

_____. *People Walk On Their Heads: Moses Weinberger's Jews and Judaism in New York*. New York: Holmes and Meier, 1982.

Schacter, Jacob, ed. *Jewish Tradition and The Non-Traditional Jew*. Northvale, New Jersey and London: Jason Aronson Inc., 1992.

_____, ed. *Judaism's Encounter With Other Cultures*. Northvale, New Jersey and Jerusalem: Jason Aronson Inc., 1997.

_____, ed. *Reverence, Righteousness and Rachmanut: Essays in Memory of Rabbi Dr. Leo Jung*. Northvale, New Jersey and London: Jason Aronson Inc., 1992.

Schweid. Eliezer. *Democracy and Halakhah*. The Jerusalem Center for Public Affairs. Lanham, New York and London: University Press of America, 1994.

Scult, Mel, ed. *Communings of the Spirit: The Journals of Mordecai M. Kaplan, Volume 1, 1913-1934*. Detroit, Michigan: Wayne State University Press, and Wyncote, Pennsylvania: The Reconstructionist Press, 2001.

_____. *Judaism Faces The Twentieth Century*, Detroit, Michigan: Wayne State University Press, 1993.

_____, Emmanuel Goldsmith, and Robert M. Seltzer, eds. *The American Judaism of Mordechai M. Kaplan*. New York: New York University Press, 1990.

Sharfman, I. Harold. *The First Rabbi: Origins of Conflict Between Orthodox and Reform*, Malibu, California: Pangloss Press, 1988.

Shapiro, Marc B. *Between The Yeshiva World and Modern Orthodoxy: The Life and Works of Jehiel Jacob Weinberg 1884-1966*. London and Portland, Oregon: The Littmann Library of Jewish Civilization, 1999.

Sklare, Marshall. *Conservative Judaism*. New York: Schocken Books, 1955, 1972.

Slomovitz, Albert Isaac. *The Fighting Rabbis: A History of Jewish Military Chaplains, 1860-1945*. Ann Arbor, Michigan: UMI Dissertation Services, 1996.

Sokol, Moshe. *Orthodox Forum: Rabbinic Authority and Personal Autonomy*. Northvale, New Jersey: Jason Aronson Inc., 1992.

Stevens, Richard P. *American Zionism and U.S. Foriegn Policy 1942–47*. New York: Pagent Press, 1962.

Stitskin, Leon D., Ed. *Studies in Torah Judaism*. New York: Yeshiva University Press and Ktav Publishing House, 1969.

Urofsky, Melvin I. *,American Zionism from Herzl to the Holocaust*. Garden City, New York: Anchor Press, Doubleday, 1975,

Warshaw, Mal. *Traditional Orthodox Jewish Life in America*. New York: Schocken Books, 1976.

Weisfeld, Israel H. *The Message of Israel*. New York: Bloch Publishing Co., 1936.

Wenger, Beth. *New York Jews and The Great Depression*. New Haven, Connecticut: Yale University Press, 1996.

Wertheimer, Jack. *A People Divided: Judaism in Contemporary America*. New York: Basic Books, 1993.

_____, ed. *The American Synagogue Transformed*. Hanover, New Hampshire and London: Brandeis University Press, 1987.

_____, ed. *The Uses of Tradition: Jewish Continuity in the Modern Era*. New York: Jewish Theological Seminary of America, 1992.

Zuroff, Efraim. *The Response of Orthodox Jewry in the United States to The Holocaust*. New York: The Michael Sharf Publications Trust of The Yeshiva University Press, 2000.

Writings by Rabbi Leo Jung

Jung, Leo. *Between Man and Man*. New York: Jewish Educational Press, 1976 (published in 1967 under the title *Human Relations in Jewish Law*).

_____. *Business Ethics in Jewish Law*. New York: Hebrew Publishing Co., Board of Jewish Education of New York, 1987.

_____. *Crumbs and Characters: Sermons, Addresses, and Essays*. New York: Night and Day Press, 1942.

_____. *Fallen Angels in Jewish, Christian, Mohammedan Literature*. New York: Ktav Publishing House, 1974. (Reprint of 1926 edition published by Dropsie College for Hebrew and Cognate Learning. Originally presented as the author's thesis, University of London.)

_____. *Harvest, Sermons, Addresses, Studies.* New York: Phillip Feldheim Inc., 1956.

_____. *Human Relations in Jewish Law*, Jewish Education Committee Press,1967

_____. *Knowledge and Love in Rabbinic Lore.* New York: Yeshiva University Press, Department of Special Publications, 1963.

_____. *Living Judaism.* New York: Night and Day Press, 1927.

_____. *Love and Life.* New York: Philosophical Library, 1979.

_____. *The Rhythm of Life: Sermons Studies, Addresses.* New York: Pardes Publishing House, 1950.

_____. *Sages and Saints.* Hoboken, New Jersey: Ktav Press, 1987.

_____. *Towards Sinai.* New York: Pardes Publishing House, 1929.

_____. *The Jewish Library Series* (N.B. The first series of The Jewish Library Series was published between 1928 and 1964; the second series began in 1968 with revised and new volumes.)

First Series

Volume 1: *Foundations of Judaism.* New York: Jewish Center, 1923.

Volume 2: *Essentials of Judaism.* New York, Union of Jewish Congregation of America, 1927, 1943, 1953.

Volume 3: *The Jewish Woman.* New York, Soncino Press, 1934.

Volume 4: *Judaism in a Changing World*, edited by Leo Jung. New York: Oxford University Press, 1939.

Volume 5: *Israel of Tomorrow.* New York: Herald Square Press, 1946.

Volume 6: *Jewish Leaders, 1750–1940.* Jerusalem: Boys Town Jerusalem Publishers, 1953, 1964.

Volume 7: *Guardians of Our Heritage, 1724-1953.* New York: Bloch Publishing Co., 1958.

Volume 8: *Men of The Spirit.* New York: Kymson Publishing Co., 1964.

Second Series

Volume 1: *Faith.* London and New York: Soncino Press, 1968.

Volume 2: *The Folk.* London and New York: Soncino Press, 1968.

Volume 3: *Woman.* London and New York: Soncino Press, 1970.

Volume 4: *Judaism in a Changing World*. London and New York: Soncino Press, 1971.

Volume 5: *Panorama of Judaism*, Part One. London and New York: Soncino Press, 1974.

Volume 6: *Panorama of Judaism*, Part Two. London and New York: Soncino Press, 1974.

Volume 7: Hyman B. Grinstein. *A Short History of The Jews in the United States*. London and New York: Soncino Press, 1980.

Volume 8: *The Path of a Pioneer: The Autobiography of Leo Jung*. London and New York: Soncino Press, 1980.

Archival Material

1. Leo Jung Collection, Mendel Gottesman Library of Yeshiva University. The collection contains 50 boxes, which include correspondence, personal material, financial records, and printed works.
2. The Jewish Joint Distribution Committee Archives, 711 Third Avenue, New York, New York 10017.
3. Jewish Center Synagogue Archives: Bulletins and Jewish Center Synagogue Annual Meeting Minutes referenced in the text are housed here.

Journals

1. *Commentary*
2. *Jewish Forum*
3. *Jewish Tribune*
4. *Judaism*
5. *Tradition*

Interviews

1. Congregants of Rabbi Jung, in discussion with the author: Martin Shwarzschild, November 11, 1996; Dora Federbush, March 4, 2002; Shelley Helfand, April 24, 2002; Sadie Silverstein, November 19, 1997.
2. Colleagues of Rabbi Jung, in discussion with the author: Former Rabbi of Jewish Center Synagogue, Rabbi Jacob Schacter, November 11, 1996; Former Assistant Rabbi of Jewish Center Synagogue, Norman Lamm, January 16, 2003.

3. Scholars, in discussion with the author: Jeffrey S. Gurock, December 17, 1996; Jenna Weisman Joselit, November 11, 1996. Email interviews with the author: Robert Agus, Judith Baumel.
4. Family, email interview with the author: Tirzah Houminer, granddaughter of Leo Jung. Written interview with the author: Rosalie Rosenfeld, daughter of Leo Jung.

INDEX

A
accommodators, 22
Adler, Dr. Cyrus, 36, 43, 80, 83, 121
Adlerblum, Nina H., 107
Agudath Harabbonim, 11, 37, 70, 82, 95, 111–112, 129, 148, 166, 217
Agudath Israel, 71–73, 92–94, 116, 143, 148, 157–158
Agus, Robert E., 111
Albo, Joseph, 105
  The Book of Principles, 105
American Beth Jacob Committee, 115, 160
American Council for Judaism (ACJ), 154
American dream, 19
American Fund for Palestine Institutions (AFPI), 159
American Jewish Joint Distribution Committee (JDC), 121, 127, 129–132, 142, 159, 180–181
American Jewish Relief Committee, 79
American Journal of Economics and Sociology, 135
American life
  disloyalty to Jewish tradition, 18–19
  freedom of religion, 17
  liberties, 16–17
  nature of lifestyle, 18
  Orthodox Judaism and, 20
  status and adjustment in, 19

American Modern Orthodoxy of 1920s, 29–30
  competition between Orthodox, Conservative, and Reform Judaism, 34–37
  concern for decorum, 48–51
  Council of Young Israel, formation of, 49
  establishment of Yeshiva College, 53–55, 74
  female emancipation, 66–68
  halakhah, modernization of, 47
  idea of "harmonious" education with Jewish studies, 43
  issue of *mehitzah*, 69
  Jewish education, 51–52
  laws of Judaism, 64–65
  merger of JTS and RIETS, proposal for, 43–47
  Mordecai Kaplan's reconstruction plan and Rabbi Jung's rebuttal, 38–43
  Orthodox organizations, strengthening of, 57–63
  privatization of Judaism, 64
  state of, 30–34
  synagogue centers, modernization of, 47–48
  trends and issues, 73–74

writings and sermons of Rabbi Jung, 55–57
Young Israel movement, 49, 52–53
Zionism and, 70–73
American Modern Orthodoxy of 1930s, 75–118
advent of the RCA, 110–112
anti-religious activities, 76–78
approach to modernity, 87–89
changes in synagogue outlook and activities, 91–92
educational outreach publications and radio, 102–107
involvement in social service, 79–84
Jewish education, 94–107
kashrut observance, 112–115
Modern Orthodox image, 90–91
new influences on Modern Orthodoxy, 84–87
new opportunities to learn Hebrew, 101–102
organizational activities, 108–115
parochial schools, 97–101
practice of opening Jewish theaters on Rosh Hashana, 77
religious leadership, significance of, 79
religious movements and emphasis on social issues, 78–79
Sabbath observance, 108–110
women, status of, 115–117
Yeshiva College, 95–97
Zionism, 92–94
American Modern Orthodoxy of 1940s
active participation of organizations, 120
age of the pioneer, 160–162
agunah problem, 163
American Jewry, new role of, 142–144
contrasting orthodox views, 157–158
decorum, 168–169
halakhah issues, 162–168
image building, 140–141
Jewish education, 144–153
kashrut supervision, 166–168
mehitzah, 164–165
Modern Orthodox Chaplain, role in war efforts, 122–127

orthodox organizational involvement in war efforts, 127–132
parochial schools, 144–145
relationship between Orthodox Jews and other Jewish groups, 141–142
resistance to Americanization by Jews, 120
Sabbath observance, 168–169
teaching Hebrew, 146
upsurge in status of religion and its institutions, 137–140
use of microphone, issue with, 165
Yeshiva College, 145
Yeshiva's role in Jewish education, 146–153
Zionism, 120, 153–162
American Modern Orthodoxy of 1950s
activities of the organizations, 176–181
agunah issue, 194, 198
Conservative *ketubbah* (marriage agreement) and *bet din* (court), 194–199
Conservative movement, 193, 198
fighting for American dream, 181–185
Halakhic Committee, 178, 189–190, 198–199
image and role of the Rabbi, 205–207
influx of orthodox immigrants, 175–176
Jewish education, 200–205
literature movement, 207–213
mehitzah, 190–193
non-Orthodox *vs* Orthodox rabbis, 213–217
relationship of Israel's leaders with American leaders, 187
religious revival, 173–175
return to *halakhic* creativity and interest, 188–194
Sabbath observance, 187
yeshiva education, 202
Yeshiva University, 203–204
Zionism, 185–188
American Orthodox Judaism, 2
American-style Orthodoxy, 15–26
anti-Semitism, 64, 82, 87–88, 92, 95, 105, 127, 134, 137, 153, 185
Aranowitz, Benjamin, 86

Ashkenazi, Rabbi Meir, 144
Ashkenazim, 159
Ashkenazi rabbi, 22

B
Baeck, Rabbi Leo, 187
Balfour Declaration, 92
Bamberger, Rabbi Bernard, 216
Baron, Salo W., 135, 187
Baumel, Judith Tydor, 82, 141
Belkin, Dr. Samuel, 106, 123, 138, 147, 150, 152, 154, 156, 164, 185, 187, 192, 203
Ben-Gurion, Prime Minister, 187
Benjamin, Rabbi Samuel, 36n39
Berkovits, Dr. Eliezer, 185, 196
Berlin, Rabbi Meyer, 32, 52, 70, 156, 160
Bermuda Conference, 128
Bernstein, Rabbi Louis, 122, 178
  Challenge and Mission, 122
Beth Jacob girls, 140, 160
Beth Jacob "Martyrs" in America, 140
Beth Jacob schools, 116
Bill of Rights, 137
Biltmore Conference, 154
Board of Education in New York City, 110
Breuer, Jacob, 4
Breuer Community, 6
Brith, B'nai, 77
Brodie, Rabbi Israel, 187
Buck, Pearl, 136
Bureau of Vocational Guidance for Sabbath observers, 110

C
CANRA (Committee for Army and Navy Religious Activities or Chaplain's Committee), 124–125, 163
Central Relief Committee, 79
Chafee Jr., Zecharia
  The Blessing of Liberty, 182
Churgin, Dr. Gershon, 204
Churgin, Dr. Pinchas, 147–148
Cleveland's Knesset Israel Congregation, 40
The Commentator, 120, 150
Conservative Judaism, 35

Council of Young Israel, 49

D
Dalai Lama, 136
Dickstein, Samuel, 62
Dickstein Sabbath bill, 62
Division of Religious Affairs Commission (DRA), 215
Drachman, Rabbi Bernard, 7, 21, 25, 37, 45–46, 51–52, 65, 99, 109
Dulles, John Foster, 186

E
Eastern European *yeshivot*, 55
Ebin, Rabbi Nachum H., 92
Eichhorn, Rabbi David Max, 215–216
Einstein, Albert, 97, 152
Elchanan, Rabbi Isaac, 44
Eleff, Rabbi Zev, 7
Emancipation, 7
Engel, Dr. Jacob, 160
Engelman, Morris, 81
Epstein, Dr. Louis, 117
Epstein, Isidore, 207
Eretz Israel, 9, 29, 57, 72–73, 93–94, 120, 153, 155–156, 158, 160
Etz Hayyim *yeshiva*, 53

F
Farbridge, Maurice, 52
Fasman, Rabbi Oscar, 67, 106
Feinstein, Rabbi Moses, 191
Feuerstein, Samuel C., 195
Finkelstein, Dr. Louis, 187
Fosdick, Rev. Dr. Harry Emerson, 136–137
Freehof, Dr. Solomon B., 124
Friedlander, Israel, 52

G
Garda, Enrico, 151
Gastwirt, Harold P., 59–60
  Fraud, Corruption and Holiness, 59
German Jewish Children's Associations (GJCA), 80
Ginzberg, Louis, 69, 164
Glatzer, Dr. Nahum, 206
Glazer, Nathan, 174–175, 201
Golding, Joseph, 151

G

Goldstein, Rabbi Herbert, 52, 54, 81, 99, 124–125, 131, 168, 206
Gordis, Robert, 216
Gottesman, Mendel, 151
Gurock, Jeffrey, 22, 34, 41, 51, 192, 217

H

Hakohen, Rabbi Israel Meir, 192
halakhic Judaism, 3
Handlin, Dr. Oscar, 187
Hapoel Hamizrachi, 155
Hashomer Hatzair, 155
Hasidim, Lubavitch, 86
Hazon Ish, 160
Hebrew Theological College, 86
Heilman, Samuel, 2
Heller, Rabbi Chaim, 149
Hertz, Rabbi Joseph H., 37
Herzog, Rabbi Isaac, 131, 160, 162
Hildesheimer, Rabbi, 8–9, 15, 116
Hildesheimer Rabbinical Seminary, 8, 14
Hirsch, Rabbi Samson Raphael, 4, 14, 116
　anti-Zionist philosophy of, 8–9
　interpretation of *halakhah*, 6
　introducing modernity in Judaism, 6–7
　Nineteen Letters, 4–5
　The Nineteen Letters of Ben Uziel, 209
　Torah im derekh eretz, 4–5, 7
Hoenig, Rabbi Sidney, 123
Hoffman, Rabbi, 15
Hofstadter-Moffat Sabbath Bill, 109
Hoover, President, 82
Hyamson, Mrs. Moses, 67
Hyamson, Rabbi Dr. Moses, 36n39
Hyman, Joseph, 130

I

Isaacs, Dr. Moses, 148
Isaacs, Moses, 89
Israel of Tomorrow, 121

J

Jewish Center Bulletin, 179
Jewish Center Day School, 98
Jewish Center Synagogue, 39, 42, 91
　in Manhattan, 33
　in New York, 25
Jewish Center Talmud Torah, 98
Jewish chaplain, 126
Jewish education
　1920s, 51–55, 94–107
　1940s, 144–153
　1950s, 200–205
Jewish Forum, 196, 211–212
Jewish Military Chaplains Association, 217
Jewish Publication Society (JPS), 105–106
Jewish Sabbath movements, 61–62
Jewish Theological Seminary (JTS), 36–37, 81, 89, 194
Jewish values, traditional, 20–21
Jewish Welfare Board (JWB), 123–124, 127
Joint Distribution Committee (JDC), 79–81, 229
Joselit, Jenna Weissman, 5, 9, 51
Jung, Rabbi Dr. Leo, 1–2, 13, 24, 64, 76, 99
　about *mikvaot/mikveh*, 66–67
　afterschool program, 100
　Americanizing Orthodoxy, 218
　on American liberties, 16–17
　approach to modernity, 87–89
　biography of, 13–15
　"cooperation without compromise," 141–142
　correspondence with Herman Wouk, 209–211
　cultural work of the JDC, 81–82
　description of Orthodoxy, 4
　on dress code, 64–65
　as editor, 56–57
　educational endeavors, 99–101, 116, 121–122, 144–146
　efforts to restore Jewish homeland, 92
　efforts to save European Jewry, 82
　Essentials of Judaism, 147
　fighting for American dream, 181–185
　Foundations of Judaism, 56–57
　goal of supporting *yeshivot* and Torah scholars, 131
　Guardians of Our Heritage, 207–208
　influence on new immigrants, 85
　Israel of Tomorrow, 137, 143, 187
　Jewish Center Synagogue of, 47–48, 50–51, 86
　Jewish Leaders, 208

Jewish Publication Society (JPS)
  projects, 105
 on Judaic marriage laws, 65–66
 Judaism in a Changing World, 106
 kashrut supervision, 113–114, 122,
   166–168, 178–180
 kedushah, 199–200
 literary work, 4–5, 55–57, 106–107,
   133, 147, 207–208, 230
 Living Judaism, 4, 56–57
 Men of the Spirit, 208
 "Modern Trends in American
   Judaism," 4–5
 Mordecai Kaplan's reconstruction
   plan and, 38–43
 movement to the right, 224–228
 and needs of the refugees, 144
 new influences on Modern Orthodoxy, 84–87
 oratorial skills, 15
 organizational efforts, 158–160
 participation in the JDC, 129
 perspective of American-style
   Orthodoxy, 15–26
 philosophy and theme in 1950s,
   199–200
 on practice of opening Jewish theaters
   on Rosh Hashana, 77
 response to World War II, 132–137
 Sabbath observance, 109–110
 schools for women, 116
 on term "Orthodox," 3
 "The Martyrs of Warsaw," 140–141
 theme in the 1940s, 138
 Toward Sinai, 56
 Woman, 106–107
 work for parochial schools, 99–101
 writings about Orthodox Judaism,
   55–57
 writings and radio addresses, 133
 Yeshiva library collections, 128
Jung, Rabbi Leo, 7–8
Jung, Rabbi Meir Tzevi, 14
Jung, Rabbi Tzevi, 8

K
Kaminetsky, Dr. Joseph, 98, 201–202
Kaplan, Rabbi Jacob, 187

Kaplan, Rabbi Mordecai, 4, 87, 91
 reconstruction of Judaism, 38–43
 study of Jewish educational conditions
   in New York, 31–32
Karelitz, Rabbi Avraham
   Yeshayahu, 160
Kasher, Menahem M., 188, 196
Kasher, Rabbi Moshe Shlomo, 195
Kehillath Jeshurun, 45, 98
Ketav Sofer, 15
Klein, Rabbi Phillip, 7
Konvitz, Joseph, 131
Kook, Rav (Rabbi) Avraham Yitzhak
   Hakohen, 14, 68, 157, 192
Kosher Law of the State of New York, 113
Kotler, Rabbi Aaron, 131

L
Lamm, Rabbi Norman, 5, 192–193, 195,
   198, 206, 219, 224
Lehman, Herbert, 95
Leipziger, Rabbi Emil W., 144–145
Levinson, Jacob, 131
Levinthal, Rabbi Bernard, 148
Levy, Rabbi Simcha, 178, 190
Levy, Samuel, 148
Lewin, Rabbi I. M., 160
Lewittes, Rabbi Mendel, 89
Lewittes, Rabbi Mordecai, 190
Lieberman, Paul, 194
Lissner, Mr. Will, 135
Lookstein, Rabbi Joseph, 52, 63, 98–99,
   106, 111, 124–125, 147, 156,
   168, 206
Lubavitch movement, 86
Luzzatto, Moses Hayyim
 Mesillat Yesharim, 105

M
Macht, Dr. Isaac, 66
Magnes, Rabbi Judah L., 52
Margolies, Rabbi Moses Sebulun, 36n39,
   63, 99
Margolies (the Ramaz), Rabbi Moses
   Sebulun, 54
Marshall, Louis, 43, 81
Mazer, Abraham, 151
McCarran, Patrick Anthony, 181

McCarran Acts of 1950 and 1952, 181–183
McCarthy, Joseph, 183
mehitzah, 69, 111–112, 164–165, 177, 190–193
Meiselman, Shulamit, 85–86
Mendelovitz, Rabbi Shraga Feivel, 7
Mendes, Dr. Henry Pereira, 99
Mendes, Rabbi Dr. Henry Pereira, 35
Mendlowitz, Rabbi Shraga Feivel, 201
Men's Club of the Jewish Center, 215
Mizrachi Land Development Corporation, 94
Mizrachi Organization of America, 33, 70–72, 92–94, 155–157, 160
    role in the development of Israel, 71
    women's organizational work, 117
Modern Orthodoxy, 1, 27–28
    American environment, effect of interaction with, 24
    defined, 3–13
    goal of, 11
    institutions, 2
    key issue in, 12–13
    norms, 220–224. *See also* American Modern Orthodoxy of 1920s; American Modern Orthodoxy of 1930s; American Modern Orthodoxy of 1940s; American Modern Orthodoxy of 1950s
    openness to new interpretations, 12
    secular world and religious world perspective, 10
Munk, Rabbi Ezra, 83

N
nationalism, 40–41
Neo-Orthodoxy, 4
New York University, 146
Noam, 195–198

O
Orthodox Jews, 4
    conflict between American rabbis and European rabbis, 21–23
    education of American Orthodox rabbi, 23
    vs socialists, 20
Orthodox Judaism, 20
Orthodoxy groups, 10
Orthodoxy of the Eastern European *shtetl,* 24
OU News Reporter, 179

P
People's Relief Committee, 79
Poalei Agudah (Agudah laborers), 158–159
Poalei Hamizrachi (Mizrachi laborers), 159
Polatchek, Rabbi Solomon, 85
Pool, Rabbi de Sola, 54, 106, 124, 126
Pool, Rabbi Dr. David de Sola, 35
privatization of religion, 64

R
Rabbi Isaac Elchanan Theological Seminary (RIETS), 7, 33, 42, 53, 71, 85, 89, 92, 112, 123, 139, 148, 204
    proposal for merger of JTS and, 43–47
Rabbinical Board of Greater New York, 33
Rabbinical Council of America (RCA), 75, 110–112, 115, 122, 155, 167, 178–180, 183, 205, 214, 217
    Halakhic Committee, 123
    war efforts, 132
Rabbonim Aid Society, 132
Rackman, Rabbi Emanuel, 9, 139, 188, 215–216
Raddock, Charles, 212
Rakeffet-Rothkoff, Aaron, 93
Ramaz, 98–99
Raphael, Marc, 49
Reform Central Conference of American Rabbis (CCAR), 124
Reform Judaism, 35
Reform movement, 5
resisters, 22
Revel, Dr. Bernard, 45–47, 54, 86, 95–96, 111, 148, 151

Revel, Rabbi Bernard, 7
Romulo, Carlos, 138
Rosenfeld, Rabbi Leonard, 216
Rosenheim, Jacob, 93, 140
roshei yeshiva, 149–150, 158, 165, 190, 206–207, 213, 217

S

Sabbath Alliance, 61–62, 109, 168
Sabbath observance, 61–63, 108–110, 168–169
Sachar, Dr. Abraham, 187
Sanrow, Edward T., 215
Sar, Dr. Samuel, 97, 144, 148
Schacter, Rabbi Herschel, 216
Schacter, Rabbi Jacob J., 41, 91n75
Schenirer, Sarah, 116
Schneersohn, Rabbi Joseph Isaac, 86
Schwartz, Rabbi Mordechai Tzevi, 14
Schwarzschild, Martin, 64
Scripta Mathematica, 147
Sephardim, 159
Shapiro, Marc B., 83–84, 197
Sharfman, Rabbi Solomon J., 192, 209
Shatzkes, Rabbi Moshe (Lomza Rav), 151
Silber, Saul, 124
Silver, Rabbi Eliezer, 93, 143, 148, 158
Sinai Campaign, 186
Sklare, Marshall, 188
  Conservative Judaism: An American Religious Movement, 188
social activism, 21
Society for the Advancement of Judaism, 91
Soloveitchik, Haym, 202, 205
Soloveitchik, Rabbi Joseph B., 86, 93, 123, 141, 149, 155–156, 178, 188–189, 193, 206–207
Soloveitchik, Rabbi Moses, 85–86, 148–149
Spektor of Kovno, Rabbi Isaac Elhanan, 53
State of Israel, 73, 153–155, 157, 162–163, 172, 185, 216
Stern, Max, 195
Stern, Rabbi Mordecai, 163

Stern College, 204
Stopes, Dr. Mary, 66
Suez War, 186
Synagogue Council of America (SCA), 214

T

Tabak, Rabbi Israel, 185, 217
Tillich, Paul, 182
Torah im derekh eretz, 149
Torah min ha-Shamayim, 12
Torah Umesorah movement, 201–202
Tradition, 211
Truman, President, 182, 184

U

Ultra-Orthodox, 10–11
Union of Orthodox Jewish Congregations of America (UOJCA), 33, 49, 57–61, 71–72, 76–77, 82, 99, 137, 145, 155, 167, 176–178
  approaches to *halakhah*, 63–70
  educational activities, 108
  facilitating Sabbath observance, 61–63, 109
  kashrut observance, 113–114
  kashrut supervision and certification, 59–60
  kosher facilities, legal fight for, 60–61
  Rabbinical Council, 110–111
  Rabbinic Council, 60
  Sabbath Committee, 63
Union of Orthodox Jewish Congregations of America Women's Organization, 117
United Jewish Appeal (UJA), 129

V

Vaad Hahatzala, 129–132, 181
Vaad Hakavod, 166
Vaad Harabanim, 33
Vaad Hayeshivot, 158

W

Weil, Frank, 124
Weinberg, Rabbi Jehiel Jacob, 195–197

Weiss, Rabbi William, 77, 99, 124, 137, 147
Weizmann, Chaim, 2
Western European Jewry, 5
White Paper policy, 128
Wouk, Herman, 2, 209–211
　This Is My God, 207, 210

Y
yeshiva, 14, 23, 47, 53–55, 86, 94, 99, 159, 181
Yeshiva College, 33, 44, 85, 89, 123, 127, 149
　library, 128
　during 1930s, 95–97
Yeshiva Orthodox, 10

yeshiva programs, 181
Yeshiva University, 8, 144, 146, 153, 162, 203–204
Young Israel Employment Bureau, 110
Young Israel movement, 49, 63
Young Israel Synagogue, 49

Z
Zeitlin, Dr. Solomon, 147
Zionism, 40
　Reform movement and, 154
　1940s, 153–162
　1950s, 185–188
　of 1920s, 70–73
　of 1930s, 92–94

www.ingramcontent.com/pod-product-compliance
Lightning Source LLC
Chambersburg PA
CBHW050105170426
43198CB00014B/2471